Fall 2001   Vol
ISSN: 0276-0045   IS

THE REVIEW OF
CONTEMPORARY FICTION

Editor

JOHN O'BRIEN
Illinois State University

Senior Editor

ROBERT L. MCLAUGHLIN
Illinois State University

Associate Editors

IRVING MALIN, DAVID FOSTER WALLACE

Book Review Editor

GREGORY HOWARD

Production & Design

TODD MICHAEL BUSHMAN

Editorial Assistants

SARA CALDWELL, SARAH MCHONE-CHASE, LAYNE MOORE

Cover Illustration

TODD MICHAEL BUSHMAN

www.centerforbookculture.org
www.dalkeyarchive.com

The Review of Contemporary Fiction is published three times a year
(January, June, September) by The Review of Contemporary
Fiction, Inc., a nonprofit organization located at ISU Campus Box
4241, Normal, IL 61790-4241. ISSN 0276-0045. Subscription
prices are as follows:

   Single volume (three issues):
       Individuals: $17.00; foreign, add $3.50;
       Institutions: $26.00; foreign, add $3.50.

DISTRIBUTION. Bookstores should send orders to:

Dalkey Archive Press, ISU Campus Box 4241, Normal, IL
61790-4241. Phone 309-874-2274; fax 309-874-2284.

This issue is partially supported by a grant from the Illinois Arts
Council, a state agency.

Indexed in *American Humanities Index, International Bibliography
of Periodical Literature, International Bibliography of Book
Reviews, MLA Bibliography,* and *Book Review Index.* Abstracted
in *Abstracts of English Studies.*

The Review of Contemporary Fiction is also available in 16mm
microfilm, 35mm microfilm, and 105mm microfiche from
University Microfilms International, 300 North Zeeb Road,
Ann Arbor, MI 48106-1346.

www.centerforbookculture.org
www.dalkeyarchive.com

THE REVIEW OF CONTEMPORARY FICTION

Call for Casebook Editors and Contributors

www.dalkeyarchive.com

Dalkey Archive Press/The Review of Contemporary Fiction is seeking editors and contributors for its new web-based casebook series: Studies in Modern and Contemporary Fiction. Each casebook will focus on one novel. It will include an overview essay on the book (its place in the author's oeuvre; its critical reception; the scholarly conversations about it) and four other essays looking at specific dimensions of the book. (Recommended length of essays: 20-25 double-spaced pages.) Also included will be a selected bibliography of critical works on the book. The anticipated audience includes professors teaching the book and graduate and undergraduate students studying it.

All casebooks will be refereed. Successful casebooks will be published on the Dalkey Archive Press website.

The duties of the casebook editor will be to write the overview essay and develop the critical bibliography, to coordinate the other essays, especially avoiding overlapping among them, and to coordinate with the series editor.

The following are the books for which we are seeking casebook editors and contributors:

Yuz Aleshkovsky
  Kangaroo
Felipe Alfau
  Locos
  Chromos
Andrei Bitov
  Pushkin House
Louis-Ferdinand Céline
  Trilogy (*North, Castle to Castle, Rigadoon*)
Peter Dimock
  A Short Rhetoric for Leaving the Family
Coleman Dowell
  Island People
Rikki Ducornet
  The Jade Cabinet
William Eastlake
  Lyric of the Circle Heart
William H. Gass
  Willie Masters' Lonesome Wife
Aldous Huxley
  Point Counter Point
Tadeusz Konwicki
  A Minor Apocalypse
José Lezama Lima
  Paradiso
Osman Lins
  The Queen of the Prisons of Greece

D. Keith Mano
  Take Five
Wallace Markfield
  Teitlebaum's Window
Harry Mathews
  Cigarettes
Nicholas Mosley
  Impossible Object
  Accident
Flann O'Brien
  The Poor Mouth
Fernando del Paso
  Palinuro of Mexico
Raymond Queneau
  Pierrot Mon Ami
Jacques Roubaud
  The Great Fire of London
Gilbert Sorrentino
  Imaginative Qualities of Actual Things
  Mulligan Stew
  Aberration of Starlight
Piotr Szewc
  Annihilation
Curtis White
  Memories of My Father Watching TV

Applicants should send a CV and a brief writing sample.

Send applications to:

Robert L. McLaughlin
Dalkey Archive Press, Illinois State University, Campus Box 4241, Normal, IL 61790-4241

Inquiries: rmclaugh@ilstu.edu

Contents

RCF Call for Contributors

The Review of Contemporary Fiction is seeking contributors to write overview essays on the following writers:

Michel Butor, Julieta Campos, Jerome Charyn, Emily Coleman, Stanley Crawford, Carol De Chellis Hill, Jennifer Johnston, Gert Jonke, Violette Le Duc, Wallace Markfield, David Markson, Rick Moody, Olive Moore, Julián Ríos, Joanna Scott, Esther Tusquets, Luisa Valenzuela.

The essays must:

- be 50 double-spaced pages;
- cover the subject's biography;
- summarize the critical reception of the subject's works;
- discuss the course of the subject's career, including each major work;
- provide interpretive strategies for new readers to apply to the subject's work;
- provide a bibliographic checklist of each of the subject's works (initial and latest printings) and the most;
- be written for a general, intelligent reader, who does not know the subject's work;
- avoid jargon, theoretical digressions, and excessive endnotes;
- be intelligent, interesting, and readable;
- be documented in MLA style.

Authors will be paid $250.00 when the essay is published. All essays will be subject to editorial review, and the editors reserve the right to request revisions and to reject unacceptable essays.

Applicants should send a CV and a brief writing sample. In your cover letter, be sure to address your qualifications

Send applications to:

Robert L. McLaughlin
Dalkey Archive Press, Illinois State University, Campus Box 4241, Normal, IL 61790-4241

Inquiries: rmclaugh@ilstu.edu

Gilbert Sorrentino

David Andrews

> He sought by stress upon construction to hold the loose-
> strung mass off even at the cost of an icy coldness of ap-
> pearance; it was the first need of his time, an escape
> from the formless mass he hated. It is the very sense of a
> beginning, as it is the impulse which drove him to the
> character of all his tales; to get from sentiment to form, a
> backstroke from the swarming "population."
> —William Carlos Williams on Edgar Allan Poe
> (*In the American Grain* 221)

There is no other American writer whose oeuvre remotely resembles that of Gilbert Sorrentino, and it is tempting to say that no
other living American can match his artistic achievement. It is the
diversity of his artistry that separates him from his peers. As a
poet, he has written works of a uniquely American flavor in the lyric
vein of William Carlos Williams and Robert Creeley; he has also
written dazzlingly baroque verse that reveals the influence of the
French symbolists and Guillaume Apollinaire. His novels comprise
his most important contribution to literature, and once again, it is
the sheer diversity that is arresting. Sorrentino has written dark,
fatalistic novels like *The Sky Changes;* hilarious satires like *Imaginative Qualities of Actual Things;* impassioned aesthetic manifes-
toes like *Splendide-Hôtel;* and towering metafictions like *Mulligan
Stew.* Yet this is just the start. To say his later fictions elude gener-
alization is to understate the matter drastically, for as an uncompromising innovator, he has pushed the novel so far that at times it
has seemed as if he were writing for no one but himself. Like his
best fiction, his criticism is austere, acerbic, and modernist in sensibility. Sorrentino has admired Edward Dahlberg for never praising
things "fit for the garbage can" (*Something* 97), so it is no surprise
that he too has denounced acclaimed authors in tomahawking critiques that recall the ferocity of Edgar Allan Poe. Through it all, his
essential inventiveness, comedy, darkness, and idiosyncrasy have
remained intact, making his work diverse in its techniques yet absolutely of a piece in tone, theme, and motif. Still, after five decades
of writing masterpieces as different as *Mulligan Stew* and "Coast of
Texas," Sorrentino continues to have trouble publishing his work,
and it is an almost trite sad-but-truism that his reputation remains

smaller than his accomplishments would dictate.

Sorrentino was born in Brooklyn, New York, on 27 April 1929 to August E. and Ann Davis Sorrentino. He attended New York public schools as a child and studied at Brooklyn College from 1950 to 1951 and 1955 to 1957. The intervening years were partly filled by his stint in the U.S. Army Medical Corps (1951-1953). During this period, he married Elsene Wiessner, whom he divorced following a cross-country trip in 1960. Now remarried to Victoria Ortiz, Sorrentino has three children, Jesse, Delia, and Christopher. Despite numerous critical successes, prestigious literary awards—including two Guggenheim fellowships, three National Endowment for the Arts grants, the John Dos Passos Prize for Literature, a Lannan Literary Award, and an award from the American Academy and Institute of Arts and Letters—and his reputation as a talented and tireless innovator, Sorrentino has never supported himself and his family solely by means of writing. Still, for the better part of four decades, the fact of writing remained central to his day jobs, first at Grove Press in the 1960s and then at the New School for Social Research and Stanford University in the 1970s, 1980s, and 1990s. Currently retired from teaching, Sorrentino lives in Stanford, California.

He has not, however, retired from writing, a career that dates back to a moment just after high school. According to William M. Robins, Sorrentino was working as a clerk at a textile-banking company during the late 1940s when he read Walt Whitman and thought, "Well, I can do that too" (279). When he left the Army in 1953, he determined "I am going to be a writer or I am going to be nothing" (O'Brien 7). His first serious attempts at publication came during his Brooklyn College years. Upon its appearance in *Landscapes* in 1956, his first short story, "Last Rites," sparked a campus controversy due to its allegedly anti-Catholic depictions. With his boyhood friend Hubert "Cubby" Selby, Sorrentino began the little magazine *Neon* later that year. Selby attributes the success of this venture primarily to "Gils [sic] creative energy" (49), which motivated those around him. "There was a tremendous sense of accomplishment," Selby writes, "a feeling that we were doing something important." Though Selby admits that some of this was naive "self-importance," what was most important for Sorrentino and him was that *Neon* got them "actively involved in the literary world."

Partly through *Neon,* Sorrentino came into contact with William Carlos Williams, Robert Creeley, Jonathan Williams, and LeRoi Jones (now Amiri Baraka), four figures who would influence his vision and help him publish its products. Then came a deluge of friends, acquaintances, and influences, including Joel Oppenheimer,

Fielding Dawson, Dan Rice, Allen Ginsberg, Peter Orlovsky, Ed Dorn, Paul Blackburn, Robert Kelley, John Wieners, Frank O'Hara, Robert Duncan, Bob Thompson, Charles Olson, and Edward Dahlberg, among many others. To read of Sorrentino's life during this period is to see a man working feverishly at the center of an incredible artistic ferment. During the late 1950s and early 1960s, for example, he was to write poetry on the periphery of three new but very different schools of poetry, viz., the Black Mountain school of Olson and Creeley, the New York school of O'Hara and Kenneth Koch, and the Beat school of Ginsberg and Jack Kerouac; he was also to interact with San Francisco poets, including Duncan. And his artistic exposure was hardly confined to the literary. Some of his most formative ties were to painters like Rice, whose work he first witnessed in the painter's loft in 1957, and Morton Lucks—and this during the ascendancy of abstract expressionism, when one might, and often did, run into the likes of Jackson Pollock, Willem de Kooning, and Franz Kline at the Cedar Street Bar. Innovators like Thelonious Monk and John Cage in music and Merce Cunningham in dance completed the feeling of a pan-aesthetic revolution. By the time *Neon* expired in 1960, Sorrentino was entrenched in the East Village scene and had formed affiliations with *Kulchur* and *Yugen,* two little magazines that suited the young writer in that their demand for quality work was just as insistent as their rejection of the "official" literary conventions of the time.

According to Sorrentino, finding journals that conformed to those two criteria was no simple thing during the 1950s. On the one hand were the established journals like the *Hudson Review* that often resisted modernist innovations. On the other hand "were the 'experimental' little magazines that would publish anything—anything at all" (*Something* 242). Sorrentino notes in "Black Mountaineering," his paean to Creeley and other contributors to the *Black Mountain Review,* that one as a result "worked in a kind of numb solitude, unpublished and unread, and, more to the point, without access to those works that could have acted as direction and buttress to one's own false starts and scribblings." But after discovering the *Black Mountain Review,* and especially after the advent of *Neon,* a publishing world that would accept him—and, equally important, that he could in turn accept—slowly opened to him. In 1958 his correspondence with Williams on behalf of *Neon* led the elder poet to excerpt a portion of Sorrentino's jazzy sketch "Bordertown" in *Paterson V.* Sorrentino's rigorous and frankly elitist opinions about then-underrated writers like Williams, Spicer, and Dahlberg found their first important outlet in *Kulchur* during the early 1960s. As for his art, Sorrentino was publishing mainly poetry. Between 1956 and 1960, his poems appeared not only in *Neon* and *Yugen* but in *Emergent, Shenandoah, Spectrum, Supplement to Now, White Dove Review, Nomad, Hearse,* and numerous collections, of which the most important was Donald Allen's *The New American Poetry* (1960).

Clearly, Sorrentino was gaining an audience in select avant-garde circles. His self-financed *The Darkness Surrounds Us* (1960) received an important if qualified review from the late Denise Levertov in the *Nation,* prompting his halting movement toward a wider audience, one that would be less automatic in its acceptance of his modernist tendencies. *Black and White* (1964), his second poetry collection and one published through his friendship with Jones, who ran Totem Press, continued this trend, as did his novel *The Sky Changes* (1966), with each successive work gaining more positive recognition than its predecessor. The publication of *Sky* marked a crucial moment in Sorrentino's career. Not only was he publishing his long-awaited first novel, he was doing so with Hill and Wang, which would promote the novel in the *New York Review of Books*— and which just missed securing a laudatory review in *Newsweek.* Though it had lost an opportunity, *Sky* still garnered more notice than Sorrentino's poetry collections, partly because of the publisher's efforts and partly because *Sky* was prose, which in America has always reached a larger audience than poetry. The notices were mostly enthusiastic, with reviewers reacting more to the emotional excruciation evinced by the novel's storyline than to its innovative techniques.

Since 1966, Sorrentino has published seven collections of poetry, thirteen works of fiction, and *Something Said,* a book of criticism. His prominence as a literary figure appears to have peaked in 1980 when he published *Aberration of Starlight,* a critical success that followed closely on the heels of two very different successes, *The Orangery* in 1978 and *Mulligan Stew* in 1979. It should come as no surprise, however, that over the past twenty years, his star has waned even as his accomplishments have broadened. During that period, mergers in the publishing world have decreased the number of outlets for serious literature and sharply reduced the willingness of editors to publish avant-garde fiction, which has, financially speaking, always been a risky proposition. That, combined with the increasing radicalism of Sorrentino's fiction through the 1980s and early 1990s, made it difficult for him to publish his work long after he had established himself as a writer. The best example of this is *Crystal Vision,* which was rejected by several publishers during the late 1970s—and which the *New York Times Book Review* did not even bother to review. Even after Grove profited from the publication of *Mulligan Stew,* a book that, among other things, parodies the publishing world, the press twice rejected Sorrentino's next, more radical novel. Not until 1981, three years after its completion, was *Crystal Vision* published by North Point, a young, relatively small press.

Despite the inevitable variations in its reception, Sorrentino's work has to this point remained consistent in its primary thematic concerns and its insistence on formal innovation. Indeed, the variation in reception is inevitable *because* of the emphasis on innovation, which in effect means that Sorrentino has rarely followed a critical success with a work that much resembles it. According to the author, he does not write in order to succeed critically, popularly, or financially. As he emphatically, even irascibly, reminds his reader, *he is not for sale*. If he writes for any reason beyond the sheer joy and relief of writing itself, he writes for aesthetic reasons, with each new venture bent on solving a formal problem of his own invention. He has pointedly complimented his favorite writers, Pound, Williams, Dahlberg, and Spicer among them, by noting that they put art before audience, which to his mind is the prerequisite and guarantor of literary freedom. All of this makes the resounding praise lavished on Sorrentino for three successive works between 1978 and 1980, three works utterly dissimilar in style, structure, and voice, the more astonishing. Now in his early seventies, Sorrentino is going strong, with his long-delayed novel *Gold Fools* having been released in March 2001 and with other projects on the verge of completion. Obviously, though, if he hasn't entered the final phase of his career, he will do so relatively soon. The time has come to begin examining his work as an established corpus so as to describe it, assess it, and place it as such.

Perhaps the most direct way of approaching Sorrentino is from the vantage of literary history. In this narrative he is the classic modernist, with his artworks at once displaying modernist and postmodernist contours. Philosophically and psychologically, he is a modernist insofar as his overall worldview remains grimly antiessentialist even as his radical aestheticism consistently flirts with essentialism and its traditional goals of truth, beauty, order, and transcendence. His antiessentialism recalls that of the late poet William Bronk. In Bronk's poetry there is the unstinting awareness that the external world is an uncaring rock that stands iron and aloof amid humanity's diverse projections of value, as shaped by hope, desire, and other internal necessities. In both his poetry and prose Sorrentino evokes the same awareness, albeit with greater a sense of passion, pain, and especially play than the serenely blunt Bronk. What makes Sorrentino more classical in his modernism is that he combines this basically existentialist view of the universe with a romantic view of art as a source of beauty and regeneration. "One should not," Sharon Thesen reminds us, "underestimate the visionary turnstile Catholicism is to Sorrentino" (57). As Thesen sees it, the atheist Sorrentino substitutes art for organized religion, and his work proposes Catholic "grace as the proper achievement of the artist at the same time that it proposes darkness and corruption as what we necessarily walk through" (57). This contradiction between antiessentialist worldview and essentialist aesthetic is typical of the modernist sensibility. Sorrentino reconciles it in the manner of Wallace Stevens and Williams, for whom art was a necessary fiction. Art is fiction in that as a product of perception and reflection it is an imaginative construct. It is necessary in that humans inescapably long for truth, beauty, and order, without which they succumb to despair. It is as if Sorrentino is suggesting that autotelic art, which as an end in itself cannot be turned against its creators, is superior to religion, philosophy, politics, and pop culture as a source of illusion. Naturally, this begs further questions. Because he never works these out in a fully logical manner, paradox remains inherent to his aestheticism, indirectly testifying to a paradox at the heart of modernism itself.

Sorrentino's working aesthetic is governed by a consistent set of principles that guide his creative activities and his criticism of other writers. First among them is his avant-gardism, which combines Williams's idea of the artist as a maker with Pound's injunction to the artist to make things *new*. This brand of modernism is linked to a second if not secondary point, his formalism. Sorrentino has been a consistent proponent of a "joyous heresy," the idea that form determines content, that form literally causes content to appear during the act of creation (*Something* 200). These twin beliefs determine the rest of his aesthetic: his emphasis on design and innovative technique; his rejection of conventional realism and its central illusion, that language can represent reality in a straightforward way; his preference for artificiality and Eliotic impersonality in art, which likewise implies his rejection of an art of self-expression or self-discovery; and the anti-interpretive stance informing numerous ideas and practices, including a preference for metonymy over metaphor, a distrust of abstraction and interpretation, and the use of his trademark lists to register the "isolate flecks" of experience.

Still, understanding either Sorrentino's philosophy and/or his modernist program does little to prepare one for the wild ride that is his art. What does that art actually look like? The simplest way to answer this is through his idea of obsession. One apparent paradox of Sorrentino's aesthetic is that he insists that art is artificial and impersonal, a matter of selection, while at the same time encouraging the artist to confront his obsessions, whether artistic or strictly personal. In *Imaginative Qualities* the narrator, who shares many of his author's opinions, asks, "Do you think for a moment that an artist selects his theme? It is all simple obsession" (61). The exact wording is instructive. The artist may select his techniques, and if he is skillful, he will wield them with rigor and detachment. But if he is also honest, he may "select" his themes no more than he may choose his memories and lifelong obsessions. Thus Sorrentino's art contains numerous motifs (e.g., unfaithful wives, dead mothers, and grandmothers of superlative wretchedness; sexualized cars; Christmas trees and tin pigs; toy zeppelins; lonely corners and departing buses; impotence; corsets and other feminine underthings; photographs; art parties; and so on) that appear and reappear with incantatory repetition. It is evident that some of these motifs have real-life models, but because Sorrentino varies his techniques from work to work, his art is neither repetitive nor autobiographical in the conventional sense. He never, that is, offers his readers his life story. What Sorrentino often does instead is recycle and reinvent through repetition, amplification, and juxtaposition the disparate elements of his past, its faces and things, its heartrending processes and emotions, its major emphases as well as its odds and ends. Central to this focus on the past are his Brooklyn relationships with his grandparents, mother, and first wife, as well as with the many acquaintances he met in the art world during the 1950s and 1960s. Just as central, however, are elements of his literary past, which in his view are no less real for being artificial. Hence Sorrentino peoples his later books with characters invented in earlier ones and reimagines images and whole scenes time and again.

Inextricably linked to Sorrentino's obsession with the past is his obsession with loss. People die, love dissolves, things are lost, and the self moves on yet remains still, captivated by imperfect memories that never quite represent the past. Connected to this type of personal loss and psychic paralysis is the linguistic loss that Sorrentino locates in debased forms of language, especially in cliché. Starting with *Steelwork,* his second novel, his fascination for cliché is abundantly clear, and this fascination runs through *Red the Fiend,* where whole conversations are fabricated from cliché without *any* specific information attached, and his most recent novel, *Gold Fools.* The point seems to be that if clichés communicate at all, they do so as ritualized forms rather than as signs pointing to particular referents. More than other linguistic forms, clichés do not represent reality; they point at nothing so much as themselves.

For Sorrentino, this is at once a source of contempt and affection. What he despises is that in saying nothing specific the cliché occludes communication and eventuates in stunted relations with oneself and others, which in turn leads to the inarticulate loss and despair that haunts his characters as well as those of Williams and Nathanael West. By contrast, what Sorrentino loves and hopes to preserve are the specifics assumed by cliché. His recurrent treatment of cliché is, then, a testament to personal and cultural loss as well as an attempt to revivify debased forms of language by paying attention to them as fragile particulars and by giving them meaningful and often brilliantly comic functions. Finally, it is a case of honesty. With Donald Barthelme, Sorrentino shares the belief that it would be dishonest to ignore cliché and other forms of waste when so much of the world is made of the stuff.

A final Sorrentino obsession worth mentioning at this stage is his fetish for metafiction. Though metafictional devices are part of the modernist legacy as handed down from writers like Joyce and Flann O'Brien, their comic use in *Imaginative Qualities of Actual Things, Splendide-Hôtel,* and especially *Mulligan Stew* once made his defiant avant-gardism almost au courant. Indeed, the emphasis he places on the multilayered, self-reflexive artifice seemed oddly in harmony with contemporaries as dissimilar as John Barth, Vladimir Nabokov, Kurt Vonnegut, and even John Gardner. Sorrentino's 1980s fiction, however, makes it clear that these resemblances are the accidents of art history. Modernism initiated the slow questioning of linguistic structures and conventions that eventuated in the popular metafiction of the 1970s. Thus a determined modernist like Sorrentino quite naturally found his way to metafiction, but what is more indicative of his sensibility is that he kept going, pushing metafiction to a kind of limit in the novels that form the trilogy *Pack of Lies*. Not only do *Odd Number, Rose Theatre,* and especially *Misterioso* resemble no other metafiction, they do not even resemble each other. What I am driving at, then, is that the postmodernism practiced by Sorrentino is an extension of modernism, modernism by another name. The deconstruction of linguistic authority, of truth and fact, is implicit to his modernism from the start and remains so, for it is crucial to his antiessentialist worldview. If Sorrentino is a postmodernist, then, he is so almost incidentally, for he never accepts the typical "postmodernist program," which is far more political or "humanist" than his modernism, which is contingent on the notion of artistic autonomy. Indeed, to say that Sorrentino is apolitical is to understate the matter. Even his most political writings are first and foremost aesthetic manifestos. In *Splendide-Hôtel,* for instance, he critiques political language as a corrupt congeries of cliché in the service of power and offsets that corruption in a small, private way by creating a thing of delicacy and beauty. Even Sorrentino's most opaque works share this aesthetic agenda, namely, to discredit cliché and other degenerate forms through the creation of art.

What follows, then, is an attempt to come to grips with seven of Sorrentino's most impressive and often underrated works by perceiving them as products of his modernist sensibility and by continually relating these works to his larger oeuvre. The discussion is divided into two main sections. The first examines *Splendide-Hôtel, The Orangery,* and *Under the Shadow,* while the second contemplates *The Sky Changes, Steelwork, Aberration of Starlight,* and *Red the Fiend.* Each of the fictions in the first group consists of a series of interlinked vignettes that largely dispenses with character development and a consistent narrative line. Thus these works foreground Sorrentino's emphasis on formal invention and penchant for impersonality and artificiality. By contrast, the novels of the second group appear to do the opposite and, partly because they contain consistent characters and obvious autobiographical elements, may be misread as conventional realism. In both sections, however, I emphasize the contradictory aspects of Sorrentino's sensibility, which result in artworks of subtlety and complexity, artworks that ultimately elude easy categorization. For example, if *Under the Shadow,* a metafiction, at first appears utterly impersonal, a case of "pure art," on second glance it betrays an interest in Sorrentino's most personal obsessions and even contains consistent characters. Similarly, in *Red the Fiend,* the characters are not only consistent, they are schematic, their ultraconsistency betraying a sadistic, unrealistic flatness. Once a novel like *Red the Fiend* reveals its basic antirealism, it is easier to perceive its cold, impersonal structure, which depends on repetition and such signature techniques as the list and the question-answer format. If the novels in the latter group seem realistic, it is not because they are not artificial or innovative or because they fulfill realism's psychological requirements, but rather because they accrete a vast number of accurate historical details.

Splendide-Hôtel, The Orangery, and *Under the Shadow*

Splendide-Hôtel was first published in 1973. The first thing that stands out about the work is its alphabetical structure, which is peculiar to the point of ostentation. Each chapter save one in this prose fiction (to call it a novel would stretch that term to meaninglessness) takes a single letter as its departure and focus. Such a precious conceit seems destined for failure, which may be why Sorrentino, who has admitted that he is "absolutely obsessed by the idea of failing miserably" (O'Brien 26), chose it, i.e., for the formal challenge, like deciding in advance to write a collection of sonnets each containing the word "orange," as he does in *The Orangery*. But above his love of artifice and his habit of inventing formal problems is his desire to make an art that sings, that works in barely perceptible ways. That the book *does* work was the opinion of most reviewers, although Sorrentino was predictably chided for using an arty structure, i.e., for neglecting the "principle that form extends from content" (McPheron 147). One reason for *Splendide-Hôtel*'s success is that its alphabetical structure and linguistic theme suit each other. Another is that Sorrentino painstakingly builds his interlinked vignettes until each one is dense with words and images that operate on multiple levels.

Before continuing, it helps to consider precisely what Sorrentino means when he asserts that form determines content, which might sound as much like a chicken-or-egg argument as its more popular converse were it not for the particulars of his meaning. Art begins as an idea or impulse within the writer. Even an adherent of automatic writing, one of Sorrentino's *bêtes noires,* begins either with the idea that such a method is a sensible way to approach the task of writing or with the sheer impulse to write, to write *now*. In other words, no art begins as form, which Sorrentino defines as the plastic, objective being of art, its appearance and sensuous surface. The form of art is the artist's objective, but because the artistic process contains so much of the spontaneous, he does not know exactly what that form will look like, what it will reveal, until it manifests itself on the page. This revelation is the content of the piece. By necessity, content exists within a viewer's mind and is subject to variations from viewer to viewer, whereas the form, physical marks on a page, remains fixed. So how does one get from an idea of form to perceived form, i.e., content? By way of technique, which also begins as an idea before becoming a kinetic, and somewhat unruly, tool of the writing process. Thus Sorrentino has described the creation of *Crystal Vision* as follows:

All I can say about my books—*Blue Pastoral,* for instance, being a rewrite of *The Sky Changes, Crystal Vision* of *Steelwork,* etc., is that I have always attempted to achieve a formal pattern decided upon before I write, that is, I don't start with the idea for a story, I start with the idea for realizing a form, e.g. how to write *Steelwork* again by using the Tarot as an organizing principle and bleeding out the temporal, while shuffling the spatial as needs dictate. OK, then I have all my *Steelwork* characters, plus all those amazing Tarot images—let's see what will happen if the two are put together. (Andrews 66)

What may surprise those who view Sorrentino as the ultimate technician, a latter-day Poe, is how integral romantic "unruliness" is to the process. Phrases like "as needs dictate" and "let's see what will happen" indicate the room he leaves for play and other mysteries. He wants a design, but it should be of the artist's own invention, and it should be "permissive of and conducive to compositional freedom" (Laurence 1):

> In Isaac Babel's famous story "Guy de Maupassant," he writes, "A phrase is born into the world both good and bad at the same time. The secret lies in a slight, an almost invisible twist. Turn your hand, getting warm, and you can only turn it once, not twice." It is that turn, that one and only turn, that I try to effect in my sentences. When the turn is just right, the sentence "works," and when it's not, the sentence is but a conveyor of information. The kicker in Babel's sentence, of course, is the remark "not twice," by which I take him to mean that the second turn is the application of craft and "professionalism" to rescue what is essentially dead. ("Sudden Diction")

In sum, Sorrentino begins with a technical "idea for realizing a form," a form that at that point is no more than raw cognition. He then lets the process unfold much as one might read a book: he waits patiently, careful not to destroy through overanalysis whatever is good in the piece, curious to see what happens.

Sorrentino has memorably described "what happens" in interviews and in "The Act of Creation and Its Artifact" (1984). In the latter he characterizes the artist-at-work in romantic terms as a semimagical being who resides within the quotidian man until the commencement of the creative process; during this process, the artist reveals to himself and others knowledge he did not know he knew (*Something* 3-12). Whatever romanticism is in evidence here is, first, consistent with his essentialist aestheticism, which remains in tension with his antiessentialist worldview, and second and more important, indicates that Sorrentino is not simply a "cold formalist" as has been purported. He does not set to writing knowing everything in advance, nor does he take a set of forms and place them "atop" content or theme—which is a bizarre, impractical idea of what an artist with formalist inclinations actually does. Reviewers who chasten Sorrentino for neglecting that "form extends from content" are themselves neglecting his use of terminology and thus spouting nonsense. How could content determine artistic form if content is defined as form perceived? Such a scenario would require a viewer whose perception of the physical artwork precedes that work rather than proceeds from it. Such critics are also neglecting that Sorrentino's overall aim differs from what they obviously think every writer's aim should be. Whereas they think that writers should, first and foremost, say something *about* something, he thinks that writers should make art.

So Sorrentino remains open during the creative act—open to themes and obsessions that return throughout his work as well as to momentary impulses. He also remains open to whatever elegant correspondences his preconceived design might wring from such obsessions. Sorrentino illustrates this process as it applies to *Splendide-Hôtel* in "The Act of Creation." Much as Poe in "The Philosophy of Composition" explains the intention and methods informing "The Raven," Sorrentino here explains the intention and methods behind the chapter titled "R" in *Splendide-Hôtel*. His point, however, differs from Poe's in that he is telling his reader that no rational account of the process will explain exactly how he came upon his graceful conclusion.

Like so much of the book, the chapter focuses on Rimbaud. It begins with Sorrentino describing the letter R as a maritime pennant since the letter derives from a Phoenician letter, which in turn reminds him of Phoenicia's legendary sailing tradition. Sorrentino then ascribes to the consonant his favorite color, orange. This serves as a bridge to Rimbaud, the synaesthete who describes the color of vowels in his celebrated "Voyelles" and to whom Sorrentino thus refers as "the monarch of colors" (43). "In the context of this work," he writes, the letter R "stands for the poet's very name." The chapter then suddenly shifts to Sheila Henry, a character "borrowed" from *Imaginative Qualities*. In that book she was a false poetess; in this one, she is a false novelist, author of "The Orange Dress," which concerns Cecil Tyrell, a *poète maudit*. Sorrentino makes clear that Sheila is as self-aggrandizing as ever. Though she writes her celebrated novel in "great bursts of energy, thirty or forty pages at a time," she maintains her pose as a fussy-aesthete by telling an interviewer that "I write very slowly, and I'm happy to do a good page in a day" (42). Once again, art is mere plaything, an occasion to play the artist, which results in art's corruption. Sorrentino closes the chapter by returning to the silent integrity of Rimbaud, the original *poète maudit* who, in pointed contrast with Sheila, turns his back on the art world, its oysters and Chablis, before his twentieth birthday. "At this point," Sorrentino notes in "The Act of Creation," "I stuck" (11). He does not know how to close the chapter but senses the presence of an ending, if only he can find it. Or remember it: "Buried in the detritus of my mind was the dim recollection of something—but what?—something I had long ago read in a biography of Rimbaud, the celebrated study by Enid Starkie." Following his intuition, Sorrentino looks up the reference, and sure enough, there it is: having given up on art, Rimbaud *sailed* to Java on *The Prince of Orange*. The chapter is thus provided the information to "snap it shut as well as coherently incorporate the elements I had already composed." Sorrentino takes a closed, impersonal pattern, the alphabet, and opens it up, allowing it to fuse with his themes, linguistic degradation and rebirth, and his own personal fetishes, e.g., Rimbaud, Sheila Henry, orange, etc., all while remaining sensitive to the words and images that will create a delicate vignette within a work of increasing density.

What is so striking about *Splendide-Hôtel* is that it is Sorrentino's most politicized statement as well as one of his most impassioned, yet this aesthetic Jeremiad is couched within the coldest of conceits. At once a sincere social critique and a subtle work of art, it masquerades as "mere" frivolity, begging to be mocked and misunderstood, as when, in the chapter devoted to the letter C, the narrator describes being showered with Coca-Cola upon reading a poem to an audience that prefers rock and roll (12). Like its author, then, *Splendide-Hôtel* is stubborn, displaying the intransigence of a man who will *not* abandon his "egoistic mumblings" and write "a manifesto that all may understand," a man who unlike Leo Kaufman in *Imaginative Qualities* does not end up a commodity like Coca-Cola and rock music. Like all manifestos, *Splendide-Hôtel* has a message, namely, that a culture whose main commodity is cliché is spurious and unhealthy:

A culture that can give no sustenance, and yet the remedies are for still more "useful skills." Useful skills, and the heart dies, the imagination crippled so that mere boys are become mass murderers or drift blindly into a sterile adulthood. The young, the young! In a stupendous rage of nonbelief—faced with a spurious culture, the art that can give life sullied or made unavailable. What art there is is cheap and false, dedicated to a quick assay of the superficial. Don't believe for a moment that art is a decoration or an emblem. It is what life there is left, though ill-used, ill-used. The young crying for nourishment, and they are given the cynical products of the most fickle market. "Look at what passes for the new," the poet says. Put a handle on it and sell it, cotton candy: to be gone in a moment and leave no memory other than the memory of sickening sweetness.

Well, so the country is dying and against its death I can do—nothing. What little I have to offer, all find useless. A government of scoundrels, a people numb with hatred and fear. Against it, I write, and write what? B? Betty Boop. Boop-boop-a-doop. Babel. Babble. The false poet has written a false novel, the language further corrupted. This rubbish will sour and destroy the soil. I write B. (9)

That Sorrentino invokes Williams here as "the poet" is apt, for *Splendide-Hôtel* has taken up the central task of *In the American Grain* and *Paterson,* artworks that diagnose the American condition by pointing to its linguistic history, that try to reverse the corruption therein the only way possible, through the creation of artistic integrity one precise, if seemingly frivolous, letter at a time. This is the point of *Splendide-Hôtel:* to make the reader see the language, which, because it is so easy to neglect during the quotidian rush, is prone to blight and casual dysfunction. On the representational level, the book provides example upon example of that dysfunction, while the book's lyricism, density, and structure are offered as antidotes neither cheap nor superficial—though Sorrentino intentionally invites the opposite judgment. He knows that a cursory glance at the book's alphabetical structure could, during the Vietnam era, be interpreted as self-indulgence, a contrivance lacking in seriousness. Nothing is further from the truth.

Like *The Orangery* and *Under the Shadow, Splendide-Hôtel* succeeds despite its abandonment of characterization and narrative development. Integral to the success of the three works is that they offer a compact system of vignettes, each a pleasure and a surprise in itself. Conventional suspense or a consistent storyline are not required to carry the reader along. The suspense lies in the invention: What will the next segment bring? In *Splendide-Hôtel* one segment provides a list of schmaltzy WWII-era songs. Another a letter to Rimbaud reimagined as a private in the American army. Another a scorecard from a baseball game in which a virtuoso pitcher records twenty strikeouts against an all-star team of politicians and politically minded writers, hacks who take their hacks. There are poems from Sorrentino as well as from others like Rimbaud and Williams. There are fake book blurbs and bits of "real" critical analysis. If any one segment disappoints, a rarity to be sure, there is no chance for boredom, for the length of each vignette will not permit it. Sorrentino has noted that, since he has trouble bringing off long poems, he instead writes serial poems, i.e., cycles of short, lyrical poems, and I believe the same principle is at work in his decision to break so many of his prose works into vignettes. Though these provide no storyline per se, they do provide a structural development that the larger work slowly teaches its reader to read. "R" provides an example of this sort of development. The chapter gradually builds the significance of its motifs through passion and subtle irony—as when Sorrentino allows Sheila to use orange, his favorite color, in the title of a mediocre novel that corrupts the linguistic soil. More important, "R" is one interesting element in an interactive system. As "B" indicates, the falsity of the popular novel is thematically established well before the reader arrives at "R," as is the regenerative significance of Rimbaud and his fellow poet, Williams.

As motifs, Rimbaud and Williams meet on several occasions, the last being in "W," which begins with the author bemoaning the fact that people love Rimbaud for the wrong reasons, that is, for his boorish behavior, his tantrums and moods (55). "In these external 'realities' they purported to see the artist," Sorrentino writes, "So that the artist becomes a waiter who deftly and unobtrusively serves what is ordered." This passage resonates in barely perceptible ways with others from *Splendide-Hôtel,* including the section in which Sheila is given what she wants, oysters and Chablis and flattery, by a waiter as she gives her interviewer what he wants, her external "reality" as a fussy, Nabokovian aesthete. Sorrentino then segues, using the artist-waiter metaphor as an excuse to discuss the waiters painted by his friend, Morton Lucks. Lucks's paintings represent a triumph of imagination in that his waiters, defeated men, are neither real nor realistic, yet they still affect our perception of reality, teaching us "to 'read' the activities of 'real' waiters acutely." "This subtlety," Sorrentino asserts, "is the artist's entire achievement. Through the employment of the imagination he lays bare the mundane." This in turn allows him to segue yet again into what I take to be the point of the chapter, a quotation from "To Elsie," perhaps Williams's greatest poem:

The painter, who may have seen the necessity for his project in the brief, single turn of a waiter's wrist, must certainly agree with the poet who writes, in a work specifically concerned with the imagination:

> It is only in isolate flecks that
> something
> is given off

So I come again to Williams, another w for this chapter.

William Carlos Williams was eight years old when Arthur Rimbaud died. It pleases me to see a slender but absolute continuity between the work of the damned Frenchman and the patronized American. (56)

Readers familiar with *Imaginative Qualities* will recognize the Williams reference as crucial both to Sorrentino's aesthetic and to the narratives themselves, in which the idea of "isolate flecks" is both a method of seeing a larger reality through an art of miniscule specifics, e.g., "the turn of a waiter's wrist," as well as a failed roman à clef by the poet-turned-waiter, Leo Kaufman, himself an isolate fleck. In other words, Sorrentino not only builds his motifs across each chapter and across each work but across his entire corpus. Even the reference to waiters, which is less important than the idea of "isolate flecks" or that of Rimbaud, resonates in this way. *Imaginative Qualities,* a work dedicated to Lucks, contains allusions to artists whose greed and ambition make them waiters serving their audience. More substantively, *Corrosive Sublimate* contains a poem called "The Insane Waiters" that is dedicated to "Mort." There waiters are metonyms of the self-destructive greed by which a culture consumes itself. Though garbage themselves, the waiters "are the entire world before us,/supplying, supplying the goods, the good/so good, good goods" (22). Thus we readers find ourselves back in Williams's native New Jersey, where sky and earth are cultural excrement, and "we degraded prisoners/destined/to hunger until we eat filth" (17). What Williams does not say directly is that we *enjoy* such filth, so Sorrentino says it for him decades later in *Under the Shadow*. In "Waiter" debased waiters oblige their hip clientele by urinating on them, but only if given advance notice. Like that of "W," the comedy is precise, accurate, and sad.

Rest assured I could have chosen "M" or "P" or most any chapter from *Splendide-Hôtel* and found equally rich ground to dig up. Believing the "great unwhispered secret" that great writers "have only a fistful of ideas" (*Something* 100), Sorrentino works with relatively few themes but transmits them through numerous motifs, motifs that are repeated and varied chapter to chapter. Consequently, almost every sentence of *Splendide-Hôtel* bursts with multiple levels of significance, each a gloss on the common themes of corruption, loss, and artistic regeneration. The same is basically true of *The Orangery,* where the burden of meaning shifts from the sentence to the short poetic lines Sorrentino writes at midcareer. As with *Splendide-Hôtel,* the structure of the book at first seems precious: the book contains seventy-eight poems, all turning on the almost unrhymable word *orange*. The greatest of these poems is the finale, "The Crown," which consists of seven sonnets, each line of which borrows from other poems in the collection. Each of the preceding seventy-seven poems is a single sonnet containing heavily stressed lines of an irregular meter and rhyme scheme. The uniformly positive reviews of *The Orangery* were less tentative than those of *Splendide-Hôtel,* despite the works' common emphasis on artifice. When *The Orangery* appeared in 1978 (some of the sonnets made earlier appearances in *A Dozen Oranges* (1976) and *White Sail* (1977)), reviewers praised the artifice of the structure and noted how deftly it interpenetrated its content. While the reviewers were correct—there is a consensus that *The Orangery* is the masterpiece among Sorrentino's poetry collections, a sentiment that Sorrentino himself shares (McPheron 34)—the contrast with their tentative praise of equally artificial prose works like *Splendide-Hôtel* and *Under the Shadow* suggests a poet is automatically given wider latitude for innovation and artifice than a prose writer.

Or it may be that *The Orangery* is a finer, more haunting example of Sorrentino's art. *Splendide-Hôtel* concerns the present, i.e., the early seventies, an era so politicized that even detached aesthetes were driven to write manifestos. By contrast, *The Orangery* concerns the past. It invents the poet's past by recombining its elements—his boyhood, adolescence, disastrous first marriage, etc.— and offers one gaudy, decontextualized image after another for the reader to interpret and enjoy. Were it not for the comedy and colors that Sorrentino uses to balance the darkness, the poetry would be overwhelmingly black, for the central point is loss: of innocence and virginity, of mother, wife, family, and friends, of moments and things. Connected to this emphasis on the past is the blunt antiessentialism, best evoked in the sonnet "To William Bronk." These two aspects of *The Orangery* are welded by artifice. The bright, steely surfaces of *The Orangery* are the persistence of hope and effort in the hard, iron world. At the same time, they are one with that world insofar as the unforgiving lines recognize that human value is, like the text itself, an artificial projection of hope, desire, and love. The most complex signifier in the text is the central one, the word *orange,* which Sorrentino uses so often as a psychic counterweight to loss and despair that it quite appropriately comes to signify those things as well as its primary referents, hope, desire, love, and artifice. Thus *orange* synthesizes all the text's main ideas into one profoundly contradictory whole.

Though *The Orangery* is replete with autobiographical information, Sorrentino has no intention of regaling us with a poetic memoir. Nor is his purpose to "redeem" a past that, because it has been fixed by death, is beyond redemption. His central purpose is to salvage the *present* by making something hard and beautiful—and thus necessarily artificial and impersonal—from the rubbish of a past that is his ongoing obsession. How much of the text is "true" to Sorrentino's actual past is impossible to ascertain. What is certain, however, is that the poems revisit images that recall the author's past as invented in several other texts. Hence we see images from a boyhood and adolescence that resemble those of *Steelwork, Aberration of Starlight,* and *Red the Fiend.* The book opens with "1939 World's Fair," which itself opens by stressing the persistence of memory: "I still hear those azure carillons/floating from the Belgium building/caroming off the Trylon/and the Perisphere" (11). The speaker's memory of himself as a boy recalls Billy Recco of *Aberra-*

tion, and his mother recalls Billy's mother, Marie Recco. It may be that writing *The Orangery,* whose publication preceded that of *Aberration* by a year, sparked the ideas that inform the novel that followed. The abrupt death of the speaker's mother in "1939 World's Fair" marks the first instance in which the past is connected to loss in *The Orangery*. The second poem, which begins, "Everybody would soon change/or die," repeats the connection, creating the text's dominant pattern (12).

Obviously, Sorrentino is not interested in subtlety when it comes to death, which he has called the single abiding fact of life. Instead, he invests his whole industry into the language and his motifs, the subtlety and density of which mark an advance over the techniques of *Splendide-Hôtel* and other collections of interconnected poems such as *The Perfect Fiction* (1968). The difficulty of reading these motifs is already apparent in the second poem, which jars the reader in its second stanza by referring to ideas and images impossible to synthesize on first encounter:

> Thin dreams of my "new life"—
> gone, gone. Thank God
> all dreams are rubbish.
> If they were not? A smell of rose oil. (12)

The end of the stanza presents a reader's block. Why "rose oil"? The peculiar function of this motif cannot be understood on a first reading unless one has read other Sorrentino works such as *Aberration,* in which Tom Thebus wears rose oil on his hair only to be mimicked by Billy, who considers its scent the "palpable manifestation of a world of beauty and delight" (4). Rose oil is one of many cultural signals by which Tom tells women like Marie that he is prosperous and attractive, thus inflaming her desire as a divorcée and Billy's as a fatherless child. Naturally, their hopes prove "fruitless" in *Aberration,* for rose oil is a pathetic commodity that cannot long hide the fact that Tom is a small-minded schmuck. But what if one has not read *Aberration?* In that case one must wait until the twenty-fifth poem, "Mr. America last seen crossing the road." There "Mr. America" is a Thebus-like figure whom the poem freezes in a moment of permanent departure, i.e., the moment in which he bursts the hopes inspired in part by "eau de Rose," "Rum and Maple," "white shoes," and a "burnt-orange slack suit" (36). Through this and subsequent reappearances of the rose motif, one may wheedle meaning from image, with rereading a necessity if one is to grasp the earlier poems fully. But even this is to reduce something whose poetic import remains beyond articulation, for the word *rose* in *The Orangery* is provided with suggestiveness by a myriad of sister motifs that refuse to stand still. For example, there is "Mexicali Rose," a woman who tends her roses in an invented Texas. Named for a popular song from the 1920s, Mexicali Rose reminds the narrator of women from his past, as do other fanciful women in *The Orangery* such as "Betsy Pink" and "Madame Mystère" (also referred to as "Madame Mystèro"). Of course, the narrator is not Sorrentino himself, and the women who obsess him are hardly ciphers of actual women. What can be said is that the rose motif is both touching and elaborate, and if its significance cannot, thank God, be pinned down, it can nevertheless usually be traced back to the book's fascination with the elusive past.

Another crucial "character" in *The Orangery* is the moon. In poem after poem, the narrator gazes at the "blank" moon only to see faces from the past. This, too, is consistent with other Sorrentino texts. For instance, in *Under the Shadow*, an astronomer named Dr. Leflave is pushed to insanity when he looks at the moon through a telescope and sees his dead parents in a bizarre sexual situation (25-26; 111-12). In *The Orangery* the moon motif is introduced in the fifth sonnet, "Fragments of an Old Song 1." The narrator recalls a stop by an Alabama cotton field with his children and wife during a trip; they are slathered in moonlight. Later, the moon appears in "Cento," this time in connection with Mexicali Rose as well as with the Alabama scene and its "white and snowy cotton" (29). What does Mexicali Rose have to do with the moon? As devices, Mexicali Rose and the moon share crucial thematic functions, for both are ways of evoking the past and its solipsistic hold on the speaker. In "Mansion of the Moon," the motifs come together. In that poem the speaker notes that "We can almost see right through the moon" (24), and Mexicali Rose is whom he sees when looking through it—and like Madame Mystère, Mexicali Rose is in turn a woman in whose face he glimpses other faces. Without sunlight, reality loses much of its objective detail and personality, which allows memory to spread the ache of subjective need and desire over all and sundry. The moon, which the narrator often characterizes as blank and white (e.g., 39, 48, etc.), yields easily to this solipsistic process. With its "hundred perfect faces" (43), the moon is an empty screen upon which the narrator projects face memory, personality, and desire.

At the center of this process is the poet's awareness that the objective world does not care about his needs and is not altered by the frenzied machinations of his subjective consciousness. He communicates this knowledge in dozens of poems, most efficiently in "To William Bronk." This poem repeats the anti-interpretive sentiment of *White Sail*'s "September in Kittery" but with a darker spin. Instead of a "white sail/On the Sound off Connecticut" (55), the incom-

parable beauty of which can only be lost through metaphor, we are
shown a "cottony and juiceless orange," which naturally the embittered narrator insists is a "cottony and juiceless orange" and nothing else:

> What did one expect the world to be?
> The world is eminently fair.
> What a bitter taste that leaves.
> If one could only rail against it. (74)

Thus the speaker's idealism ends in cynical bitterness—as displayed through his use of negative details, which ironically undercuts the objective tone that the poem pretends to take. Theodicy,
which makes cruelty, idiocy, mud, and evil part of a benevolent design, the speaker depicts as a desperate sophism, an attempt to redeem humanity's place in a world of iron neutrality. If all human
values are empty signifiers, all is quite literally "fair" in the sense
that no one "deserves" anything and all fates are equally arbitrary.
Suddenly the poem reveals the irony in the title of *The Orangery*'s
first poem, "1939 World's Fair." As a naïf, the speaker looked on the
fair as a "Magic land," the product of a nation that like himself still
believed in progress. But ironically, the loss of these ideals is en-
coded in the project's name from the start. Adding subtlety and contradiction to this darkness is the fact that the poem, which insists
on an anti-interpretive, antimetaphorical stance, communicates
through metaphor: the world *is* a cottony, juiceless orange. This is a
gloss on a metaphor established earlier in "Remember the story of
Columbus and the orange?" Whether or not the contradiction is intentional is difficult to gauge. Regardless, it is in accord with contradictions seen elsewhere. The speaker's disdain for metaphor is
rooted in his belief that the trope is false and artificial in a world in
which things are what they are despite our hopes and dreams,
which so rarely accept the world as is. In other sections of *The
Orangery,* however, falsehood and artificiality, as well as hopes and
dreams, are seen as essential, even inevitable, aspects of existence.
The speaker therefore does not always meet them with the blunt
contempt of "To William Bronk." Perhaps by using metaphor to
drive home an antimetaphorical statement, the author is purposely
undercutting his speaker's bitterness, in effect telling his reader
that though metaphor is false, it is also inescapable.

The subtle contradictions that add wholeness to the bitterness of
"To William Bronk" also inform a much more complex and central
aspect of *The Orangery,* the word *orange* itself. Three times the narrator refers to himself as "immured in a situation symbolized by
orange" (19, 93, 94). By "situation," I take him to mean the whole of

life, the world, everything. Thus in the elegiac "A Word for Paul Goodman" the narrator notes it "is not the beautiful/one wants to save but save it all," to which he adds, "These oranges hold it all" (80). How can an unprepossessing word like *orange* encompass the complexity of human experience? The only way to answer this is to look at the rich and varied ways in which Sorrentino uses the word. First, he uses it in the title and in each poem as a playful source of unity and shape. Next, in a book in which color is *almost* as important as idea, he uses orange as the gayest daub on his palette, a sweet spot balancing the visual tones of a book containing so many grays and blacks. This, of course, is allied to the conceptual balance provided by orange. In *The Orangery* gray and black are associated with depression, cruelty, nothingness, pain, death, loss; most crucially, they are associated with reality itself. By contrast, orange is allied with love, sweetness, anaesthesia, hope, and more crucially, art and artifice. This final association is implicit from the start in a book in which *orange* is used in every poem. The different colors, then, evoke a set of intellectual opposites in tenuous equipoise.

This visual and conceptual play is apparent in "Provence," a poem haunted by the memory of Paul Blackburn. "Provence" begins by twice invoking the gray, impressionist misery of sleet and rain and ends by twice referring to brightness and love:

> orange love seems what it always was,
> impossible
>
> and orange, love, seems
> what it always was. (69)

The sonnet achieves visual balance, the two light orange stanzas precisely offsetting the grays of the heavier first two stanzas. By contrast, the poem at first seems conceptually imbalanced, with the miserable grays crushing the sweet oranges, and calling into question the very possibility of love through the fanciful mirage, "orange love." But if the poem teeters on the edge of total conceptual oblivion, it never quite falls over, for the final stanza must be read in a number of different ways at once. The first is dark: "and orange, *i.e.,* love, seems what it always was, *i.e., impossible.*" But two other readings insist on the reality of love. The first is simply a twist on the dark reading: "and orange, love, seems what it always was, *i.e., love.*" The second is brighter yet, since it implies a conversation with a loved one whose very presence confirms love's reality: "and orange, *my dear* love, seems what it always was, *i.e., love.*"

These readings must not be thought of as mutually exclusive, for that would vitiate Sorrentino's vision of a world alive with contra-

diction—a world most directly and playfully invoked in the non se-
quiturs of "Seminar" and paradoxes of "To David Antin." The darker
terms dominate the visual and conceptual dynamics of "Provence,"
which suits the death-obsessed *Orangery* as a whole. To keep black
from "winning" the game, however, Sorrentino enthusiastically
fixes the fight, placing a point of color in every poem, which subverts through color the idea proclaimed by so many of the poems,
i.e., that life is a grayness that terminates in utter blackness.

What really keeps the tension alive and active is the fact that
artifice and reality are no more exact opposites than orange and
black. "Nothing is the thing that rhymes with orange," the speaker
repeats, and he means it conceptually as well as sonically: nothingness has affinities with artifice and love. The poems tell us that
though they are artificial they are also real, one with the reality
they decorate. For that reason, they embrace pain and darkness.
Thus the poems juxtapose orange and black so frequently that the
colors come to imply one another. Life is bittersweet. If there is always "a dead fly" in one's orangeade, there is, likewise, always some
color in the darkness of America (46, 40). At the same time, the poems recognize that artifice is *not* "realistic." The power of artifice to
reflect reality is in the most unflinching analysis the power to refract and invent. The poems delight in acknowledging this through
fanciful surfaces and bizarre characters. Still, this recognition in no
way undercuts the reality of these illusions. It only undercuts their
truth value. The speaker's "images persist snow crystals/brilliant
upon this iron world" because his memories and poems are constructed from the same iron stuff as the world (95). Art is necessity,
as are love and hope. We do not choose them. They are also necessary, morphine in a world of hurt. Hence drunks "cry with shame
and delight/for a miserable dime they get that/putrid muscatel they
fill their heads/with buzzing and crippled memory all/orange orange orange orange" (70).

Published thirteen years after *The Orangery*, *Under the Shadow*
borrows many of the techniques of *Splendide-Hôtel* and *The
Orangery* while taking the latter's emphasis on contradiction and
antirealism several crucial steps further. Like those works, *Shadow*
consists of a series of interdependent vignettes, each entitled by a
single noun such as "Tree" or "Hat." Like those works, *Shadow* is
organized according to an external structural principle, with the
fifty-nine vignettes each a gloss on H. A. Zo's drawings for Raymond
Roussel's *Nouvelles Impressions D'Afrique*. And like *The Orangery*
in particular, the work concludes with "Things," a sort of crown that
offers a generalized summary of what has preceded it. Thus
Shadow depends more on the structural and thematic development

of motifs than on narrative and character development, just like *Splendide-Hôtel* and *The Orangery*. What distinguishes *Shadow* from the other two works is the hyperartificiality of the world represented in its pages. While *Splendide-Hôtel* and *The Orangery* delight in juxtaposing imaginary constructs like Rimbaud's Hotel Splendide or "Betsy Pink" alongside the hard-edged things of the actual world, in the end they both concentrate directly on that world. *Shadow,* however, is more consistently surreal, and it is not at first obvious what its focus is. The text assembles an atemporal, off-kilter collage dominated by dreamy tableaux of partially clad women and "spheroids" that recur with disturbing frequency. In this wholly fictive world, the "I" of the author or his proxy disappears altogether, and with it, it seems, any connection to or concern with objective reality. Consequently, it seems we have, as the jacket asserts, entered "the realm of pure art." But this is another of the work's artful illusions, for this uniquely metafictional novel invents subtle new ways to register its lingering obsession with the past, and it offers further insight into Sorrentino's inquiry into the nature of language and its connection to concepts like "fact" and "truth."

Again, like all innovative works, the work insists that the reader read it on its own terms. I once tried to make sense of *Odd Number* by tracing the seemingly random references to each of the many characters, characters that seemed "realistic" because they had been used in semirealistic ways in books like *Imaginative Qualities*. My hope was that these references would add up to a coherent set of relationships, thus revealing the book's "true" plot. I quickly gave up. The thankless project led me deeper into disorder. In *Fact, Fiction, and Representation* Louis Mackey contends that this is part of Sorrentino's strategy in *Pack of Lies:* the author deliberately short-circuits the literary conventions by which truth is thought to manifest itself in novels in order to amplify the fact that truth and fact are *never* literally made manifest by an art of representation. In *Shadow,* his first book after *Misterioso,* Sorrentino embraces a similar challenge, but on a smaller scale and using different methods. Unlike the more radical *Misterioso,* the book contains characters whose presence tempts the reader into expecting a fully realized plot. Again, *that* plot never materializes. There are dozens of characters, and their incredibly complex interrelations preclude the emergence of a unitary narrative. Still, this does not suggest that one should dispense with conventional reading techniques altogether. Though character references are arranged more for their formal value than their psychological (or "realistic") value, several characters develop through a subtle rounding process that humanizes what at first seem like the flattest of characters.

Jonathan Tancred, the paranoiac who sets fires in a desperate attempt to destroy "official memories" (8), exemplifies my point. At first, the arsonist seems a cartoon. He is suspicious of everything and finds ways to set fires even under maximum security. Tancred's paranoia is also misogynistic. He tortures his psychiatrist, Dr. Sydelle Lelgach, by claiming to see through the "doctor costume" she wears to hide "filthy EVIDENCE" (81). As a result, she becomes increasingly unstable and compulsively pulls down her skirt, a gesture echoed by other female characters. Tancred also influences his fellow patients, who join him in doing his "joy-fire dance" during exercise periods (80). After his transfer from Lelgach's hospital, he tells a committee of psychiatrists that he has taken to wearing a pillowcase-hat so as to protect his brain from the perverted messages of Lelgach, who has an "awful machine between her legs" that generates the messages (121). The final reference to Tancred involves a paranoid, misogynistic letter he has sent to her from his new hospital. While listening to patients dance and chant under Tancred's spell, Lelgach reads the letter, which she had hoped would be a romantic letter from her lover, Stephen Alcott. Realizing her mistake, she experiences nausea, then vomits.

Though ascribing realistic motivations to characters in an anti-realistic fiction is tricky, in this case it is necessary, for it is undeniable that Tancred is made recognizably human. His paranoid monomania clearly derives from sexual frustration and the religious fanaticism that exacerbates it. In this reading, the absolute revulsion that Tancred feels for the "official" past is psychic escapism, a way of eluding the traumatic memory of some nameless event or events that have determined his psychosis. And despite his aggressive behavior, Tancred seems at bottom a vulnerable child; for example, when the committee decides to confiscate his pillowcase-hat, he begins to cry, whining, "I need my hat" (123). But if Tancred is made understandable and human, he is no more a candidate for pity than is Red in *Red the Fiend*. Like Red, he is a sexist as well as a racist, and it is this further dimension that makes him seem more in tune with reality than "the touching victim" so popular in contemporary realism. Many other character histories in *Shadow* can be read in this familiar manner. Clearly, though, characterization is not the crux or the author would have spent more time developing fewer characters. I point to Tancred mainly to suggest that Sorrentino does not necessarily abandon the conventional technique when experimenting with the unconventional. Despite often dismissive statements regarding character, plot, and setting, he usually expands the novel's range through addition rather than

shrink it through subtraction. And if *Shadow* does not totally abandon conventional illusion making, neither does it fail to emphasize
actual reality, though in a less direct manner than *Splendide-Hôtel*
and *The Orangery*.

Like *The Orangery, Shadow* is obsessed with the past in general
and with Sorrentino's past in particular. *Shadow* also registers
many other Sorrentino obsessions, which suggests that its impersonal surface is yet another illusion created from the shards of the
personal. As Tancred's story suggests, *Shadow* approaches such
material from odd angles. The narrator opens "Fire" by noting that
the publishing mogul Emiliano Soreau has already begun figuring
out a way to profit from the destruction of his warehouse by com-
missioning a hack journalist to write a story about the fire,

someone with flair and intelligence and a respect for the public's well-de-
fined taste, someone to evoke the day itself, the events leading up to the
disaster, the people and accidents and coincidences, as well as, of course,
as Mr. Soreau puts it, "the blunders and heartaches, the heroism and cowardice, the self-sacrifice of so many plain, ordinary people, the laughter,
the tears, the joy and the agony, the searing questions and shocking answers, the sober postmortems, the *why.*" His colleagues nod and smile at
the sound of these familiar, comforting words. Once again, they realize
what a wondrous business they serve. (8)

The satirical tone of this narrator differs slightly from that of the
wise-guy narrator of *Imaginative Qualities,* but the object of his satire is often the same: false artists, false publishers, false critics,
false audiences. It is this intertextual recognition that allows one to
locate a greater and basically antipsychological (or antirealistic)
significance in Tancred's madness. As in *The Orangery,* this significance refuses to stand still in the fabled manner of unitary meaning
and depends for its richness on a nexus of motifs. Tancred wants to
destroy the past because he thinks that "official memories," which
he equates with Soreau's inventory of middlebrow fiction, stand in
the way of the new. Razing the warehouse "would allow a new past
to be born, a wholly different past" (8). Tancred's madness sounds
suspiciously similar to that of the modernist artist, who, in burning
down the official literary establishment, blazes a future for art.
However, this more symbolic reading of Tancred's history, which is
no more or less "correct" than the psychological reading already discussed, is in many ways ill-matched with that reading, which shows
Tancred to be completely insane and utterly unconcerned with any
cause beyond the religious fanaticism that sublimates his sexual
desire. What makes this picture stranger and more complex is that
the specific memories Tancred wants to destroy (e.g., of "a blue

metal laundry hamper, a half-opaque-glass bathroom door which would not close completely, a toy zeppelin, and three young women in luminous white dresses by the shore of a dark lake" (8)) include images that, first, *may* refract Sorrentino's actual past, second, definitely recur throughout *Shadow,* and third, resonate with similar images in other Sorrentino texts. In an odd sense, then, Tancred wants to destroy the same materials Sorrentino, a true modernist, uses as material for his own art, which is quite consciously a rejection of official literary conventions. None of this fits together neatly, nor does it seem intended to. Just as the text self-consciously refuses to make a single coherent context from the many characters and their confusing entanglements, it also refuses to forge a single coherent meaning from interconnected details such as these. Thus the text provides more suggestiveness than stability, forcing us to depend more on emphasis, i.e., repetition and variation, than on psychology and symbol.

Two particular images form repetitive patterns that dominate *Shadow.* The first, featuring a seminaked woman washing at a sink, draws on material introduced in *Steelwork.* In a chapter entitled "The Old Witch" a six-year-old boy accidentally barges in on his mother, who, topless and wearing only "step-ins," is washing some underclothes at a bathroom sink. Embarrassed and angry, the mother sends her "dirty" child out into the yard and decides to punish him if he interrupts her again. When the boy, frightened and confused, does so, she plays a trick on him. From behind the door, she tells him that an "old witch" has taken his mother away. Though she doesn't disguise her voice, the agitated boy takes the message literally and falls "on the floor in terror and hysterics" (94). The second pattern, featuring three nubile women in white dresses near a lake, draws on material introduced in "Silences" (see *Black and White).* The poem suggests that the image derives from a picture that hung in the author's childhood household. The import of that image is less clear, particularly since the speaker claims to "know" that the original figures were white "sails," not white dresses—although even that knowledge is modified by a crucial "perhaps." As usual, the meaning of the image may have more to do with the subject beholding it than the reality behind it. Variations on these images appear in other works. *Red the Fiend,* for example, reenacts the naked mother scene (189-90), and "The Disappearance of Oilcloth" reworks the lake scene (*Selected* 256). However, no text repeats these images with the hypnotic frequency of *Shadow,* which contains dozens of variations. The seminal images get broken into barely recognizable bits, as when Alcott, Lelgach's lover, intentionally distorts "a blinding recollection of a strange woman, dressed in a dazzling white dress, or slip, who emerged from the darkness of a closet or cellar to speak to him, in his mother's voice, of the disappearance of his mother" (30). Conversely, they may resemble the seminal image with utter clarity except for a few crucial changes. Hence, in "Mother" a young unhappy mother is washing her breasts at a sink when she notices the confused eyes of her three-year-old at the door (78-79). She ejects him from the house. When he comes back in, she is gone. Has she been kidnapped by an old witch? The text gives no definitive answer.

These and other patterns—a minor one, for example, involves a sexualized toy zeppelin, another seemingly autobiographical element that appears frequently in other Sorrentino works—replace the plot as the novel's primary source of structure. But, as with the story of Tancred, these patterns do not translate into precise symbolic or allegorical messages. Critics like Paul Emmett have applied Freudian theory to texts such as *The Sky Changes,* and the Oedipal scenes that litter *Shadow* would invite the same treatment if the text weren't so self-conscious—and if it didn't mock psychoanalytic jargon and academicisms in general as narrow expressions of the critic's own desires. Apparently, the novel's patterns are to be enjoyed as one enjoys the art of fugue, for the cleverness of the counterpoint and the sheer joy of repetition and variation. Still, while the text provides little in the way of exact allegorical meaning, it is extraordinarily rich in suggestiveness. The particular nature of the patterns suggests an intense fascination with voyeurism. The text concentrates on three types of voyeurism: voyeurism regarding the female form, voyeurism regarding the past, and voyeurism regarding documents and texts. In a text obsessed by the difficulties of reading and perception in general, it is apt that the result of voyeurism is usually guilt and increased confusion.

Of course, the voyeurism is also the reader's, so it is also apt that the reader's desire to understand is destined to end in disquieting confusion if he insists on traditional routes to meaning. A metafiction that routinely refers to language as "false systems of hierarchy and constantly eroding signifiers" (136), *Shadow* is most self-conscious, and most subtle, in this regard. As in *Odd Number,* the incidents described in *Shadow* are destabilized by ambiguities built into their telling. The majority of them are presented to the reader as having been drawn from blurry memories, falsified documents, careless gossip, and outright lies. Heavily subjective methods of communication continually obscure whatever "objective" reality lies behind the incidents. "Clues," an especially opaque vignette about a set of apparently scandalous events puzzled over by a nameless town, ends with one "rather singular piece of information: for each of the clues in and of itself, and for all of them in combination with certain, or all, of the others, there is always to be discovered a person who, aghast, reads in them the hidden secrets of his or her own life" (15). As in *The Orangery,* the subjective consciousness continually projects its past onto other elements of reality in a desperate and ultimately solipsistic attempt to reconnect with that past. Other chapters provide more emphatically self-reflexive comments on the difficulties of seeing and reading. For example, in "Fountain" a seminude woman hiding her bare, soapy breasts behind a tree suddenly reacts "to the importunate encroachments of the prose" that examines and describes her in her hiding spot (43). Self-conscious, embarrassed, she attempts to cover herself. Like her, this sly chapter with its arch allusions to the French symbolist Paul Verlaine is self-conscious in its gestures, all designed to suggest the elementary point that signifiers cannot present, or make *present,* the things of the past that they only more or less represent: "The descriptive prose pokes around behind the trees, which quietly rustle near the 'jets d'eau sveltes,' but the woman is nowhere to be found. The prose describes, and yet again describes, but to no avail. The woman is, simply, not there" (44). Were the chapter to end on that note, it would have little beyond its wit to recommend it. But the final two sentences point to the chapter's broken heart: "Perhaps she never left her bathroom at all, although her son swears that she disappeared forever. At least for him."

Over and over, the book tells us that the language from which it is itself constructed is a series of arbitrary symbols with no essential meaning, just as the things around us are arbitrary objects with no meaning beyond themselves. The final sentence of "Things," the chapter that reprises the whole in generalized terms, sums this up as follows: "The stars, in their trillions, shone on these people and phenomena, on these credos, tears, and *things,* on this vast desire, shone and shone, meaningless" (137). Yet as the ending of "Fountain" indicates, this idea is only half the point. The other half is that loss, pain, and desire have always and will always drive otherwise lucid people to ignore the elementary. Witness Sorrentino, who continually directs his own and others' attention to the past despite his manifest knowledge that such attention cannot produce that past through visual or verbal means. Taken together, these two ideas create a text haunted by an overwhelming futility and pathos. The anonymous "she" who hides behind the tree could refer to the absent mother of Stephen Alcott or of a half dozen other male characters whose mothers disappear; it could even, for that matter, refer to the mother who disappears in *Steelwork* or to Sorrentino's own mother, whose absence is the overt theme of *The Perfect Fiction*. The "she" can function this way because Sorrentino has designed his text and his entire oeuvre to allow it to do so. Why? Partly for purely arbitrary aesthetic reasons. Like many modernists, he finds ambiguity and repetition pleasing in themselves. He also does so because the generalities they imply often ring true. Mothers repeatedly disappear; sons repeatedly search for them to no avail.

Thus we see that the urge to create "pure art," an urge that *Shadow* and the entire Sorrentino oeuvre manifests, is peculiarly if paradoxically suited to the kind of content that *Shadow* conveys. Like their author, the characters repeatedly strain and fail, strain and fail, to find the past and its contents in decontextualized images and repetitive phrases. Sorrentino is suggesting that there is no such content, for there is no such thing as *objective* content, just as there is no such thing as a signifier that makes present its signified. No matter how we poke around, no matter how we stare, whatever meaning we find in the repetitive, contrapuntal images we see outside us is not really there but forever locked inside our heads. On the other hand, what should be obvious is that *Shadow* is not "pure art" if by that designation one means an art purified of meaning or content. The fact that it manifests an urge to create such an art is already enough to make it somewhat "impure." *Shadow* is only relatively "pure" insofar as it clearly seeks to maximize formal pattern and minimize its reliance on conventional representation.

Although Sorrentino does not use the term *pure art* himself, he does use other holdovers from the aesthetic movement such as "art for art's sake" (e.g., O'Brien 27). He also regularly insists on art's uselessness and the primacy of form in a way that might lead one to frame him as an idealistic aesthete. Still, while some of this rhetoric is attributable to his aesthetic idealism, most of it is practical in function. Throughout his career, Sorrentino, like Williams and so many modernists before him, has created a space for himself as a writer of innovative fiction. In this endeavor he has had to battle the whims of the public and the publishing houses that serve it. What this public wants is conventional realism, predictable novels neither innovative nor difficult nor terribly negative. Such novels typically depend on the continuous representation of experience. Sorrentino's aestheticism needs to be placed in this historical continuum. He is not in favor of an art purified of meaning but against a tedious conventionalism that knows but one way to convey its interests. In *Something Said* Sorrentino characterizes his "artistic necessities" as "an obsessive concern with formal structure, a dislike of the replication of experience, a love of digression and embroidery, a great pleasure in false or ambiguous information, a desire to invent problems that only the invention of new forms can solve, and a joy in making mountains out of molehills" (265). Obviously, works like *Splendide-Hôtel, The Orangery,* and *Shadow* are products of such a program. On first glance, they appear artificial not because they are in some absolute sense more artificial than conventional fictions but because readers have been conditioned to associate the term *realistic* with just one type of artifice. That these works highlight artifice by parting with conventional illusions does not, then, mean they exemplify "pure art" in the idealistic sense. Each manifests an interest in reality's patterns, processes, and limits, and each uses conventional forms of representation to achieve its ends. What they do not seek to do is replicate experience through a continuous accretion of psychological details so as to create a reasonable illusion of the passage of time. Nor do they provide "touching" characters and palatable messages. In other words, Sorrentino refuses his reader the interpretive and philosophical comforts of conventional realism.

Sorrentino has never written a novel that might be categorized as conventional in this sense. However, he has written several novels that mimic conventional realism in that they follow a limited set of characters who exist in fairly detailed, specifically American twentieth-century contexts. These novels, which include *The Sky Changes, Steelwork, Aberration of Starlight,* and *Red the Fiend,* are also his most straightforward presentations of autobiographical material. Still, if these works make their concern with American reality and with content in general more obvious than do *Splendide-Hôtel, The Orangery,* and *Shadow,* they are not necessarily less artificial or innovative. It is just that Sorrentino, especially in later works like *Aberration* and *Red the Fiend,* so deftly cloaks his works in illusions of reality that the antirealistic structures basic to each may seem beside the point. This is a misperception. As the next section argues, such structures are in fact crucial to the formal and intellectual achievements of each work.

The Sky Changes, Steelwork, Aberration of Starlight, and Red the Fiend

In *The Sky Changes* Sorrentino transforms the disintegration of his first marriage during a 1960 cross-country trip into the stuff of art. The autobiographical resonance of this first novel is difficult to ignore or dispute and has been confirmed in print by several acquaintances of the author, including Hettie Jones and Robert Creeley. McPheron notes that Sorrentino wrote the first forty pages after his wife left him, which perhaps explains the wrenching immediacy of the writing. This quality is especially obvious in comparison with his other works, most of which place a premium on aesthetic distance even when dealing with personal material. Nevertheless, as Sorrentino reminds us, it is *very* possible to overstate the issue. Though *Sky*'s fatalism is charged by the personal, the dark tone is still a calculated result achieved by the exclusion of any light elements that, regardless of the reality "behind" the book, would have vitiated the overall effect. Indeed, even amidst *Sky*'s lyrical seething, it is evident that Sorrentino has not yielded to automatic writing or the jazzy, Beat techniques that are manifest in his earliest writing (see, for example, "Bordertown," the sketch excerpted by Williams in *Paterson V* (214-15)). Even in his first novel, then, it is possible to find the structural signposts that predict the emergence of a different artist, an innovator who cherishes rigorously structured prose.

The most obvious evidence of this development involves the overall structure. *Sky* is a spatial collage. It juxtaposes a number of different American locales, most of which represent stops on a cross-country journey that the protagonist mistakenly thinks will breathe life into his marriage. Thus a scene from Drakestown, New Jersey, follows one from Memphis, Tennessee, which follows one from Gallup, New Mexico, etc. Though this by necessity makes the chronology nonlinear, the literal sequence of events is easy to determine as one proceeds, so the realistic illusion is not deeply disrupted. The main effect of this structure is to reinforce the book's most striking feature, its fatalism. It does this, first, by revealing the protagonist's bad faith. The protagonist understands the hopelessness of his journey but refuses to confront it, instead choosing the comfort of the warm lies he tells himself and others. The author uses quick cuts in time and space to highlight the protagonist's dishonesty, and the overall effect is to suggest the essential dishonesty of hope itself. The novel's idiosyncratic structure, then, aids characterization and defuses suspense, an effect contingent on the possibility of change. The collage also reinforces the fatalistic tone by connecting the sterility of the protagonist's marriage to that of the American landscape. "I selected specific locales to show specific instances of disintegration," Sorrentino notes in his interview with John O'Brien (9). "It was a conscious attempt on my part to parallel a kind of desperate, sterile quality about this country with the desperate, sterile quality of this marriage."

Another obvious if somewhat less successful departure from convention involves the absence of character names. This, too, is designed to reinforce the overall sense of hopelessness. "The characters are nameless or only have initials for names," Sorrentino notes, "because the characters are all hopeless; they're really dead, they're zombies" (O'Brien 11). The anonymity works well with the husband, wife, children, and driver because each is defined by his or her function in a hopeless situation. As noted by the book's reviewers, the technique works less smoothly with the husband's friends, who are given capital letters (J, C, etc.) in lieu of names. The main problem is that the device sticks out in an otherwise naturalistic narrative. The friends have rudimentary personalities as well as organic roles in the narrative, so the author's contention that giving them names would have given the novel a "cachet of reality which I did not want" (O'Brien 11) seems at odds with the novel itself, which depends on such "cachet" for its effectiveness.

Thus the novel's two most obvious departures from convention do not disrupt the illusions of reality most basic to conventional realism, i.e., those of character psychology and historical context, and all of the innovations are meant to reinforce the crushing sense of changelessness so that the book becomes "a plunge from a dark gray to black" (O'Brien 10). *Steelwork,* Sorrentino's second novel, is more innovative than *Sky* but no less dark and no less reliant on realistic illusions. Like *Sky,* it has a collage structure, but whereas the earlier novel is a spatial collage that jumps from locale to locale but has a fixed central character and a fixed temporal context, *Steelwork* is a temporal collage that jumps from decade to decade and character to character but remains fixed in its spatial context, namely Brooklyn. The effect is to make the Brooklyn neighborhood the central character, or, more precisely, to have the neighborhood fill the function usually filled by such a character. This does not, however, mean that we watch Brooklyn change over time. We neither watch its gradual rise in fortune nor trace it as a figure of decline. Like the husband in *Sky,* the neighborhood is already debased and wounded when the book begins and remains unchanged in that regard throughout. The novel cannot, then, explain the cause of the debasement, which has seemingly existed forever, nor suggest its remedy. Instead, the novel focuses solely on the specifics of the debasement it documents through character vignettes that span the years between 1935 and 1951.

One effect of this narrative strategy is to minimize the illusion of a plot, which depends on change. In *Sky* the central character undergoes great psychological trauma but little development. By the end, he has gained neither wisdom nor despair. But because the reader has a central character to follow through time and space, the illusion of a plot remains even though the collage structure reveals early on that this character will remain static. *Steelwork,* which lacks a human protagonist, disrupts the illusion of plot more fully and is thus more difficult for readers accustomed to conventional fiction. Why does Sorrentino choose a narrative strategy that minimizes narrative? Ultimately because he demands more "actuality" from his work than do conventional realists. In the conventional novel the reliance on plot dictates a reversal, or series of reversals, in the main character's fortune. Thus most stories are either stories of success or failure. The crucial issue facing the writer of such a story is where to begin and end the plot. This is a matter of selection, of artifice, and has little to do with life, which knows no boundaries outside birth and death. At the same time, this artifice, which is untrue to actuality, claims to be realistic. In books like *Steelwork* Sorrentino eschews success and tragedy, which please readers who recognize these ideas as comforting signals of a predictable, comprehensible world. Sorrentino avoids ideas of success and tragedy by creating stories in which the main characters do not change. Thus the stories do not yield "realistic," i.e., conventional, plots. In this regard Williams was Sorrentino's mentor:

His entire body of work is a record of continual observation, of the revelation of what he calls the "isolate flecks" in which the whole meaning of a life, or of a cultural milieu, may be contained. . . . Nothing fooled him for long because he refused to let "ideas" govern his work. He is sprawling, confused, unfinished, and at the same time brilliant, succinct, crafted—and unfailingly, unerringly dark. Not dark with the tragic, but with the endless defeats of life and—nonetheless—its tenacity. Without sentiment about God, politics, love, the working man, nature, the family, marriage, or children, he is yet uncynical. People are born and live in recurrent confusion; the overwhelming majority of their days is wholly without meaning. In America, this happens in a specific way, a way which makes us specifically American. The imagination, only the imagination, Williams says, will free us from the waste and despair that America has hidden under its continual smile. It is the flight, or the heartbreaking attempt at flight, of the imagination that he seeks to pin down and isolate in all his work. (*Something* 23-24)

Sorrentino could be talking about his own work here. According to Sorrentino, the result of Williams's persistence and ingenuity is that works like the Stecher Trilogy have remained unfathomable and unknown, for not even the "the literary" can understand narratives that do not depend on sentimentalized ideas of success or failure.

If Sorrentino has a thematic focus in *Steelwork,* it is the clichés that dominated the novel's Brooklyn milieu during the thirties, forties, and fifties. Because he refuses to submit to literary clichés when examining working-class clichés, Sorrentino refuses to create a conventional plot with conventional characters. Instead, vignette after vignette concentrates on the hollow lives of these Brooklyn characters, most of whom are dominated by petty American ideas of success in romance, war, business, and religion, as well as by the ethnic prejudices that allow even those at the bottom of the socio-economic ladder to feel superior to some group of others. The book also avoids convention by avoiding the didacticism of most social fiction. The detached, analytical novel champions no idea, for like Williams, Sorrentino refuses to let sentimentality of any political stripe govern his work. Neither does he sympathize with characters or places. For example, the book ends with "The Lot," which is dated 1939. In it, a boy eats mickeys in a cold, deserted lot while contemplating the construction equipment that is changing the face of the neighborhood by building parkways, harbingers of a new commuter culture. "It was sad to see the park going" (177), the narrator comments, indirectly conveying the boy's thoughts. It is not possible to read this nostalgia as coming from the author. The vignette, like the book as a whole, shows no sadness at the destruction it limns. What the boy does not realize is that the parkways signal continuity rather than change. They are the visible resurgence of the "American dream" at the end of the Depression, a dream that will profit by the slaughter of the Second World War and the Korean War. The new neighborhood may look different, but it will be driven by the same processes, by the same clichés of success and failure, as the old. The seemingly elegiac ending is, then, a reprise of what goes on throughout the novel: people and places are enslaved to and destroyed by clichés and false cultural signals, and there is little hope for "progress."

This is not to suggest that the book is endlessly dour. *Steelwork* is more comic than *Sky,* though the humor is necessarily black. One of Sorrentino's most successful comic techniques is his signature, the list. The technique, which, because of its emphasis on specificity and concreteness, owes as much to Williams as to Whitman and Joyce, makes its first appearance in *Steelwork* in the chapter "Sexology: 100 Facts." This celebrated compendium of the clichés typical of sexually frustrated boys in Brooklyn, circa 1940, begins with a rather suspect "fact": "If you jerk off you get hairy palms." It ends ninety-nine entries later with "Girls shoot a load like men when they come" (46, 49). Though "Sexology" is a catalog of juvenile misinformation, it is "realistic" insofar as its hilarious clichés and misogynistic distortions are the "isolate flecks" of an actual time and place, bits of Americana "utterly true to the environment they inhabit" (*Something* 118). According to Sorrentino, the naked specific is often funny:

I came to see that a list somehow strips all verbosity from the usual narrative paragraph and distills all that, removes the fact or the truth about Joe Bush from all the impedimenta of his life. Now, if you isolate specific things that way, you often see the comedy in all our absurd pretensions towards civilization and intelligence. . . . The impedimenta of life inhere in narrative and if you can rip all that garbage away and get the fact, you have an odd, comic quality about a man or woman. (O'Brien 19)

Lists isolate flecks of experience without obscuring them through writerly conventions. The list is, then, appropriate to *Steelwork* insofar as the entire novel attempts to avoid literary clichés in order to expose the clichés that dominate its Brooklyn milieu. Since the novel as a whole is clearly about language, and because the novel cannot be read for its conventional plot, "Sexology" is an organic part of the whole rather than an aberrant verbal artifice such as, say, the use of initials in *Sky*. Consequently, Sorrentino reconciles two seemingly polarized aspects of literary form, which is at once something to see through and something to be seen. Through the list, he provides his readers with a clear window onto actual experience without forgetting that words are artifactual, that is, simultaneously artificial and factual. Critics who accuse him of self-indulgence for using such antirealistic techniques implicitly neglect that conventional techniques are always artificial. Artificiality, then, is not a valid criterion for disapproval. The question is not whether to be artificial, but what kind of artificiality suits one's purposes.

Sorrentino often uses variations on the list to complement more conventional narrative techniques of plot and characterization. This is especially true of the three quasi-realistic novels, *Steelwork, Aberration,* and *Red the Fiend,* all of which more or less concern the same historical time period. Consider, for example, the loosely autobiographical character, Grandma. Grandma is one of Sorrentino's most memorable characters. To use a phrase Sorrentino often mocks, she "walks off the page." Because Grandma is often depicted in lists, her characterization over the course of Sorrentino's career provides a case study of his development of the list as a novelistic form. Grandma first appears in *Sky,* where she is referred to as a "woman who had made, who had spent her life making, one perfected hell into which the shattered family all were drawn inexorably" (27). But in *Steelwork,* where she is first presented in list form, Grandma comes to resemble the Grandma characters of *Aberration* and *Red the Fiend:*

She sat in the broken Morris chair, her leg over one arm so that Red could see up her pale-blue-veined leg to the twisted reddish hairs of her crotch. She squinted through her glasses, the nose piece held together with adhesive tape. She chased him around the dining room table with thin patent leather belts from her crepe de Chine dresses. She rifled the dumbwaiters for yesterday's papers, so that everything they read in that house smelled of garbage. She made head cheese and boiled potatoes for supper once a month. She fried eggs so that the whites were black and elastic and the yolks underdone and scummy. (101)

This passage, a list of Grandma's characteristic behaviors shorn of all plot, continues for two more brilliant pages, every sentence a specific evocation of hell. Though it is not one of Sorrentino's classic lists in that it is not limited to nouns, the repetitive phrasing makes obvious its affinities with that form. What makes Grandma so memorable is not that she is credible in a conventional sense, but that she is psychologically flat yet intricately detailed in terms of behavior and accoutrements. In this sense she is well-suited to the list format, which is always flat on the page yet absolutely specific. This is an unsettling combination: the specificity is so persuasive that it gives a character who might otherwise be dismissed as a contrivance, a grotesque sight gag, an illusion of reality. Though not "round" in the Forsterian sense, she is a complicated character, at once fearsome and fearful, humorous and humorless. She is also the perfect metonymical emblem of her time, a woman whose narrowness is fed by the Depression it in turn feeds.

Reconfigured as Bridget McGrath, Grandma returns in *Aberration*. Though Bridget is dead at the time of the novel's action, she continues to warp three of the four main characters by way of memory. Many of these memories are conveyed by listlike passages from which Sorrentino squeezes more illusions of reality. Take, for example, the distillation of clichés spouted by her "shanty Irish" relatives at her funeral:

That she looked wonderful; that she looked beautiful; that she looked better than she did alive; that she looked as pretty as she did when she was a girl; that she looked alive; that she looked as if she'd open her eyes and talk bejesus; that it was all for the best; that she was with God in heaven; that she had gone to a better place; that she was spared a lot of suffering going when she did; that she didn't suffer at all thanks be to God . . . that Bridget was so young a woman; that the good always die young; that poor Marie was motherless too now; that the poor grandson didn't know what to make of it all, God save the poor little cockeyed runt of a thing. . . . (172)

This passage evokes the suffocating atmosphere of Bridget's funeral without resorting to conventional techniques. It is a scene, but one that is about cliché rather than being a cliché itself. The "shanty Irish" relatives voicing these clichés are indirectly represented; their larger but still empty relationship to Bridget is indirectly captured; and the confusion of the boy Billy, which adds delicate pathos, is indirectly realized. The specifics themselves narrate the scene, and no more is needed to realize the imaginary space of the funeral. At the same time, the passage remains defiantly artificial, a list enclosed within a question-answer section that recalls Joyce and O'Brien. In other words, realistic illusions can be conjured from antirealistic techniques.

This is certainly true of *Aberration* as a whole. The most stunning achievement of the work is that it weaves a coherent illusion of reality from a great variety of modernist innovations, many of which are highly unconventional, i.e., not "realistic" in the literary sense. Part of this success stems from the fact that it follows a consistent cast of characters. More important, however, is its claustrophobic focus on events that take place over a few days' time at a New Jersey boardinghouse in the summer of 1939. Like so many of Sorrentino's works, *Aberration* is a lean work with a rigorous structure. It comprises forty chapters that are divided into four sections. Each section is devoted to a single character: ten-year-old Billy Recco; his divorced mother, Marie; her would-be paramour, the divorced meat-cutting-machine salesman Tom Thebus; and Marie's father, widower John McGrath. What makes *Aberration* more intricate in its perspectivism than *Rashomon* or *The Sound and the Fury,* works to which it is compared, is that each of its four sections is divided into ten types of document, each of a different style, and each matching the style of a correlated document in the other three sections.

All of the four main sections begin with a short, third-person piece that focuses on the character whose consciousness is the center of the section. This is followed with a short letter from that character to a character outside the confines of the boardinghouse. Then comes a chapter of pure dialogue. After that, the novel takes an openly modernist turn by including a Joycean question-answer section, with many of the answers couched as noun-heavy lists. The fifth section is a fantasy letter written in the present tense from the center of consciousness to a character for whom the fantasist harbors rather complicated feelings. The sixth is also wish fulfillment, a brief third-person fantasy that depicts how the center of consciousness would tailor the future, while the seventh is a fantasy that represents a similar attempt to mend the broken past. The eighth and ninth sections are devoted to the main action of the plot, a date between Marie and Tom, with the eighth section concerning what happens before and during the date, and the ninth concerning the events that immediately follow. The final section is a collage, another repetitive, noun-heavy, plotless narration that indirectly characterizes the center of consciousness in terms of his or her personal obsessions.

As this summary suggests, only the eighth and ninth sections provide plot details in a conventional way, and these sections focus on the events of only a few days, yet the effect of the four correlated sections is to create a profoundly lush picture of each of the four characters' lives, portraits that spiral in and out of the past. The fantasy sections are crucial given the stress on perspective. Sorrentino is emphasizing not just that perception is subjective but that perception is determined by desire. The central characters see what they want to see, flattering themselves so casually that the reader must examine each from all four perspectives to get a sense of the central character's "true" reality. For example, both Tom's and John's sections reveal that Marie is beginning to show her age, but in her fantasies this can only be inferred from her overweening vanity. What Sorrentino's perspectivism does *not* suggest, however, is that desire creates objective reality. Like *Sky* and *The Orangery*, *Aberration* paints a picture of an unyieldingly objective universe, one that squeezes each character in its grim iron grip. Excluding Billy's, each character's fantasies are ineffectual forms of escapism fabricated from cliché and vanity. The author indicates the existence of an objective reality most clearly in the question-answer sections, where he answers questions about the central characters from an omniscient point of view. These answers, though filled with Jamesian qualification, are to be taken as the literal truth about these characters, an objective truth that subjective limitations keep them from seeing for themselves.

It is odd, then, that the reader takes away from *Aberration* a perfectly coherent whole in which all the perspectives and all their distortions coalesce into one illusion of objectivity. Because of the rapid shifts in point of view from section to section as well as within each section, the savvy reader is conditioned to perceive each character as a perceiver captured in the act of perceiving, so the shifts seem consistent and rarely confuse. The subjectivism clearly belongs to self-absorbed characters, not to an author bent on aesthetic solipsism. The incredible specificity of the piece, which evokes its Depression-era setting through nouns rather than sentiment, further undergirds the illusion through its accuracy, precision, and concreteness. Consequently, even the novel's most artificial aspects, including the humorously intrusive marginalia that presumably issue directly from the author, fail to disrupt the illusion. It is as if Sorrentino set out to prove that a carefully contrived stylistic tour de force can be hyperrealistic while jettisoning the cliché and sentimentality associated with conventional realism. This blend of blatant artifice and trompe l'oeil illusionism is reflected in numerous favorable reviews, which lavish praise on both aspects of the novel in equal measure.

The same cannot be said of Sorrentino's thirteenth novel, *Red the Fiend,* which received some rather rough notices. *Kirkus,* to cite one example, disapproved of the antirealistic characters, which the reviewer calls "caricatures, not flesh and blood." This criticism, which Sorrentino has repeatedly endured since the publication of *Imaginative Qualities,* is false in at least three regards. First, it assumes that some characters are more real than others and that if enough psychological motivations are included, the letters of the words comprising the literary construct grow flesh and blood. Second, it narrowly assumes that the *only* worthwhile thing for a novelist to do is to create this one type of illusion. Finally, it assumes that Sorrentino was trying to make something other than caricatures, or as he calls them, "humors," and failed—which is not the case.

Another odd thing about the negative reviews is that *Red the Fiend* is clearly a reworking of the characters in the critically praised *Aberration.* Published fifteen years and seven novels later, *Red the Fiend* transfers these characters from pastoral New Jersey to the Brooklyn of Sorrentino's childhood. This shift in setting, along with the renewed prominence of the Grandma character, explains the grittier tone of *Red the Fiend,* which is Sorrentino's bleakest, most wrenching novel since *Sky.* But if *Red the Fiend* is equal to *Sky* in emotional impact, its artifice is far more subtle, innovative, and comic. In brief, the novel focuses on four characters, with Red the center of consciousness. The other three are all named in relation to him: Mother, Grandma, and Grandpa. A fifth major character is Father, an alcoholic largely absent from Red's life. The plot, which takes place during Red's early pubescence, is episodic and largely unswerving as it charts the increase in his depravity and the decrease in his hopes and dreams, which, as the omniscient narrator makes clear, are shrunken and false from the start. By the end of the novel, Red is both brutalized and brutal, a figure ruled by cruelty, nihilism, and an imagination warped by cultural clichés. The primary engine of his misery is Grandma, who also tortures Mother and Grandpa, two classically passive-aggressive, static characters whose contempt for Grandma, unlike Red's, never blossoms into defiance. The plot traces the gradual increase in this suicidal defiance, which is a function of his hopelessness. The novel comes to an abrupt halt with a parody cliff-hanger that evokes the advanced despair of the protagonist, who through his relationship with Grandma has become a sadomasochist who frequently longs for death. This longing is reflected when he writes "DIRTY OLD

CUNT" on one of Grandma's treasured photos then "goes in to sit on the couch, to wait quietly for Grandma and Mother. Ecstatic, he feels the world on the edge of obliteration" (213). The overall structure of the novel, whose model, according to the author, is "a rather obscure French novel of the late 19th century" (Letter, 22 June 1996), suggests that "sustained misery . . . can function according to permutations as elaborate as those of a fugue" (47).

Due to their gritty urban settings and plots that focus on working-class Catholics, *Steelwork* and *Red the Fiend* have been compared to the works of pioneering American naturalists, works that include Crane's *Maggie* and Farrell's *Studs Lonigan*. And it is true that along with the naturalists, Sorrentino emphasizes nurture. Like Grandma, Red is a product of his environment, too weak, unimaginative, and corrupt from the start to rise above it. Still, Sorrentino resists the comparison, noting that the naturalists depend on convention. According to him, *Red the Fiend* "can be construed as conventional narrative/illusion only by the most willful ignoring of the formal aspects of the book, and, especially its people!" (Letter, undated). He is suggesting that the book is not conventionally realistic, and that, besides its parody, which makes comparison to naturalism problematic, the novel's antirealism has two distinct components. First, the book is blatantly artificial, even schematic, in its contrapuntal structures. That is, it differs from conventional realism in its stubborn refusal to let its form disappear from the reader's view. His second point, about the book's "people," construes the word *realistic* in a different sense: unlike *Aberration, Red the Fiend* is unrealistic in that its events are often implausible and its characters intentionally flat. "[H]ow," the author asks, "could a Realistic Red survive such unbelievable batterings? With heavy, sharp implements, etc.?" These antirealistic qualities are the result of Sorrentino's creative intention. "Red is a literary construct," Sorrentino asserts, "made so as to posit a set of forms that are unrelievedly and claustrophobically (I hope!) cruel and vicious" (Andrews 67).

The overall point made by the myriad structural inventions, which vary from chapter to chapter, is that violence and cruelty are intricate, repetitive, and largely empty of meaning. Although their forms vary, their essence is static. For example, in chapter 8, Red suffers an unspecified injury. This injury causes a ritualized disturbance in the household: Grandma berates Red for his clumsiness while she makes Mother feel guilty for wanting to waste Grandpa's money on doctor visits. What is clear is that Grandma enjoys the disturbance, which provides her with an excuse to manipulate and torture Red and Mother. Binding the chapter together is the narrator's curt repetition of the sentence, "It doesn't matter." What doesn't matter, the narrator is saying, is the exact nature of the injury, for regardless of specifics, ritual cruelty is timeless and unchanging. The narrator does, however, offer an exquisitely exhaustive set of possibilities: "It's a ripped-open knee, pebbles, dirt, grease, and wood embedded in the bloody flesh; a deep puncture beneath the arm caused by a fall on a rusty picket; a purplish-blue knot on the forehead, its center a nucleus of black blood" (24). What makes this device interesting is how the "unimportant" possibilities create an illusion of depth, continuity, and recurrence. The concreteness of the possibilities cloaks their hypothetical nature in unique verisimilitude. In them, the reader discerns a hundred unnamed situations. This has all happened before and will happen again.

Many of Sorrentino's structural inventions attempt to mirror through verbal artifice the ritualized quality of Grandma's cruelty. As the above suggests, the artifice often takes on a listlike form so as to capture both the repetitiveness and the specificity of each re-enactment of the ritual. Time and again, the narrator notes that the specificity does not matter, for every detail leads to the same things, pain and despair. Yet for the reader, the detail is absolutely the point, for it not only conveys the hopelessness of Red's situation, it gives an otherwise grotesque, implausible story a foundational illusion quite different from that of conventional fiction, which, as noted, often depends on "rounded" psychological portrayals. Thus Sorrentino combines blatant artifice, melodrama, and a wealth of concrete detail in a chapter that starts rhythmically and almost playfully, "Anything that disturbs Grandma's fragile composure is ultimately the fault of Red, the lout, the miscreant, the ungrateful: he on whom charity is wasted, he who is rotten to the very core" (110). What follows is a four-page list of abusive behaviors: "When Grandma makes her egg too soft and runny, she strikes Red so hard that he shits himself. When Grandma's corset makes it difficult for her to breathe, she cuffs Red on the nape of the neck so violently that he pisses his pants. . . . When Grandma bitterly considers that Grandpa no longer cares to see her naked, she bashes Red's ribs until he begs for mercy" (110). The catalog continues until, halfway through, the sadism pivots: "When it occurs to Grandma that Mother and Grandpa may outlive her, she swats Red across the face until he blithers like an idiot; and when it then occurs to Grandma that she may outlive Mother and Grandpa, she pastes Red in the mouth so that he again blithers like an idiot" (111). The second half of the chapter retraces the first half, with Grandma abusing Red for all the opposite "reasons." It ends by inverting its beginning: "If Grandma realizes that she is pleased that Grandpa no longer cares to see her naked, she belabors Red with kitchen implements until he begs for mercy. . . . If Grandma's corset makes her feel lumpy and unattractive, she batters Red so relentlessly that he pisses his pants. When Grandma makes her egg too hard and dry, she pummels Red until he shits himself" (112-13). There is no logic behind Grandma's violence except the aesthetic logic of pattern and repetition. Every thing or idea, contradictory or not, becomes an excuse to continue the cycle of waste; only the sky changes. The ultraspecificity suggests no meaning beyond itself: like reality as a whole, it simply is. If Grandma beats Red with a wooden spoon because her mother beat her with a switch, it is implied that Grandma's mother was beaten by her own mother with something else. Why? It doesn't matter.

The theme of specificity and its absence also plays a role in illuminating Red's corrupt imagination. One way Sorrentino conveys the characters' reliance on cliché is to portray monologues in which specifics are all but absent, so enmeshed are they in clichés. Thus in the following passage the only salient narrative detail is that Father perceives Grandma as being jealous of his daughter's early marital happiness: "Father tells Red that you never know, it can happen no matter what, it's a long road that has no turning, time will tell. That a penny saved, a rolling stone, a stitch in time, a face that would stop a clock all have a silver lining. That it's the God's honest truth, it tells no lies, Grandma, the old witch, old bitch, was jealous, everything comes out in the wash" (99). Here Father is trying to say something significant to his son Red, but that something is so mired in optimistic clichés and received wisdom that his language becomes hopelessly inefficient and inarticulate. The result? Red learns to ignore his father and inadvertently begins to filter out the lonely specifics, as indicated by Sorrentino's frequent ellipses. Sometimes the same effect is achieved through sentence fragments: "Red is not to worry. Every dog will have and the world is his oyster. If Father knew what was in store. No need for Joe Walsh. A hell of a nice woman. No reason to blame Mother. No. No. A saint. Some day when he's a little older he'll" (206). The final consequence of this process is that Red himself becomes unable to talk and think without relying on cliché. This leaves him with an imagination enfeebled by cliché, as well as the rage of the inarticulate, the kind so often seen in drunks. The degradation of his imagination is made clear when he tries to imagine one of his Grandmother's malicious monologues: "Grandma says that somebody is a horse's ass, that somebody else is the cock of the walk, that somebody else is a greenhorn trying to pass himself off as a real American, and that somebody else is a shameless tramp no matter that she's also some kind of holy roller Baptist with her Bible under her oxter and the Sunday-school medals all over her coat" (181). Here Sorrentino exemplifies what he says of Williams, i.e., that it "is the flight, or the heartbreaking attempt at flight, of the imagination that he seeks to pin down and isolate in all his work" (*Something* 24). Red does now and then struggle against the forces of cliché that surround him, as when, despite the manifest lovelessness of his world, he nevertheless "wishes to Christ that he could, that he could, that he could what? He thinks to reach over and touch his father's thick useless hand" (207). But it comes to the same: "No soap." Ultimately these forces—which emanate from the movie screen and the radio as well as from his social relations—are too much, so Red submits, becoming one with them, learning to enjoy the ritualistic cruelty they demand. What makes passages like those quoted above such an achievement is that they remain utterly specific even when they are about the characters' failure to be specific. From Sorrentino's perspective, the clichés themselves, many of which are antiques lost to time, are absolute cultural specifics unique to the book's setting. Their historical exactitude, along with the precise yet always inventive function they play within the narrative, testifies to the author's transcendence of cliché, the complete control he wields over it rather than vice versa.

Again, there is no sentimentality here, no victim who is not also a victimizer, no social idea, no solution, no comfort. Though Sorrentino's worlds are comic worlds, their comedy is almost always welded to cliché and insult, misogyny and ethnic hatred, waste and despair. Some of *Red the Fiend*'s reviewers seemed unhappy that the book features comedy, parody, and antirealism, as if themes of child abuse and urban corruption are too intrinsically serious for such treatment. But that is quite literally *their* problem. Comedy, parody, and antirealistic techniques are utterly serious, and *Red the Fiend* is a serious work by a quintessentially serious artist. The problem is that many reviewers, like many novelists, trust just one type of seriousness and one type of realism. Another reason for such criticism lies in the failure of the book to provide a hopeful message, which is typical of books containing similar themes. Sorrentino systematically refuses to provide anything progressive. Take for example a particularly interesting trio of chapters, each of which offers a slight structural twist on the other. The first begins, "Red might be able to understand Grandma if he ever discovers how she has been obstructed by . . ." (171). The chapter then provides a list of Grandma's "obstructions." The next two chapters concern how Red might sympathize with Mother and forgive Father if he knew certain details about them, details that the chapters proceed to enumerate. The chapters seem to be leading to a breakthrough, to some ray of hope. But since Red does *not* know these things, each chapter culminates with a blank fact: "Red may see only that which he may see" (173, 176, 179). People are closed to one another. As a self-protective impulse, they hide that which might allow others to understand, sympathize, and forgive. Since this and other Sorrentino texts show us with utter clarity why someone might adopt a self-protective posture even within the "secure" confines of the family, there is no solution. This, Sorrentino almost says to his reader, is simply how it is.

There is, then, no final difference between Sorrentino's "artificial" works and his "realistic" ones. All of his works, including those not covered here, are consistent in that they find subtle and inventive ways to manifest their artificiality *and* to register their fascination with the objective reality that is refracted in, and remade by, their surfaces. None of Sorrentino's works is conventional, although some create the illusion that they are through a multitude of historical specifics. In none is the author's bleak vision interrupted by comforting literary clichés or hopeful messages.

In a sense, then, the way I have grouped these texts is false. Of course, the works in each group do share resemblances. For example, the works in the second group are apparently more autobiographical than those in the first. Some borrow characters from each other. These, however, are borrowings of models only. The Red of *Red the Fiend* has a number of models, including the Red of *Steelwork,* Billy of *Aberration,* and perhaps even the young Sorrentino. If Mother is the fictional echo of Sorrentino's own mother, so is she the reworking of other fictional echoes in *Sky, Steelwork, The Orangery,* and *Aberration,* as well as of various mother-figures in *Under the Shadow.* It would, then, be as theoretically wrong to say that Mother "is" Marie Recco as it would be wrong—not to mention insensitive and insulting—to say she "is" Sorrentino's mother. Such a mistake is made when the critic Paul Emmett, in a pioneering essay on the Freudian references in *Sky* and *Aberration,* asserts that Billy "is" the husband of *Sky* "as a youth" (125). Though one familiar with Sorrentino will know what Emmett means, the imprecision invites misreading. Regardless of historical models, each character is a singular literary construct designed to fulfill a fictional purpose specific to each text, which makes each work true to itself rather than to any of its precursors. Besides, most of Sorrentino's works contain autobiographical resonance, and they are interconnected by subtler means than setting and characterization alone. An intricate set of motifs interweaves his entire oeuvre, motifs whose complexity I have only touched on here. As one delves deeper, rereading the works, setting- and character-based categorizations seem less tenable, until even distinctions between the poetry and the prose seem arbitrary. Is *Splendide-Hôtel* prose, poetry, or prose poetry? Is *Under the Shadow* "really" less realistic than *The Sky Changes?* And what does it matter? Each of Sorrentino's works has the same impetus, to be art, to be beautiful and precise, to be sui generis yet still connected through recurrent motifs to the whole that is his oeuvre, through innovation to the whole that is modernism, and, through the mystery of metonymy, to the whole that is the world.

Sadly, an overview like this cannot treat every work in equal detail, especially when the writer is as prolific and complicated as Gilbert Sorrentino. Because Sorrentino is also so underrecognized, I have made the difficult choice of skipping works already treated in detail by other critics. These include some of his funniest, most popular works, including *Imaginative Qualities* and *Mulligan Stew,* as well as some of his most radical and challenging, including *Blue Pastoral, Crystal Vision, Odd Number, Rose Theatre,* and *Misterioso*—all of which, incidentally, are also animated by the comic. Critics have dealt with the first two metafictions in numerous articles and dissertations; of the second group, the last four are the subject of Louis Mackey's monograph, *Fact, Fiction, and Representation: Four Novels by Gilbert Sorrentino.* The only book devoted to Sorrentino alone, Mackey's study is an excellent introduction to the philosophical dilemmas posed by the author's most uncompromising novels. Mackey concludes that *Pack of Lies,* which includes *Odd Number, Rose Theatre,* and *Misterioso,* is, despite its lack of a continuous narrative, a legitimate trilogy in that it develops a skepticism regarding notions of "fact" and "truth" that is both consistent and cumulative. Mackey begins his work with an essay on *Crystal Vision,* which he views as the trilogy's intellectual precursor in that it, like the later works, "problematizes the art of fiction, destabilizes the concepts of truth and reality, and in the process brings literature and philosophy to a new consciousness of their common preoccupation with the powers and paradoxes of language" (1). What makes this philosophical bent appropriate is that ultimately philosophical realism and literary realism depend on the same Platonic illusion. The antiessentialism explicitly evoked by so many of Sorrentino's novels and poems is, then, of a piece with his antirealism, which, as Mackey rightly notes, reaches its apotheosis in *Pack of Lies.*

Still, viewing *Crystal Vision* as the trilogy's precursor ignores the fact that Sorrentino first "problematizes the art of fiction" through *Sky*'s self-conscious devices. This antirealistic imperative becomes the dominant feature of *Imaginative Qualities,* in my view making this roman à clef *the* breakthrough in Sorrentino's oeuvre. All of the novels after *Imaginative Qualities* manifest the same unstinting freedom, whether such license manifests through the self-imposed alphabetical constraints of *Splendide-Hôtel,* the picaresque adventures in language of *Blue Pastoral,* or the demonology of *Misterioso.* His poetry also underwent liberating shifts, becoming less idea-oriented, far more comic, and more blatant in its artifice, with line structures that increasingly depend on baroque repetitions for force and meaning. What is curious about the trajectory of his career is that his four most durable successes, *Imaginative Qualities, The Orangery, Mulligan Stew,* and *Aberration,* all of which reject conventional literary forms, were praised for their formal ingenuity. Yet it is this same formal ingenuity that reviewers would complain about during the 1980s when struggling with works like *Crystal Vision* and *Misterioso.* This is not to suggest that his later books were critical flops. By the 1980s, the attention generated by his earlier works had earned him automatic respect. But the respect is often grudging, with reviewers typically paying lukewarm homage to the author's originality and virtuosity before noting, in McPheron's paraphrase, that the work in question "provides less fun than literary sweat" (187).

Since the 1980s, Sorrentino's literary presence has diminished. Though Dalkey Archive, Sorrentino's consistent ally in the publishing world, has been steadily reprinting his work, it seems fair to say that an author who achieved an international following after the publication of *Mulligan Stew* is again on the verge of obscurity. Most of his readers divide into three main groups. The first includes a handful of academics who perceive his work as exemplifying various poststructuralist theories of literature. These readers typically became acquainted with Sorrentino through *Imaginative Qualities* and *Mulligan Stew* and are typically unfamiliar with his poetry. They also pay little attention to his aestheticism, choosing instead to read him as a postmodern novelist of ideas. I am thinking, for example, of readers like May Charles, who in "A Postmodern Challenge to Reference-World Construction: Gilbert Sorrentino's *Mulligan Stew,*" an essay that appeared in 1995, argues that, in novels like *Mulligan Stew,* "rather than pointing to a referent beyond the signified, the words become obstacles to the construction of a reference world" (240). While her thesis is correct and interesting in itself, Charles uses it, unfortunately, to argue that Sorrentino is up to much the same thing as all-those-other-postmodernists, which is neither correct nor interesting. Jerome Klinkowitz—one of the few high-profile critics to have written on Sorrentino at some length in books like *Literary Disruptions, Literary Subversions, The*

Self-Apparent Word, and *Structuring the Void*—takes a similar approach, albeit without resorting to the deconstructive systems and literary jargon that Sorrentino so often pokes fun at in *Pack of Lies, Under the Shadow,* and other fictions. The second group includes older living writers such as Hubert Selby, Robert Creeley, and so on. Many of these readers are familiar with the entire output, including the poetry and the criticism. These readers, some of whom have been reading Sorrentino for three or four decades, typically appreciate him for his comedy and humanism. Generally, they comment on the darkly comic web of relationships visible in his texts and admire his artistic devotion before noting the vertiginous, self-reflexive innovations determined by that devotion. Richard Elman speaks for this group when claiming that the author's aestheticist rhetoric constitutes "a persona that should be contemplated for what it is: the means by which an artist of great seriousness, and talent, and ability, has shaped the pain of experience to animate the language and show the limitations by which we live, and the dramatic breaks, and small startling changes, and terrible betrayals" (156). According to John O'Brien, the third and largest group comprising Sorrentino's audience is made up of younger readers who have come across his work by chance, often by working in the very bookstores that have for decades failed to promote Sorrentino's works. (That his books do not sell well is unfortunate and undeserved yet sadly appropriate, given his penchant for praising writers like Pound and Dahlberg who in his words are not for sale.) Due to the efforts, then, of small publishers like Dalkey Archive, Green Integer, Black Sparrow, and others, Sorrentino remains on the shelves, awaiting general discovery and critical revival.

It is telling that in 1981, when Elman made the above observation, *Mulligan Stew* was still the measure of difficulty in Sorrentino's work. Since then, that role has been usurped by *Pack of Lies,* which makes *Mulligan Stew* look something like a cupcake. But it would be unfair to characterize Sorrentino as a radical novelist intent on creating works of greater and greater difficulty, works that focus primarily on the indeterminacy of signs. While *Under the Shadow* is a difficult novel, its unity, comedy, and relative brevity make it highly readable. Though it is concerned with linguistic instability, that warhorse is hardly the focus. A parody of naturalism as well as an experiment in contrapuntal structures, *Red the Fiend* is also a difficult novel but of a much different stripe, and it, too, is an enjoyable novel engineered to make the reader laugh. In other words, though Sorrentino does not cater to "the general reader," neither is he trying to alienate him. He is instead intent on creating art. That is why he risks alienating his reader by refusing to stuff inspiration

into the restrictive molds of convention. Unfortunately, if the reviews of *Red the Fiend* are an indication, critics are still (!) demanding Forsterian "roundness" while evincing an inability to understand parody or even to recognize that narrators do not necessarily
speak for authors. With luck, this will change with the reception of
Sorrentino's recent novel *Gold Fools*—whose characters are every
bit as flat, if not more so, as those of *Red the Fiend*—but don't, as it
goes, hold your breath.

Gold Fools is a fond and wildly comic burlesque of a 1924 boys'
adventure book. Though the novel consists entirely of interrogative
sentences, the plot is surprisingly clear. As is typical, however, the
point is language rather than plot. Framed in the clichéd locutions
and literary structures of "the Old West" of both popular and literary culture, each question allows Sorrentino to question the meaning and etymology of its component words and phrases. Naturally,
this moves author and reader further and further from the plot's
central cliché, a quest for gold in the Gila Desert (which is as dry,
sort of, as the characters' laconic speech), and allows for a dizzying
array of ludic subtexts. One such subtext, for example, involves the
pervasive homoeroticism that Sorrentino locates in many stock
situations and Westernisms, while another tracks the movement of
the nonsensical yet still comprehensible phrase, "Wa'al, I vum!"
(16)—which is, it seems, a completely artificial locution emblematic
of the characters' inarticulateness, not to mention that of the adventure books that Sorrentino is parodying throughout. The author
ratchets the comedy of cliché ever higher as the adventure
progresses by mixing in pat phrases culled from a variety of contemporary sources, particularly academia and the media, generat-
ing a brilliant gibberish, ironic and allusive, that highlights the
humorous emptiness of ordinary speech as observed in "all walks of
life." Among Sorrentino's works, *Gold Fools* most resembles *Blue
Pastoral,* another playful quest-novel centrally concerned with
cliché. And like *Blue Pastoral, Gold Fools* has a clear place in the
Sorrentino canon. Not only does it grind, albeit interrogatively, all
the usual axes, it also incorporates many of his central themes and
motifs—though it does not include the recurring characters such as
Sheila Henry that enliven many of his fictions.

This is to say that the author's most recent work has him in fine
form and is a promising indicator of Sorrentino works to come. *Gold
Fools* also shows the author to be as innovative, literary, and uncompromising as ever when it comes to language and structural effects. But since these compliments describe most of Sorrentino's
works, many of which have been abused by reviewers and ignored
by the general public, one wonders whether another artistic success

will translate into the large-scale commercial success that might in turn spark a well-deserved revival in critical interest.

Perhaps, though, it is unnecessary and even unseemly to bother overmuch about the vicissitudes of literary and commercial fashion. Given that the artistry of Sorrentino's greatest work is unquestionable and his place in literary history prominent and influential, it seems reasonable to expect that his underappreciated works, especially his poetry collections and his later novels, will someday gain a recognition commensurate with their merits. If so, a wider audience will become familiar with an astonishing artist and comic genius who has far more original things to offer than postmodernist ideas.

> Poe's work strikes by its scrupulous originality, not "originality" in the bastard sense, but in its legitimate sense of solidity which goes back to the ground, a conviction that he can judge within himself.
> —William Carlos Williams (*In the American Grain* 216)

WORKS CITED

Andrews, David. "The Art Is the Act of Smashing the Mirror: A Conversation with Gilbert Sorrentino." *Review of Contemporary Fiction* 21.3 (Fall 2001): 60-68.

Charles, May. "A Postmodern Challenge to Reference-World Construction: Gilbert Sorrentino's *Mulligan Stew*." *Style* 29.2 (1995): 235-61.

Creeley, Robert. "Xmas as in Merry." *Review* 157-58.

Elman, Richard. "Reading Gil Sorrentino." *Review* 155-56.

Emmett, Paul. "*The Sky Changes*: A Journey into the Unconsciousness and a Road into the Novels of Gilbert Sorrentino." *Review* 113-29.

Jones, Hettie. *How I Became Hettie Jones*. New York: Grove, 1990.

Laurence, Alexander. "Gilbert Sorrentino Interview." *The Write Stuff: Interviews* 1994: 7 pp. Online. Dec. 2000. http://www.altx.com/int2/gilber.sorrentino.html.

Mackey, Louis. *Fact, Fiction, and Representation: Four Novels by Gilbert Sorrentino*. Columbia: Camden House, 1997.

McPheron, William. *Gilbert Sorrentino: A Descriptive Bibliography*. Elmwood Park, IL: Dalkey Archive Press, 1991.

O'Brien, John. "An Interview with Gilbert Sorrentino." *Review* 5-27.

"*Red the Fiend*." *Kirkus Reviews*. 1 Oct. 1994: n. pag. Online. Dec. 2000.

Review of Contemporary Fiction. "Gilbert Sorrentino Number." 1.1 (Spring 1981).

Robins, William M. "Gilbert Sorrentino." *Dictionary of Literary Biography V5: American Poets since World War II (Part 2)*. Ed. Donald Greiner. Detroit: Gale Research Company, 1980. 278-84.

Selby, Hubert. "Gilbert Sorrentino." *Review* 48-51.

Sorrentino, Gilbert. *Aberration of Starlight*. 1980. Normal, IL: Dalkey Archive Press, 1993.

——. *Black and White*. New York: Totem Press, 1964.

——. *Blue Pastoral*. San Francisco: North Point Press, 1983.

——. *Corrosive Sublimate*. Los Angeles: Black Sparrow, 1971.

——. *Crystal Vision*. San Francisco: North Point Press, 1981.

——. *The Darkness Surrounds Us*. Highlands, NC: Jonathan Williams Publisher, 1960.

——. *A Dozen Oranges*. Los Angeles: Black Sparrow, 1976.

——. *Gold Fools*. Los Angeles: Green Integer, 2001.

——. *Imaginative Qualities of Actual Things*. 1971. Normal, IL: Dalkey Archive Press, 1995.

——. Letter to the author. 22 June 1996.

——. Letter to the author. Undated, 1996.

——. *Misterioso*. Elmwood Park, IL: Dalkey Archive Press, 1989.

——. *Mulligan Stew*. 1979. Normal, IL: Dalkey Archive Press, 1996.

——. *Odd Number*. San Francisco: North Point Press, 1985.

——. *The Orangery*. 1978. Los Angeles: Sun & Moon, 1995.

——. *Pack of Lies*. Normal, IL: Dalkey Archive Press, 1997.

——. *The Perfect Fiction*. New York: Norton, 1968.

——. *Red the Fiend*. New York: Fromm, 1995.

——. *Rose Theatre*. Elmwood Park, IL: Dalkey Archive Press, 1987.

——. *Selected Poems: 1958-1980*. Santa Barbara: Black Sparrow, 1981.

——. *The Sky Changes*. 1966. San Francisco: North Point Press, 1986.

——. *Something Said: Essays by Gilbert Sorrentino*. San Francisco: North Point Press, 1984.

——. *Splendide-Hôtel*. 1973. Elmwood Park, IL: Dalkey Archive Press, 1984.

——. *Steelwork*. 1970. Elmwood Park, IL: Dalkey Archive Press, 1992.

——. "Sudden Diction." *Feed* 1999: n. pag. Online. Dec. 2000. http://www.feedmag.com/book/dialog_intro.html.

——. *Under the Shadow*. Elmwood Park, IL: Dalkey Archive Press, 1993.

——. *White Sail*. Santa Barbara, CA: Black Sparrow, 1977.

Thesen, Sharon. " 'in the song / of the alphabet': Gilbert Sorrentino's *Splendide-Hôtel*." *Review* 56-61.

Williams, William Carlos. *In the American Grain*. New York: New
Directions, 1956.
———. *Paterson*. New York: New Directions, 1963.

Gilbert Sorrentino
Photograph by Thomas Victor

A Gilbert Sorrentino Checklist

Fiction

The Sky Changes. New York: Hill and Wang, 1966; San Francisco: North Point Press, 1986; Normal, IL: Dalkey Archive Press, 1998.

Steelwork. New York: Pantheon Books, 1970; Elmwood Park, IL: Dalkey Archive Press, 1992.

Imaginative Qualities of Actual Things. New York: Pantheon Books, 1971; Normal, IL: Dalkey Archive Press, 1991; rpt. 1995.

Splendide-Hôtel. New York: New Directions, 1973; Elmwood Park, IL: Dalkey Archive Press, 1984.

Flawless Play Restored: The Masque of Fungo. Los Angeles: Black Sparrow Press, 1974.

Mulligan Stew. New York: Grove, 1979; rpt. 1987; Normal, IL: Dalkey Archive Press, 1996.

Aberration of Starlight. New York: Random House, 1980; rpt. 1981; Normal, IL: Dalkey Archive Press, 1993.

Crystal Vision. San Francisco: North Point Press, 1981; Harmondsworth, England: Penguin, 1982; Normal, IL: Dalkey Archive Press, 1999.

Blue Pastoral. San Francisco: North Point Press, 1983; Normal, IL: Dalkey Archive Press, 2000.

Odd Number. San Francisco: North Point Press, 1985.

A Beehive Arranged on Humane Principles. New York: Grenfell Press, 1986.

Rose Theatre. Elmwood Park, IL: Dalkey Archive Press, 1987.

Misterioso. Elmwood Park, IL: Dalkey Archive Press, 1989.

Under the Shadow. Elmwood Park, IL: Dalkey Archive Press, 1993.

Red the Fiend. New York: Fromm, 1995.

Pack of Lies. Normal, IL: Dalkey Archive Press, 1997.

Gold Fools. Los Angeles: Green Integer, 2001.

Poetry

The Darkness Surrounds Us. Highlands, NC: Jonathan Williams Publisher, 1960.

Black and White. New York: Totem Press, 1964.

The Perfect Fiction. New York: Norton, 1968.

Corrosive Sublimate. Los Angeles: Black Sparrow, 1971.

A Dozen Oranges. Los Angeles: Black Sparrow, 1976.

Sulpiciæ Elegidia: Elegiacs of Sulpicia. Mt. Horeb, WN: Perishable Press, 1977.

White Sail. Santa Barbara: Black Sparrow, 1977.

The Orangery. Austin: U of Texas P, 1978; Los Angeles: Sun & Moon, 1995.

Selected Poems: 1958-1980. Santa Barbara: Black Sparrow, 1981.

Criticism

Something Said: Essays by Gilbert Sorrentino. San Francisco: North Point Press, 1984; rev. ed. Normal, IL: Dalkey Archive Press, 2001.

The Art Is the Act of Smashing the Mirror: A Conversation with Gilbert Sorrentino

David Andrews

The following interview was conducted by mail during the summer and early fall of 1996. It was completed in early 2001.

DAVID ANDREWS: In the preface to *Something Said* you note that you "no longer hold many of the positions taken here; many of them are, in a word, embarrassing." Could you give a broad sense of what you meant when you wrote this in 1984? Have there been major changes in your critical thinking over the years?

GILBERT SORRENTINO: Speaking broadly, as you suggest, it's not so much particulars or specifics that are embarrassing or annoying but, in certain pieces, a kind of overt partisanship, often coupled with a very heated prose. The positions, I'd say, are by and large not bad, but the way they're defined can, in retrospect, look gauche and unconvincing. Of course, I can cop a plea and say that virtually all of these pieces were written to interest an audience in writers I liked, or conversely, to drive an audience away from writers I disliked. They were also written pretty quickly, rarely laboriously revised, and, paramount in these enterprises, written with little or no concern with what people would think of them or me. Put these things together, and there is a real possibility of winding up with egg on the face. As for changes in my critical thinking, I don't think so. I still distrust analogy and comparison, I still have no idea how words seem to represent the world, even as I know that this is quite impossible. Little theory has dented me, it all seems to come down to the mysteries of language, and the results of such investigations are what writers have always known: language will kill you if you give it an inch; a "good sentence" is so only in context; and words are things that refuse to stop changing.

DA: Many of your works contain obvious autobiographical resonance. Could you describe your view of the relationship between your past and your art?

GS: Let's assume you're looking in a funhouse mirror, there you are, David Andrews, and yet . . . you don't really look that way. Now you take a hammer and smash the mirror, and look again. You don't look *that* way, in spades! Yet there you are, really, right? OK. The past is you; its memory is the image in the mirror; the art is the act of smashing the mirror. The past is simply a mine from which one draws ore, and then does this and that with it. The closer "this and that" seems to be to the past facts, the more it is thought to be auto-biographical. On the other hand, *Mulligan Stew* may well be my most "autobiographical" work. But the "this and that" of the book is relentlessly foregrounded, twisted, distorted, tortured into weird shapes, and artificialized, so that no one has ever said a word about its autobiographical elements. That's saved for *Sky* and *Aberration,* which look Really True. As for my short stories, oh boy! Many of them are written in the first person, so that readers, even sophisti-cated readers, simply cannot or will not accept that "I" as a charac-ter. Nothing to be done about it.

DA: Do you consider yourself an aesthete? How do you feel about *aesthete* as a term? The word is so often associated with pejoratives like *mere* and *naive* that it almost seems pejorative itself.

GS: "Aesthete" is fine by me. Oddly enough, or maybe not so oddly or enough, the people who scoff at aesthetes are those who go all weak in the artistic knees when presented with "deep" stuff. They love things that don't seem to mean what they say, as if the artist went out of his way to "fool" them into taking his work at face value—but they'll not be fooled! Look at all the crap that's been written about the cetology chapters in *Moby-Dick*. Why are they there? What does it all mean? The novel is so richly symbolic, so redolent of hidden meanings, etc., etc., that these chapters must have a metaphorical/symbolic function, too! Whereas they seem to me to be rigorously metonymic, absolutely conceived as a series of complex signifiers that point to the great signified of Moby Dick himself. However—and it's a big however indeed—when we've fin-ished all these chapters, and the white whale arrives, not one goddamned thing that we've learned helps us to understand him. He slips out from under his putative role as the book's signified and becomes another empty signifier. It's a very profound investigation, via these beautifully wrought chapters, of how nothing in life pre-pares us for the "next thing." So all this is right on the surface, and yet to deal with it as such seems to be the aesthete's contemptible position. We learn to distrust the oddness of the surface, but chil-dren know better. If you read a book to a child—and I speak from long experience as the father of three—no matter how odd or roiled or impossibly weird the tale, children take it as it's given. They never, *never* ask, so to speak, "but what does the little elf with the funny name stand for—what does he mean?" The little elf is the fiend, Rumpelstiltskin, and he is evil and terrifying and quite crazed. That would seem to be enough for kids. Peel away his layers if you must, but he is still this mysterious figure, unknowable. Like Iago. The most profound example of surface complexity, at least in this century, is Leopold Bloom, about whom we, arguably, know more than we do about any other character in fiction. And when we finish *Ulysses,* we have no idea of the most important thing in his life: Why do he and Molly love each other so deeply? Of course, the great beauty of *Ulysses* is that it is nothing but surface. Or should I say, "mere" surface? Which reminds me that somebody recently said, apropos *Mulligan Stew* and Alexander Theroux's *Darconville's Cat,* that they were examples of "mere literary genius." Now *that* is a mouthful, no?

DA: Americans, even American aesthetes, typically find art and beauty suspect. This doubt in art may in part be a reaction to artists like Leni Riefenstahl, who still uses aestheticism as a way of explaining her complicity with Nazi politics. Yet you never evince doubt in art. Your *Imaginative Qualities of Actual Things,* for example, seems a critique not of aestheticism but of the art world.

GS: Yeats said, of Wilfrid Owen, that "the poetry is not the pity." Williams sympathized with young radical/communist strikers, but said that their writing was weak and ill-formed. Barthes mocks the literary taste and work of political radicals as being petit-bourgeois. And so on. Beauty is form. There are no beautiful ideas. Form does everything, changes everything, influences everything. If I write a limerick about the Holocaust, the Holocaust is thereby cheapened and insulted. Pornography exists because of its transparent linguistic form: to place tortuous and occluded language between the reader and the sexual acts being described subverts pornography, so that it is no longer pornography. Leni Riefenstahl is basically full of shit not because of her Nazi-glorification, but because she thought that her Nazi-glorification was an *idea!* The idea subverted her film as art—it's propaganda. Very good propaganda—like Pepsi commercials. Speaking of commercials, they're much more visually interesting and adventurous than the shows that interrupt their relentless flow. So what? Are they, as they say, art? I don't think so. They are products of an extra-artistic agenda. Art is form in the service of, if you will, nothing. Or as Pound says, in the *Cantos,* "The temple is holy, because it is not for sale." The characters in *IQAT* have problems, as you say, because they want to be artists—not make art.

DA: One aesthete whom you've had fun with is Vladimir Nabokov. Not only have you borrowed his characters, you've borrowed him, as in your dead-on parodies of him as an interview-subject (e.g., Dick Schiller's interview with Thomas McCoy in *Mulligan Stew*). Yet the opinions *you* express in interviews are often indistinguishable from those expressed in *Strong Opinions*.

GS: Nabokov became a kind of convenient straw man for me to delight in knocking over, mostly because I took out on him the idiocies of his crazed admirers. To be clearer: in the mid-seventies there sprang up a kind of "idea"—for want of a better word—about Nabokov as The Great Artistic Innovator. This was all the rage among the intelligentsia clustered about such publications as the *New York Review of Books,* etc. What was intolerable about this, at least to me, was the smug and strangely provincial conviction that Nabokov was a lonely avant-garde figure, more or less single-handedly inventing the postmodern novel. This revealed an almost unbelievable ignorance of what had been happening in American letters since 1945 and even earlier. So I "used" Nabokov as a club to beat his admirers with. Now, I rarely think about him, and haven't read a word by him in many years. One might consider him an American, save for his grimly bourgeois Europeanisms, as if he, every once in a while, thinks that Thomas Mann invented him. He, of course, became a kind of icon of High Art—surely OK, but again, what to say of Nabokov living at the same time as Robert Duncan? John Ashbery? James Schuyler? William Gaddis? Were not these writers as unswervingly inventive or avant-garde? Could it be that they were just too "American"? As for our aesthetic ideologies converging, this is not so rare, not rare at all, really. Artists say many things, but the proof of the pudding, right? I agree with Allen Ginsberg and, God help me, John Updike on many things, but write like neither of them.

DA: In your novels of the 1980s and early 1990s, you also seem to have a good deal of fun with deconstructionists. Yet deconstructionists continue to use your novels as examples of an intentional deconstructive strategy put into practice. Any comment?

GS: I never quite know what to think of any trends, critical or otherwise. Deconstruction gives us some very useful ways to think about writing—it can also be utterly dumb and as middle-class as a Republican picnic. The problem, and this is certainly not a startling "insight," is that deconstruction and all that it implies and includes is like psychoanalysis in that for every first-rate practitioner, you have a hundred schleppers. This has always been the case, at least in the world of academe, so that by the time *Of Grammatology,* say, has been run through a thousand dissertations, its "message" is pretty stale. Academics find what they want where they want it, and are great masters and mistresses of tunnel vision. If Ronald Firbank, for instance, disturbs their vision of, let's say, "the British comic novel in the twentieth century," then Ronald Firbank is as good as nonexistent. Which is, of course, why you get these dreary books entitled *Gloom Triumphant: The Postmodern Strategies of Barth, Updike and Morrison.* It's enough to make a cat laugh.

DA: *Red the Fiend* describes a boy, who, in trying to fathom the banality and malice of his world, gives up attempting to interpret his world in a fit of despair, opting instead to be one with its cruelty. It seems you promote an anti-interpretive stance in your essays, yet Red's abandonment of interpretation at the close of his novel seems symptomatic of his despair and corruption. Are you suggesting that life is, in the end, justifiable only as an aesthetic phenomenon?

GS: Your questions are too complicated for me to address in an interview. I could say that my books are the answers to your questions, but that seems frivolous. I'm baffled by your remark that Red "abandons interpretation" at the close of the novel, whereas his writing of a clear message on the photo of Grandma seems an indication of, if you will, writerly intrusion and invention. I don't think that life is justifiable only as an aesthetic phenomenon; I don't think life is justifiable at all. Life is simply life, its meaning is what one does each day and every day from birth to death. Life is neutral, surely far, far from the "unfairness" of the current cliché. To say that life is unfair is to imply that life is sentient and "cares" about us. This leads to sentimentality and mawkishness and, with many people, murderous fury at what life has "done" to them. Then these folks take it out, not on "life," but on the unsuspecting neighbors. Life, as I say, is just life. The same "life" that gives your mother cancer wins your wife the lottery: Which "life" is not fair?

DA: I guess I was fishing for the Nietzschean answer you're offering: life is just as unjustifiable as a work of art. One can, in the end, only look at its surface in shock and wonderment. As for Red "abandoning interpretation," what I meant was this: throughout the novel, Red tries to understand Grandma, who, for the most part, remains opaque. At the end, it appears that, to some extent, he gives up on this task and, through his "writerly intrusion and invention," steals some of Grandma's opacity. He takes the upper hand, so to speak, by writing his message to Grandma, a message that places him in a position to evoke the same shock and wonderment in Grandma that Grandma evokes in him throughout the novel. In this way he completes the claustrophobic pattern of destruction and banality that Grandma, who had a Grandma-like mother herself, follows in her own life.

GS: OK, your reading of Red's "taking power" at the close of the book seems reasonable, only this appropriation of power (if we can commit the unpardonable sin of speaking of that which is not in the novel) opens up the probability of wholesale disaster—for Red! Is it suicidal, masochistic, sadistic, a gesture of hopelessness, is it what they now sadly and querulously call "empowerment"? It's up to the reader, surely, to decide what Red has let himself in for. And there are more things operative, of course, than the blasphemy of the dirty word, there is also the disrespect for Grandma's property, and her nostalgia-hazed past. Red is really pushing, and knows how to push! Yes, he completes the claustrophobic pattern, etc., etc., as you say.

DA: Paul Mariani notes that William Carlos Williams chose to climax *In the American Grain* with the emergence of Poe rather than with that of Whitman because Poe attempted to clear the field of European imitators more radically and acidly than Whitman. He also notes that Williams admired Poe's formal precision but had reservations about Whitman's free verse and the sprawl of his measure. Williams expressed the same reservations about Allen Ginsberg's poetry. Would it be presumptuous to assume Williams would admire your attachment to innovation and formal precision the way he admired Poe's? I ask in part because it seems Williams sets up a curious contrast—or antagonism—by juxtaposing Ginsberg's letter against your sketch in *Paterson V.*

GS: I think you're right about this. Williams admired Allen because of his courage, his openness, his willingness to smash icons, to take on the dead establishment of poetry, etc. By the same token, he was wary of what he took to be Allen's return to Whitman's long, sprawling line, and his fondness for the catalog as a representation of American life—very different indeed from Williams's metonymic positing of minuscule specifics as lenses through which to see us and how we are: "No one/to witness/and adjust, no one to drive the car." Very different from the lamentations of "Howl." As for the contrast between me and Allen in *Paterson,* Williams never mentioned this to me, nor to anyone else that I know of. It may be simply coincidence—the necessities of the poem at that particular point in its composition.

DA: Do you view your life or your art as a political act in any practical way?

GS: I don't think in any "practical" way, although the current cant will have it that "everything" is politics—a strange kind of blanket statement that, upon investigation, means virtually nothing. It's more or less like saying, "everything moves toward *death!*" Yeah? I mean, it's so dimwitted as to be unassailable in its smug truism. I buy a loaf of bread, the yeast in which can be traced to its source in the stoop labor of somebody in the Sudan. What to do about this? I mean, sure, buying the bread is a political act—I am, in a very real way, subsidizing stoop labor in the Sudan. In a really A to B barter society, this is easily remedied, but here we are in a world in which money and power are inextricably intertwined: *And* politics. But politics *is* aesthetic in that language is involved in all of it. I grant you, the language is a debased one, a congeries of old and new clichés, references to linguistic signs (the flag, babies, family, etc.), and very few concrete nouns, so that while we are promised Peace, we are not promised Steak. But writers are political in the oddest ways, and can't be trusted to be faithful to a Cause. I think Blanchot says that politicians are absolutely right in their distrust of writers, since writers are faithful to words and forms, i.e., *how* to say something.

DA: On first glance, it seems Williams affected your poetry more than your fiction. Looking more closely, there appears something of a division in your work. On one hand are those works that, like *Mulligan Stew* and *Blue Pastoral,* "hold reality cheap"; on the other, those works that, like *The Sky Changes* and *Steelwork,* hold reality dear. Is it the latter kind that Williams influenced? Incidentally, it's interesting that Williams's own prose divides between avant-garde inaccessibility and the relative accessibility afforded by a style that approximates, or parodies, conventional realism: e.g., the Stecher trilogy.

GS: I wish I could answer this question cogently, but I can't. More than one person has pointed out the fact that my books are of (at least) two "sorts"—and they're probably right. I tend, as you may well know by now, to rewrite my books, my scenes, and recall my characters over and over again. Sometimes they have the same names, sometimes they're in disguise. All I can say about my books—*Blue Pastoral,* for instance, being a rewrite of *The Sky Changes, Crystal Vision* of *Steelwork,* etc., is that I have always attempted to achieve a formal pattern decided upon before I write, that is, I don't start with the idea for a story, I start with the idea for realizing a form, e.g. how to write *Steelwork* again by using the Tarot as an organizing principle and bleeding out the temporal, while shuffling the spatial as needs dictate. OK, then I have all my *Steelwork* characters, plus all those amazing Tarot images—let's see what will happen if the two are put together. By the way, I know what you mean by WCW and his varied prose—and yet, his most accessible prose almost always does something very fresh and iconoclastic in terms of narrative and plot—and characterization. For instance, where is the truth to be found in "Old Doc Rivers," where all data are second-, third-, and fourth-hand? Why is "The Knife of the Times" a stunning collection of clichés, one strung upon another? How come Jean Beicke disappears in "Jean Beicke" so that the story is about something else? And so on. Williams once said, if I am recalling this properly, that his short stories and his novels were extensions of his poetic by other means. Of course, writers will say anything to justify their work, but it is quite true, I think, that Williams is really of a piece. How amazing it is to find "Of Asphodel"'s techniques posited in the poems of *Spring and All*. Clear as day.

DA: I: Could you describe how your poetry has changed over the last forty years?

GS: My poems have become more artificial.

DA: Your descriptions in *Something Said* of the title character in *J R* remind me of Red. Do you judge Red to be "touching" in spite of his viciousness? If so, how do you separate this sentimentality from the sentimentality you describe as central to James T. Farrell's conception of another title character, Studs Lonigan? Is it possible to create a "touching" character without resorting to sentimentality? Does the matter-of-fact tone of *Red the Fiend* help you avoid the sentimentality that the more pretentiously tragic tone of *Studs Lonigan* creates?

GS: First off, yes, "touching" characters can be created without the sentimental. Hubert Selby does it in virtually all his work. Fellini created the brute Zampano, and made him touching without ever making him soppy. As for Red, he is really a monster of a character, and the novel is far from the realistic—for instance, how could a Realistic Red survive such unbelievable batterings? With heavy, sharp implements, etc.? No, Red is a literary construct made so as to posit a set of forms that are unrelievedly and claustrophobically (I hope!) cruel and vicious. I don't think Red is "touching," but I have no authority over my readers. As for Red and J R, sure Red is "based," so to say, in Depression Brooklyn, a place about a million light years from 1960s suburban Long Island. If we want to think of both books in political terms, say, Red, in a brilliantly depraved dictatorship like Nazi Germany, would be a brownshirt, a headbreaker with the S.A., whereas J R would no doubt be an officer in an S.S. Death's Head battalion, married, devoted to his wife and children, and, no doubt, an admirer of Mozart, Goethe, Heine, and Carole Lombard. Just a regular guy until he goes to work. Red, on the other hand, would be in street fights two or three times a week. *Studs Lonigan* was not in my mind when I wrote my novel, certainly not consciously, and so I wasn't cutting against the grain of that character. I might add that many people really disliked *Red the Fiend,* REALLY! How deeply we want to care, unequivocally, for the brutalized figure, and how hard it is to do so when he is a really corrupted figure like Red. It's like trying to feel bad for Popeye because of our understanding of his childhood. Well, all right, but this is the guy who fucked Temple Drake with a corncob!

DA: You've noted that your works are often organized according to external principles. Is this true of *Gold Fools?*

GS: *Gold Fools* is closely written (as to characters, plot, and narrative line) after a boys' adventure book (featuring the Boy Ranchers), published in, I believe, 1924. I've burlesqued the original, fondly, I think, since I loved such books when I was a kid, and written the whole in interrogative sentences. You can see the sort of mischief that one can get up to considering that questions that have little to do with furthering the narrative are asked, often prompting more questions—these piled-up questions divert the narrative and often create new or sub-narratives.

DA: What are you working on now, and how do you see it and other recent work as fitting into your work as a whole?

GS: I've written a new book, *Little Casino,* which will be published by Coffee House Press in Spring 2002; I've just completed another book, *Painting the Moon,* which I'm letting sit for a while before I read it again; I've written three new short stories; and I've put together a MS of short stories written over the past thirty years. I've also added twenty-five critical pieces written since the publication of *Something Said,* which will be added to an expanded edition of that book and published by Dalkey Archive in 2001. I have absolutely no idea of how any of these projects fit into my work as a whole.

DA: Have your difficulties publishing your work shaped the work itself in substantive ways? If yes, could you describe how?

GS: I don't believe so, not substantively, but maybe in small ways. It is hard to keep one's focus on a new book when an earlier book is still looking for a publisher. There are many writers who have never had to deal with this—happy souls!—but those writers who have gone through it know how hard it can be. What sits maliciously in the mind is the possibility that the book you've finished will not find a publisher and that soon to join it will be *another* book that will not find a publisher. It's difficult to concentrate on the work at hand when this is the case; one tends to become distracted, and, of course, discouraged. This has happened to me on more than one occasion, the most pointed being those merry days when both *Mulligan Stew* and *Crystal Vision* were being regularly (one wishes to say automatically) rejected—often by the same editors at the same houses for the same reasons—while I was working on *Aberration of Starlight.* (You might note that *Crystal Vision,* although written before *Aberration,* was published after it.) All three books were, of course, published, finally, by three different publishers. This came about because none of the publishers wanted all of the books. The only thing, of course, that makes this sort of thing palatable is the millions of dollars in advances that I'm regularly offered.

William Gaddis

John Beer

Most serious readers of contemporary fiction today know William Gaddis's name. Many could identify him as the author of *The Recognitions,* a predecessor to such massive and difficult fictions as DeLillo's *Underworld,* Pynchon's *Gravity's Rainbow,* and Wallace's *Infinite Jest.* Far fewer, though, have worked through Gaddis's novel, which retains, as William Gass observed in an introduction to the Penguin edition, something of the odor of the cult about it (vi). When Gaddis died in 1998, it was noted in most of his prominently placed obituaries that he remains an author more respected than read. Mel Gussow summarized the situation in the *New York Times:* "He was often considered one of the least read of important American writers. But his books have become contemporary classics."

For all the late attention, Gaddis remains a novelist neglected by both readers and critics. This neglect is deeply regrettable and is not alleviated by ritual invocations of his importance or uncritical adulation. In four novels totaling over twenty-four hundred pages William Gaddis made an honest and brave attempt to assay the way we live now. A master satirist, he both scorned and relished the absurdity of a culture which pays a book it does not read the empty compliment, "contemporary classic." The difficulty of Gaddis's books stems less from their shows of erudition than from their embrace of the awkward and evasive speech out of which each of us makes a self to meet the selves we meet. Like his fiercely difficult and untimely predecessors Melville and Faulkner, Gaddis demands of his readers that they match his stake of industry, courage, and intelligence.

Though Gaddis insisted repeatedly upon the irrelevance of writers' lives to the understanding of their works, his life presents a constant temptation to the allegorist. His life seems to illustrate in sequence the artist's possibilities in America. As a young man, he is a bohemian, thrown out of school, drifting around Europe and Greenwich Village. His encyclopedic denunciation of the falseness of contemporary civilization receives brickbats from the critics and yields royalty checks of $4.70. Gaddis in middle age is an American Kafka, flacking for Pfizer and other commercial leviathans while working steadily through nights and weekends on the labyrinthine *J R*. Finally, Gaddis enjoys the kind of old age normally reserved for faithful political lieutenants, mediocre poets, and college presidents: he is showered with encomia and foundation money and honored as one of America's most distinguished living authors, even if on the whole his novels remain unread.

Born in Manhattan on 29 December 1922, Gaddis spent his early childhood in Massapequa, Long Island. This community was later to serve as the setting for the Long Island sections of *J R*. In fact, the ultimate disappearance of the Bast home in that book has its roots in the Gaddis family's struggles with the Massapequa school board. Gaddis told Dinitia Smith in a magazine profile, "I wrote *J R* in revenge against Massapequa" (38). Gaddis's parents divorced when he was three years old. His mother, an executive with the New York Steam Company, a forerunner of Consolidated Edison, sent him to board at the Merricourt School in Berlin, Connecticut, at the age of five. Though his loneliness at this school may be reflected in the dismal recollections of Jack Gibbs in *J R* ("End of the day alone on that train, lights coming on in those little Connecticut towns stop and stare out at an empty street corner" (119)), Gaddis also expressed gratitude later in life for the rigorous, traditional education which he received there.

At the age of thirteen, Gaddis returned home and attended public high school on Long Island. During high school, he contracted "a tropical fever of unknown origin" (Smith 39). Like his character Wyatt Gwyon, Gaddis was diagnosed as suffering from *erythema grave*. This diagnosis means only "extreme irritation and redness of the skin"; it is the name of his symptom, not of the symptom's cause. Whatever its origin, the disease was severe enough to reduce Gaddis's weight, again like Wyatt's, to seventy-nine pounds. Gaddis was subjected to a barrage of medical procedures and finally recovered. However, the treatment for this illness turned out to cause kidney dysfunction, which eventually rendered him unfit to serve in World War II.

Gaddis entered Harvard in 1941. His literary talents found an early outlet at the *Harvard Lampoon,* and he became its president in his senior year. Gaddis's sketches for the *Lampoon* showed flashes of the absurdist wit and fondness for both recondite knowledge and vulgarity that would later animate the great novels. One piece notes that wartime ship production has outpaced the store of admirals' names with which to christen them, and so future destroyers will end up bearing names like "Blatz" or "Boy Scout Troup No. 71 of Oakdale" (Peter Koenig 6). Another purports to translate for lazy French students Guillaume Ravenkill's *Putains Que J'ai Connues* (Kuehl and Moore, *In Recognition* 4). On the whole, though, Gaddis's time at Harvard, its classrooms emptied by a war he could not join, seems to have reinforced a sense of isolation and singularity engendered earlier by the Connecticut boarding school and lengthy illness. Gaddis left Harvard in his senior year without graduating. An alcohol-inspired encounter with Cambridge police drew the attention of the local newspapers and a resulting invitation to withdraw from the dean of the college.

Gaddis found a congenial position at the *New Yorker* as a fact checker, work he later described as the ideal training for a writer. At the same time, he commenced initial sketches of what, ten years later, would become *The Recognitions*. Toward the end of 1947, he left New York to travel. He went to Panama City with hopes of working as a journalist, hopes soon dashed by his struggles with Spanish. Instead, he worked on the canal, sorting bolts and running cranes. The outbreak of war in Costa Rica led the adventurous young Gaddis to San Jose, and his account of his experience there merits quoting in full:

The fighting was out around Cartago, where I was handed over to a young captain named Madero and issued a banged-up Springfield that was stolen from me the same day. We leveled an airstrip out there for arms coming in from Guatemala. Life magazine showed up and rearranged the cartridge belt for an old French Hotchkiss over the blond sergeant's shoulders before they took his picture beside it, and when the arms came in we celebrated with a bottle of raw cane liquor and the sergeant took us home for dinner where I met the most beautiful girl I've ever seen and passed out at the table. When it was all over I stayed around San José for a while, and I never saw that sergeant's sister Maria Eugenia again, and finally came home [like Otto Pivner] on a Honduran banana boat. (Moore, *Reader's Guide* 304)

Gaddis spent the following summer living at his family's house on Long Island, traveling frequently into New York to prowl the bohemian haunts of Greenwich Village, despairing at the spectacle of immense talents and energies squandered for lack of a coherent purpose that could guide and organize them, vying for the affections of the eccentric poet and painter Sheri Martinelli, gathering material for what would become *The Recognitions*. He soon moved on to Spain, where he lived for two years. There he met Robert Graves and began serious exploration of the mythological underpinnings of his novel. Stints in Paris, North Africa, and back in New York followed. Finally, in 1952 he secured an advance for the novel and retreated to an isolated farmhouse to complete it over the winter. He also met Jack Kerouac during this period, who memorialized Gaddis as Harold Sand in *The Subterraneans*.

Harcourt, Brace published *The Recognitions* in 1955. Gaddis told an interviewer decades later that "I almost think that if I'd gotten the Nobel Prize when *The Recognitions* was published I wouldn't have been terribly surprised" (Abadi-Nagy 58). Famously, this was not the case. The initial reception of *The Recognitions* has frequently been described as a low point in American book reviewing, though it perhaps pales in comparison to the hostility directed at *Moby-Dick* or *Pierre*. Jack Green published a series of amusing analyses of and diatribes against the book's reviews in his underground newspaper *newspaper;* these have been collected as *Fire the Bastards!* Green catalogs such questionable judgments as "The outside world of modern American life, which is surely a legitimate subject for the novelist today, is described so imperfectly, [*sic*] and so superficially as to make us feel that the novelist himself has never known it" (33), "One flat statement about the book can be made with confidence: Entertainment is not a primary objective" (9), and "What is 'The Recognitions' about? Really, I have no idea" (5). Green notes that the few ardently hostile reviews are outweighed by the mass of noncommittal ones. Critical indifference proved sufficient to sink sales of *The Recognitions*. In a 1986 interview Malcolm Bradbury told Gaddis that he and his friends in graduate school in the 1950s had eagerly read the novel and considered it a work of major importance; Gaddis tartly observed that they must have been passing around a shared copy of the novel, based on his sales figures.

Shortly after the publication of his novel, Gaddis married Pat Black. The couple had two children, Sarah and Matthew. With a family to support and hopes for literary fame dashed, Gaddis began working in public relations, initially for the pharmaceutical company Pfizer International. Over the next decade, Gaddis held several corporate writing jobs. He wrote film scripts for the army until his growing concern about American involvement in Vietnam led him to resign. He worked for a year on a book for the Ford Foundation about television in the schools, but this project was never completed. He wrote speeches for corporate executives. At the same time, he was engaged in several writing projects which remained incomplete, but fragments of which surfaced in his later novels: *Once in Antietam,* a play about "Socrates in the US Civil War" (Kuehl and Moore, *In Recognition* 12), a work about automation and the arts presumably called *Agape Agape* and focusing upon the player piano, and a screenplay for a Western. Toward the end of the 1960s Gaddis resumed work on an novel about business which he had set aside some ten years before, the novel that would become *J R*. During the same period, his first marriage ended, and he married Judith Thompson; the couple moved to a Carpenter Gothic house in

Piermont, New York.

Appreciation for Gaddis's achievement in *The Recognitions* had slowly built through the 1960s. The book was reissued in paperback by Meridian in 1962, and both sales and reviews were markedly stronger than in 1955. Gaddis received a grant from the American Institute for Arts and Letters in 1963. The poet Karl Shapiro planned an issue of the journal *Prairie Schooner* devoted entirely to *The Recognitions,* though this plan was scrapped after Shapiro quit his job over an unrelated censorship controversy. In the early 1970s *The Recognitions* gained increased attention from critics such as Tony Tanner and became the subject of several doctoral dissertations. The sixties and early seventies also saw a turn away from the midcentury's predominant social realism in American fiction. The dark comedy and metafictional pyrotechnics of authors like Pynchon, Vonnegut, Coover, and Barth created a context more hospitable to Gaddis's writing.

J R was published in 1975, twenty years after Gaddis's first novel. It won the National Book Award, judged by William Gass and Mary McCarthy, and garnered generally favorable critical attention; two prominent dissenters from this praise were George Steiner, who proclaimed the book "unreadable" in the *New Yorker,* and John Gardner, who predicted that Gaddis's fiction, diagnosed as the pessimistic productions of a crabbed spirit, was doomed to eventual oblivion. Although the press was more favorable than previously, *J R*'s sales proved disappointing: "the promise was not fulfilled as I hoped it would be," Gaddis later said (Smith 40). He was able to leave behind his corporate writing assignments, however. As a visiting professor at Bard College, he taught a seminar on failure in American life and literature, with a prominent place given to that bête noire of *The Recognitions,* Dale Carnegie's *How to Win Friends and Influence People*. During this period, Gaddis's second marriage came to an end, and he met Muriel Oxenberg Murphy, a Manhattan curator, television producer, and socialite, to whom *A Frolic of His Own* is dedicated.

His financial security finally guaranteed by awards from the Guggenheim and MacArthur foundations, Gaddis spent the early eighties working on *Carpenter's Gothic,* a comparatively brief work (262 pages) by his standards. The form of *Carpenter's Gothic,* Gaddis told several interviewers, was an exercise he set for himself in obeying dramatic unities and revivifying stock plot elements: the mysterious stranger, the adulterous affair. The novel's content is more clearly tied to contemporary events than those of its predecessors; Gaddis parodies mercilessly the religious fundamentalists and fervid cold warriors of the Reagan Revolution. The novel, published in 1985, garnered lavish praise from Cynthia Ozick in a front page *New York Times Book Review* article. The *Times*'s daily reviewer proclaimed it the first Gaddis book he could read with pleasure and in fact the first he could finish, though this had not stopped him from reviewing *J R*.

By the time *A Frolic of His Own* appeared in 1994, Gaddis's position as an elder statesman of American letters was secure. The novel was greeted with a torrent of praise and a second National Book Award, placing Gaddis in the rarefied company of Saul Bellow, John Updike, and Philip Roth. Mario Cuomo named Gaddis the official writer of New York State. A growing number of book-length studies of Gaddis's work appeared, led by Steven Moore's essential scholarship. Even though the heavy cigarette smoking featured throughout the novels had begun to take its toll on their creator, it seemed as though Gaddis had finally achieved the literary recognition that had eluded him through lonely decades of obscure toil. William Gaddis died of prostate cancer on 17 December 1998. At the time of his death, he was working on a manuscript entitled *Agape Agape*. This project, originally envisioned as a nonfiction work on automation and the arts, centering on a history of the player piano, eventually was transformed into a fictional monologue in the style of Thomas Bernhard. It is not clear presently when or if this manuscript will be published, although a forty-page translated excerpt was broadcast as *Torshlusspanik* (an allusion to *J R)* on German radio in 1999.

Of the critical work now extant on Gaddis's oeuvre, Moore's remains the best starting point. Moore has performed indispensable philological labors on all Gaddis's books. His *Reader's Guide to William Gaddis's "The Recognitions"* not only provides background on the book's countless allusions but also identifies the references on which Gaddis relied. Moore has performed similar studies for Gaddis's other novels; these annotated guides are available on the Internet at the *Gaddis Annotations* website. This site also contains Moore's exhaustive Gaddis bibliography. His *William Gaddis* is a useful thematic overview of Gaddis's writing up to *Carpenter's Gothic*. Finally, he and John Kuehl edited the seminal *In Recognition of William Gaddis,* the first collection of critical essays devoted to the author. Of particular interest in this collection are John Leverance's "Gaddis Anagnorisis," a rhetorical analysis of Gaddis's style as a pastiche of "seventeenth-century loose baroque prose" (Leverance 33), Steven Weisenburger's "Paper Currencies: Reading William Gaddis," an inventive discussion of the interplay of art and currency in *The Recognitions* and *J R,* and David Koenig's "The Writing of *The Recognitions.*" This last essay is adapted from

Koenig's dissertation "Splinters from the Yew Tree," a study of the structure and composition of *The Recognitions*. Koenig had access to Gaddis's notes and manuscripts in the preparation of his thesis, making this an invaluable exploration of Gaddis's creative process, although in a later interview with Kuehl and Moore, Gaddis disputes Koenig's interpretation that Harcourt, Brace insisted upon substantial cutting of the manuscript.

Critical interest in Gaddis expanded alongside the large-scale importation of French theory into American English departments. Since many of Gaddis's characteristic obsessions—counterfeiting, art and the cash nexus, the duplicity of language—mirror theoretical concerns, it is unsurprising that some sympathetic critics have read Gaddis as an illustration of theory, just as more conservative critics condemn Gaddis and theory as springing from the same decadent and obscurantist impulse. *Carnival of Repetition,* by John Johnston, and *The Ethics of Indeterminacy in the Novels of William Gaddis,* by Gregory Comnes, provide examples of both the benefits and the perils of such an approach. Both studies do illuminate Gaddis's work, but they pay short shrift to the aspects of Gaddis's fiction that resist theory's linguistic vertigo. While characters like Basil Valentine and Cates might delightedly agree that "there is nothing outside the text/system," it is less clear that Gaddis would endorse this conclusion. Christopher Knight's *Hints and Guesses: William Gaddis's Fiction of Longing* serves as a useful corrective to this theoretical turn, and its rich cultural contextualizations of the novels are an essential resource for any serious study of Gaddis.

Any attempt at an overview of Gaddis's work is bound to be incomplete, given its complexity and grand scale. Suitably caveated, though, we may begin exploring his work by examining three pairs of master concepts about which the novels incessantly inquire: tradition/innovation, realism/artifice, interpretation/misinterpretation. Each of these pairs (we can call them binary oppositions if we must) define a dimension of conceptual space which Gaddis explores both thematically and formally throughout his career. For example, the interplay of tradition and innovation is considered thematically through the omnipresence of technology and its effect upon art. This subject, the focus of both the unfinished monograph *Agape Agape* and Gaddis's first published work outside the *Harvard Lampoon,* "Stop Player. Joke No. 4," haunts all the novels. In a casual conversation between Wyatt and Esther in *The Recognitions,* we find "(a discussion: did the coming of the printing press corrupt? putting a price on authorship, originality)" (92). Oscar Crease's central struggle in *A Frolic of His Own* concerns the usurpation of his play by the movies; he only sees the movie itself when it is played on television, an even more technically sophisticated and commercially degraded medium. A stream of advertisements, radio commentary, and telephone conversation provides the sonic backdrop to all the novels.

But while Gaddis is clearly skeptical of enthusiasts for technological "progress," he is not a simple reactionary. It is, after all, surprising when he declares that *J R* is "in many ways a traditional novel" (qtd. in Knight 20). *The Recognitions* does reflect a nostalgia for the situation of the Flemish painters, who "found God everywhere. There was nothing God did not watch over, nothing, and so this . . . and so in the painting every detail reflects . . . God's concern with the most insignificant objects in life, with everything, because God did not relax for an instant then, and neither could the painter then" (251). But this nostalgia is coupled with an awareness that the harmonious marriage of form and content available to the Flemish painter has ruptured beyond repair. As a result, an artist who, like Gaddis, refuses to settle for an art in service of the modern gods of self or commerce cannot simply retreat into imitation of received forms, the sort of unsuccessful strategy pursued by new formalism in poetry, for example. Such a strategy will result only in a counterfeit of the original impulse. Instead, Gaddis embraces innovative form, featuring liberal employment of parody, pastiche, collage, and distancing devices, in the service of such traditional, if contradictory, ends as the accurate representation of reality, the creation of an autonomous artifact, moral instruction, and entertainment. This tension between form and content, coupled with the incompatibilities discernible within the novels' guiding intentions, accounts for much of the mixed brio and pathos of Gaddis's creations.

Gaddis gives our second theme, the nature of reality, a similar dialectical treatment. His work cannot be described as simply realistic, although one can find in it painstakingly accurate descriptions of the minutiae of counterfeiting, high finance, and the law, as well as close observation of the conversational patterns of contemporary Americans. Neither is it pure artifice, turning its back upon the world to signify nothing but the bare wealth of its own intrinsic patterning, even if the novels both separately and as a whole are marked by intricate structures of conceptual rhyme and self-reference. Gaddis's approach to the question of realism might be most accurately described as naturalistic means put to non-naturalistic ends. Gaddis disliked the work of Vladimir Nabokov, but his writing has a closer affinity to Nabokov's than to that of many writers more commonly cited as Gaddisian. Both writers successfully convey a sense of a cosmos governed less by ironclad laws of causation than by cruel and whimsical relations of coincidence, paradox, and irony. But while their universes are arbitrary, their descriptions of it are not. Only through obsessively careful attention to the specific data of the actual world, Marianne Moore's real toads in imaginary gardens, can these two master conjurers create their poetic alternate realities, these worlds recognizably ours even when most askew.

Much of the difficulty in Gaddis's texts can in fact be traced to one or the other of these impulses. In the service of naturalism, the authorial presence, already attenuated in large swaths of *The Recognitions,* virtually disappears from the later novels. Almost all of the action of these novels is related through dialogue; what narration there is tends to description, if lyrical, of the natural world. Psychological motivations and causality must be inferred from the behavior presented to the reader. On the other hand, these patterns of motivation and causality are tangled in the extreme. Seemingly insignificant details can assume major importance through the mysterious operations of a chance essentially identified with fate through its "unswerving punctuality," as a phrase occurring in all four novels observes (*R* 9; *J R* 486; *CG* 223; *F* 50). These intricate plots, communicated as they are inferentially through dialogue and scattered observations, make intense demands upon a reader's concentration. Though Gaddis is avowedly a difficult author, he is rarely obscure; for the most part, close reading will yield the significance of the initially darkest passage.

A passage from *J R* may help clarify our consideration of the interplay between realism and artifice. The frustrated writers Tom Eigen and Jack Gibbs are talking with Beamish, the attorney for Triangle Products, a company in which their suicidal friend Schramm had large holdings:

—Jack damn it look take that off will you? and just let Mister Beamish leave if he . . .

—Wait shut up Tom look, twelve million only get about nine after capital gains though right Beamish? Fixed assets seven and a half million look, somebody gives you two million one hundred thousand on that and you get eighty percent of the difference what you ask and what they pay back from taxes, two, three, four hundred wait, God damned many zeroes, million, four million three hundred twenty thousand, wait let me got a pencil?

—Jack God damn it will you just take that off and let Mister Beamish get . . .

—No this ah, this sounds interesting Mister Eigen, I . . .

—Getting all this down Beamish? Wait damn it . . .

—Look now you've split it, what the hell did you . . .

—Three million Beamish can't be right, inventory three million Beamish?

—Yes I'm afraid inventory control had been rather poor until . . .

—Poor must have been God damned nonexistent, all right you take ninety percent of that two point seven million get eighty percent of the difference back on taxes for two hundred forty thousand add it up . . . here Tom, drop in on Mrs Schramm give her these . . . he'd reached under the bed, —still plenty of good wear in them . . .

—What in hell is . . .

—Add it up your asking price is four and a half million and four and a half back on taxes you've got nine all you'd get anyhow, write off some of those accounts receivable as bad debts and you might cut off another half a million, how's that. (395)

At first, such a passage presents serious difficulties for the reader, not the least of which is figuring out what is going on. Even disregarding the liberal use of direct address to indicate the direction of the conversation, however, it is fairly easy to identify the various speakers by their distinctive patterns of talk: the deferential tones of Beamish, the profane irascibility of Eigen, and the drunken bravado of Gibbs. The characters do tend to name each other more frequently than is normal. But this single concession to readability is far outweighed by the acute fidelity to real speech patterns demonstrated in the abrupt, lurching interruptions of self and other which only intermittently yield to coherent statements of complete thought. I find particularly sublime in this passage Gibbs's clipped "God damned many zeroes" as he calculates a possible tax write-off.

The details of that calculation offer the other realistic aspect of the scene. Like the other financial intricacies of *J R,* like the legal niceties of *A Frolic of His Own,* and like the historical, anthropological, and pharmacological arcana of *The Recognitions,* Gibbs's plan for selling Triangle Products successfully turns out to be factually accurate for the most part. Although the book value of the company is, Beamish assures the men, substantially over $12 million, the company has been difficult to unload, in part because its investments in tobacco and wallpaper appear to have been ill-timed. Gibbs argues that selling the company for four and a half million turns out, after taxes, to be equivalent to selling it for twelve million. Capital gains taxes reduce the twelve million to a net nine. Tax breaks on losses of $5.4 million on fixed assets and $300,000 on inventory, on the other hand, add an additional $4.56 million to a sale price of $4.5 million.

While *J R* documents late-twentieth-century financial and linguistic practices quite faithfully, it is also a densely plotted network of symbolic meanings. Throughout the book, several characters' clothes, initially definitive of identity, deteriorate and migrate from one character to another. This process represents one strand in the larger theme of entropy, a theme signaled by the name Gibbs (Willard Gibbs formulated the second law of thermodynamics (Abadi-Nagy 74)). When Tom Eigen rebukes Gibbs for rummaging through their dead friend's wardrobe, we are given one more fleeting moment in a sequence that also contains: the tear in Gibbs's pocket from the subway (243); the loss of Gibbs's shoe, loosened when its lace burst into flame, to the renegade taxi driver Hardy Suggs (272); Gibbs's, Vogel's, and Glancy's purchases from the thrift store to which Dan diCephalis's daughter has sold his suits for Brownie points (319); and Amy's gift to Gibbs of Joubert's old summer suit (484).

The scene, in its casual glimpse of this ceaseless downward spiral of clothing exchanges, exemplifies several of Gaddis's most characteristic artifices. First, as Johnston has detailed for *The Recognitions,* Gaddis's characters take part in elaborate systems of mapping and mirroring. Gibbs, for instance, by being caught up in the clothing exchange, is linked to Bast (whose shoe he borrows), diCephalis, and Joubert. And these characters all share deeper resemblances to Gibbs. Bast and diCephalis are also working on major projects, though Bast is able to continue working by reducing the scale of his musical work, and diCephalis enjoys institutional support for his conformist work on measurement. Gibbs is linked to Joubert through Amy, not just by being her lover, but by ultimately disappointing her.

While the intensity with which Gaddis pursues these systematic resemblances between his characters is distinctive, one might stop short of Johnston's assessment that "the proper name in Gaddis's fiction designates not so much a subject as something happening among a set of terms or elements" (139). It is rather the *tension* between the opposing perspectives of characters as psychologically motivated actors and as products and pawns of impersonal systems, discursive and otherwise, that Gaddis exploits. His work as a whole bears implicitly the message that the simultaneous necessity and impossibility of reconciling this tension is a, perhaps *the,* crucial issue for contemporary life. We must not delude ourselves about the possibilities for individual action in a world governed by vast corporate-military-governmental bureaucratic structures, by entropic natural law, and by the vagaries of chance. But at the same time, the realism that such a systemic view entails must not become acquiescence. A meaningful life is still possible, though by no means easy, as Gaddis's own example makes clear.

The clothing interchange also provides an example of the rich layers of interconnection which link all the novels. Through recurrences of character and incident, the three later novels in particular create an imaginary New York metropolitan area to rival Faulkner's Yoknapatawpha County; such interconnections include the revelation that Christina Lutz (from *Frolic*) and Elizabeth Booth (from *Carpenter's Gothic*) were schoolmates. The novels are also thematically interconnected: not only by the large-scale themes of tradition, artifice, and interpretation, but by lower-level topics to which Gaddis returns repeatedly. So we could see the gradual deterioration of suits and shoes as they pass from character to character as one more illustration of Gresham's Law, the principle that bad money drives out good, a principle often mentioned in *The Recognitions*. Gaddis clearly believed that the law applied not only to its immediate economic context, in which people tend to hoard coinage of greater purity and circulate coinage of lesser, but to systems of exchange in general.

Finally, Tom Eigen and Jack Gibbs both serve as figures for Gaddis himself. Eigen has invested seven years in writing "one of the most important books in American literature" (417) according to Gall, himself another Gaddis stand-in. The book, however, was neglected by its publisher and attracted a small audience indeed. He supports himself and his family with corporate writing jobs and continues to work on a play about the Civil War; the fragment of the play we are given (262) turns up again in Oscar Crease's Civil War play *Once in Antietam* (*Frolic* 70). Gibbs, in turn, has labored unsuccessfully for years on an opus about mechanization in the arts entitled *Agape Agape*. Similar figures for the author abound in the other novels: besides Oscar Crease, these include Willie, the novelist working on an arcane novel intended for "a rather small audience" (373) in *The Recognitions,* as well as that novel's Otto, who shares Gaddis's youthful affectation of keeping his writing arm in a sling, and McCandless in *Carpenter's Gothic*. Is it paradoxical for an author so insistent upon the divide between writers' lives and work to inscribe himself repeatedly in that work? Gaddis, after all, in response to inquiries about his life, has cited Wyatt Gwyon's "What did you want of him that you didn't get from his work?" (*Recognitions* 95). But from this authorial reticence arises no inconsistency, just as the wealth of allusion in his work does not belie Gaddis's impatience with questions about influence. In each case he objects to the search for reductive explanations of the novels which seek to evade their essential fictionality, substituting putative knowledge of the work's "real sources" for the complex and elusive experience of the novels themselves.

The question of interpretation provides the final grand theme of Gaddis's writing. This issue gets its fullest exploration in *A Frolic of His Own,* which takes as its subject the arena in which interpretation has its most visible consequences in America, the legal system. Justice Oliver Wendell Holmes appears as a guiding spirit for that book's Judge Crease, as Norbert Wiener does for Gibbs in *J R*. Holmes's pragmatic legal realism denied the recurrent fantasy that proper interpretations of the law, and in particular the American Constitution, can be reduced to an automatic divination of original intent, a legal fundamentalism that in contemporary times often allies itself with the biblical fundamentalism attacked in *Carpenter's Gothic*. Rather, Holmes viewed legal interpretation as an always provisional process of finding living meaning in the dead letter of the law by balancing the competing claims of intent, precedent, and present context: "as the law is administered by able and experienced men, who know too much to sacrifice good sense to a syllogism, it will be found that, when ancient rules maintain themselves . . . , new reasons more fitted to the time have been found for them, and that they gradually receive a new content, and at last a new form, from the grounds to which they have been transplanted" (qtd. in Knight 220). Interpretation, Gaddis and Holmes would agree, is a human necessity, always fraught with peril, for which, as Eliot said of criticism, there is no method but to be very intelligent. Perhaps the greatest danger is a rigid insistence upon one's own perspicacity.

Examples of the deceptive certainty which attends misinterpretation abound. More sophisticated versions of the biblical fundamentalists include the power brokers who believe they discern the real workings of the world, men like Recktall Brown and Jack Cates, and to a lesser degree Paul Booth. Supremely confident in their ability to read and direct events in their own interests, all suffer eventual falls from their heights of influence. *The Recognitions* is replete with comic misreadings and misunderstandings. Some are mere snapshots: "He's been talking for simply hours about the solids in Oochello. Wherever that is" (570). Some have weightier significance, as when "Dick" sends Reverend Gwyon's ashes in an oatmeal can to the Real Monasterio de Nuestra Senora de la Otra Vez. And a cascade of misinterpretations accounts for the book's most hilarious scene, Otto's attempt to meet his father, Mr. Pivner, for the first time. Mr. Pivner tells Otto to wear a green scarf, so that Pivner can identify him. Unfortunately, Frank Sinisterra has given identical instructions to his partner in counterfeiting, whom he is meeting in the same hotel bar.

Another moment of misinterpretation in *The Recognitions* anticipates a set piece in *Carpenter's Gothic*. While visiting his lover, Esther, who is married to Wyatt Gwyon, Otto indicates a drawing on the wall of Wyatt's studio. It is, he asserts, a "magical diagram," led to this conclusion by an earlier conversation with Wyatt about alchemy. Esther corrects him, explaining that the diagram is only a study in perspective (129). Similarly, in *Carpenter's Gothic,* Paul Booth sketches out for his wife the web of influence which he expects to navigate. Later, the Mormon missionary-turned-spook Lester interprets the sketch as an illustration of the battle of Crécy (147). While McCandless, himself no slouch at interpretation, makes light of Lester's certainty ("Always get it right don't you, Lester"), Lester's misinterpretation does get a note of support from the narrator, who, forsaking his usual neutrality, likens the arrows on Paul's sketch to those that darkened "the skies over Crécy" (107). And Lester's reading carries a seed of truth, if we accept the apocalyptic intimations of the final pages: just as Crécy inaugurated the use of firepower, the forces sketched by Paul have brought about its apotheosis. Even if misinterpretation is ubiquitous, it may fortuitously lead us to the truth, just as the worthless painting concealed under a forged Titian may itself conceal a real Titian (*Recognitions* 450).

American novelists, a cranky, unreasonable bunch as befits an unreasonable and cranky country, continue to cobble together impossibly grand imitations of life in bicycle shops and ivy-eroded faculty offices long after the great American prospectus eclipsed the novel as a measure of youthful ambition. Even as this odd guild cherishes the novels of William Gaddis for models of crafty accomplishment, the least savvy among us must recognize with what consummate grace the fates have deigned to replace reality as we once knew it with a Gaddisian simulation. Sadly, Gaddis did not live to see missile strikes in Khartoum and impassioned exhortations for impeachment occasioned by the lingual exertions of a young Revlon PR rep, missed the instauration of the amiably dull scion of the Texas Bushes certified per curiam in the dead of night, never heard waitstaff and computer technicians angrily denounce the death tax which robs Rockefellers and Waltons alike of the fruits of their forebears' labors. But had Gaddis lingered to view the latest rigged trials of our heralded missile defense system, he might have repeated the questions with which he closed his 1981 piece for *Harper's,* "The Rush for Second Place": "Will anyone be left to sing the day's hit song, 'Yes, We Have No Mananas'? Will anyone have been accountable? And will it, any of it, have been worth doing well?" (39).

The Recognitions (1955)

On the infrequent occasions when *The Recognitions* is discussed, it is often described as a novel about forgery, an observation as cogent as that *Moby-Dick* is about whaling. The central character, Wyatt

Gwyon, is a talented painter who turns to forging Old Masters when his attempts at original painting prove unsuccessful. Gaddis began the novel as a parodic retelling of *Faust,* and the novel retains at its core the story of Wyatt's temptation by the Mephistophelean Recktall Brown, his ensuing mental and spiritual deterioration, and his eventual redemption. But like Melville's meditations on the whale ship *Essex,* Gaddis's parody of Faust grew into a labyrinth which encompassed a critique of contemporary society, a reflection on the nature of art, and an allegory of the ultimate nature of the cosmos.

The novel opens with the death of Wyatt's mother, Camilla. Crossing the Atlantic with her husband, a Calvinist minister, Camilla is taken ill and dies as the result of a botched appendectomy performed by the counterfeiter Frank Sinisterra, posing as a ship's doctor. Reverend Gwyon has Camilla buried in Spain and, after a period of travel, returns home to his young son. Gwyon is a distant father, preferring to pursue the studies in the pagan roots of Christianity, particularly Mithraism, which exert a growing power over his thought. Under the pious scrutiny of his Aunt May, Wyatt develops a talent for painting, exercised in copying European masterworks; in particular, Wyatt works on a likeness of the Hieronymus Bosch tabletop which Gwyon brought back from Europe. He does not finish this piece before leaving home to study for the ministry, just as he cannot finish a copy of his mother's portrait, or any original work. In the years that follow, Wyatt abandons his theological studies for art, rejects an offer from the unscrupulous art critic Cremer, who promises favorable reviews in return for a percentage of sales, and settles in New York with his wife, Esther, where he works as an architectural draftsman and restorer of paintings.

This atmosphere of promise unfulfilled is transformed upon the arrival of Recktall Brown, apparently conjured by Wyatt with a spell from the *Grand Grimoire* (Moore, *Reader's Guide* 126). Brown, a vulgar, mysterious businessman, convinces Wyatt to forge works by such Flemish masters as van der Goes and Bouts. They are abetted in this scheme by Basil Valentine, a renegade Jesuit, secret agent of Hungary, and connoisseur of art. Valentine publicly raises doubts about the authenticity of these works and then confirms their provenance. As models for these "rediscovered" paintings, Wyatt uses his own image, captured in a mirror, and the poet and heroin addict Esme. Esme, to whom Wyatt feels an increasing erotic attachment, is explicitly linked to Wyatt's lost mother; she serves as the model for the completion of Wyatt's copy of his mother's portrait, and in a final encounter, she dons Camilla's earrings before entering Wyatt's bed.

Wyatt's growing doubts about his enterprise with Brown and Valentine come to a head when he informs Valentine that he has kept fragments from the forgeries, in order to prove his authorship should the occasion arise. At Valentine's suggestion, Wyatt turns these fragments over to him before leaving New York. In a state of mental disorder, mirrored in a stream-of-consciousness narrative, Wyatt returns to his father's house, in a confused attempt to return to the ministry. The Reverend Gwyon, however, lost in arcane studies and schnapps, takes his son for an aspirant to the Mithraic priesthood, arrived to undergo the twelve trials of fortitude, including death at the hands of the Pater Patratus. After destroying the forged Bosch tabletop that he had substituted for the original years ago, Wyatt returns to New York. There, at Brown's Christmas party, he tries to expose their forgery ring, only to find that Valentine has destroyed the evidence left in his keeping. At the height of the party, Brown dies, falling down the stairs in a suit of armor he had donned as a frolic. The party quickly disperses, leaving only Valentine and Wyatt to squabble over the corpse. When Valentine tries to seduce him into a renewed partnership, Wyatt stabs him with Brown's penknife. He then flees to Europe, echoing his father's dictum: "Spain is a land to flee across" (429).

At the cemetery in San Zwingli, where his mother was buried decades ago, Wyatt encounters her killer, Frank Sinisterra. Sinisterra, who has taken the name "Yak" (the name of the quarry of Mr. Inononu, a Hungarian associate of Valentine's), has read that an Egyptologist named Kuvetli (Inononu disguised) seeks a lost mummy; he plans to fake a mummy using a body from the cemetery. Sinisterra is aware of his responsibility for Camilla's death, and, in recompense, he offers Wyatt a forged passport ("Stephan Asche") and enlists his aid in the mummy hoax. He keeps a watchful eye over "Stephan," fruitlessly trying to dissuade him from carousing with prostitutes, including the innocent Pastora. Frank makes a mummy from the body of a martyred little cross-eyed girl, mistakenly placed in Camilla's tomb; the girl's putative body, en route to the Vatican for beatification, had been remarked upon for its large size. Stephan and Frank travel together to Madrid, the mummy in tow; at the train station, separated momentarily from Frank, Stephan flees when he hears that the police are searching for a North American "falsificador."

He finds refuge at the Real Monasterio de Nuestra Senora de la Otra Vez ("Our Lady of the Second Time"), where his father had stayed years ago, and where the rapist-murderer of the little cross-eyed girl does penance as the janitor. Here he is discovered by Ludy, a relentlessly middlebrow novelist writing a piece on religion for a popular magazine (the style of Ludy's drafts suggest Henry Luce's *Time).* Confronted by Ludy, who took him for a thief, he introduces himself as Stephen (the name his mother intended for him). During their conversation, he explains his practice of "restoring" the monastery's paintings by scraping away their surfaces, while he and Ludy eat the grayish bread which the monks have unwittingly baked out of the Reverend Gwyon's remains. He tells Ludy of his adventures in North Africa, where he shot in self-defense Han, his companion from student days. In his last conversation with Ludy, Stephen, freed finally from his legacies of familial guilt and loss, makes Thoreauvian resolutions to "simplify" and "live deliberately," and then he is gone.

Though Wyatt is the central character of *The Recognitions,* this synopsis of his story cannot do justice to the book, considering that he figures only intermittently in the action of the book's middle five hundred pages, often disappearing for close to a hundred pages at a time. Aspects of Wyatt's situation are mirrored in the novel's myriad lesser characters, a circumstance signaled by the vanishing of Wyatt's name after the third chapter. Gaddis wrote during composition: "he [Wyatt], the no-hero or not-yet-hero, is what the other person might be: in Valentine's case, the self-who-can-do-more, the creative self if it had not been killed by the other, in Valentine's case, Reason, in Brown's case, material gain; in Otto's case, vanity and ambition; in Stanley's case, the Church; in Anselm's case, religion, &c. &c." (qtd. in Koenig 100). All of Wyatt's heroic and antiheroic actions take place against a vividly drawn background of artists, frauds, would-be artists, would-be frauds, and critics. These include Arthur/Anselm, the scat-obsessed writer who hides Tolstoy's *Kingdom of God* inside a girlie magazine, and who eventually castrates himself before joining a monastery; Stanley, the pious composer who perishes in the novel's final lines, as the cathedral at Fenestrula collapses around him; Max, the fraudulent painter who offers a torn workshirt as abstract expressionist canvas and publishes Rilke's first Duino Elegy as his own; Big Anna, the gay sunburned Boy Scout fancier; and Mr. Feddle, last seen holding a copy of Dostoyevski's *Idiot,* its dust jacket hand-lettered with his own name.

Of all these, the most central to the novel is Otto Pivner, Harvard graduate and aspiring playwright, introduced to us as he insinuates himself into Wyatt and Esther's domestic life. Otto cadges many of his lines, both for conversation and for his play, from Wyatt; Gaddis describes Gordon, the protagonist of Otto's play, as "a figure who resembled Otto at his better moments, and whom Otto greatly admired, [who] said things which Otto had overheard, or thought of too late to say" (121). After a brief affair with Esther, Otto heads for Central America. He returns from this adventure sporting a sling, which, he claims, he got during an outbreak of revolutionary violence. Like Wyatt, Otto has a troubled relation with his father; in fact, he has never met Mr. Pivner, a meek diabetic. A meeting arranged between them leads, through a hilarious series of mishaps, to Otto mistaking Frank Sinisterra for his father, being mistaken for Frank's counterfeit pusher, and thereby receiving $5,000 in counterfeit twenties. Distributing this unexpected largesse freely, Otto is responsible for Stanley's arrest. Shaken by this revelation, he meets Wyatt shortly after the scene at Brown's party. Wyatt, however, is interested only in the fate of his model Esme, committed to Bellevue after a suicide attempt. Otto abandons New York for Central America again. This time, he is caught up in a real revolution. In the tumult he is knocked unconscious; revived, he is amnesiac and states that his name is Gordon.

Even this woefully brief summary of Otto's career makes plain how large a role the idea of recurrence plays in *The Recognitions*. Although this concept is most evident in the theme of counterfeiting and forgery central to both the main plot and the embroidery of subplots, it is not restricted to these local themes. Rather, it comes to work as a principle at the level of plot and action itself. The dramatic structure of *The Recognitions* is essentially at war with itself. On the one hand, as the above synopsis displays, Wyatt's story follows a traditional narrative plan of linear progress; Wyatt succumbs to temptation, experiences various trials and setbacks culminating in the climax of Brown's death, and eventually finds a kind of redemption in his Thoreauvian resolve. But Gaddis's growing discomfort with this very traditional structure is indicated by his change in plan regarding its resolution. Initially, he planned "a final chapter in which Wyatt would be 'at last redeemed through love' " (Koenig 36). By returning to the prostitute Pastora and their daughter, Wyatt would achieve narrative closure to rival anything offered by Oprah's book club. In turning away from this dream of dramatic fulfillment, Gaddis inevitably foregrounded the other principle at work throughout the book, that of static recurrence. The tension between these two principles is not a flaw in *The Recognitions;* rather, it is an essential strength of the book that it creates a space for the coexistence of the principles of progress and of stasis, each with their own truth, their own enduring grip upon the imagination.

An apparently trivial example of what I mean by the principle of static recurrence is provided by the joke of Carruthers and his horse. Moore helpfully provides the joke, which is never given in full, in his *Reader's Guide:* "two stuffy British majors are discussing the latest scandal: 'Heard about Carruthers?' 'No.' 'Been drummed out of the army.' 'God, what for?' 'Caught in the act with a horse.' 'Ghastly! Mare or stallion?' 'Mare, of course—nothing queer about Carruthers!' " (Moore 97). While the joke has obvious thematic relevance, given the mingled homoeroticism and homosexual panic that suffuses the text, I am more interested here in the effect of its repetition. We encounter the joke at pages 66, 306, 631, and 941. These appearances give us glimpses of the joke's development: at 631, we learn that Carruthers had a mare, while at 941, we get the punchline—"Nothing queer about Carruthers." In a sense, then, the course of the joke through the length of the book gives us a narrative development. A joke is, after all, a model of narrative writ small. Stripped of such fripperies as symbolism, mood, and character development, a successful joke gives rise to the pure rising tension and sudden release which narratologists have long discerned at the heart of plot. But the periodic recurrence of the joke over the course of this immense, insanely complex novel produces a different effect: not one of progressive discovery, but of familiar recognition. This recognition in turn gives rise to a disturbing and uncanny sense of ennui. One does not admire the tellers of the joke for their wit. Instead, they appear almost like automata, pointlessly shifting about chits in an endless linguistic exchange. As Ed Feasly puts it, "finally we're all just parodies of each other" (614). Like Rilke's angel, Carruthers hovers changelessly over this absurd social panorama, ceaselessly pursuing his equestrian delights.

This may seem an overinterpretation of what is, after all, a minor joke in the vast framework of the novel. But its pattern, in which apparent action is transformed by repetition into stasis, recurs at all levels of the novel. Verbal echoes are omnipresent, both within characters' speech and in the narration: for instance, the critic's inevitable answer to "Did you read it?" "No, but I know the son of a bitch who wrote it" (179, 936); or the duplicate descriptions of San Zwingli, which appears "suddenly, at a curve in the railway, a town built of rocks against rock, streets pouring down between houses like the beds of unused rivers" (16, 776). Actions in the novel also frequently mirror earlier actions. All the cocktail parties end in violence: Herschel striking Hannah, the critic slugging Anselm, Wyatt stabbing Valentine. Conversations between Otto and Esther parodically replicate earlier conversations between Wyatt and Esther (147-48, 619-22). Finally, Wyatt's project of forgery is intended as an attempt to replicate a lost Golden Age. By abandoning the contemporary demand for originality and obsessively reconstructing the material processes of the old masters, Wyatt hopes to recover a spiritual purity to which they had access. If this attempt is determined to fail by the inherent vice of his materials and models, necessarily tainted with timeliness, it is also continuous with his father's effort to reconstruct through scholarship the primordial roots of monotheism underneath the accretions of Christianity.

This unmasking of apparent activity as mere repetitive status lies at the heart of the novel's theory of history. The characters who, unlike Max, reject the bad faith of our time universally suffer from malaise. Though the patent roots of this malaise vary from individual to individual, Gaddis implicitly diagnoses a single latent root: modern historicist self-consciousness. Historically naive eras could experience the narratives which gave meaning and direction to life as necessary and progressive. But in our contemporary plight, we are doomed to see all narratives, and hence all values, as contingent; our lives come to seem stale repetitions of earlier forms, once vital, now drained of meaning. The figures of Gwyon, Wyatt, and Stanley warn us that simple nostalgia is no remedy for this problem. We cannot choose to live in simpler times. In fact, as Valentine reminds Wyatt, even our impression of these times as simpler is a sentimental fantasy: "your precious van Eyck, do you think he didn't live up to his neck in a loud vulgar court? In a world where everything was done for the same reasons everything's done now? for vanity and avarice and lust?" (689-90). Transcendental meaning was never easily won; and to the extent that earlier eras did afford traditions within which such meaning could be found, these traditions cannot be reconstructed through individual fiat.

Were those first reviewers justified, then, who criticized Gaddis for his harsh, despairing view of life? Put aside the question whether "heart-warming" is the highest term of critical praise, whether James Herriot beats *King Lear*. Gaddis's work does offer hope. While Gaddis himself located the hopefulness in his work in the destinies of his characters ("Wyatt has been part of the corruption, but at the end he says we must simply live it through and make a fresh start" (Abadi-Nagy 64)), I think it is more usefully discerned in the accomplishments of the novels themselves. It is often remarked that Gaddis's novels are littered with failed artistic ambitions. Too often the quick conclusion is drawn that Gaddis himself recommends something like Wyatt's retreat into antiart, scraping away the painted surfaces, or Bast's gradual diminution of his musical project, as though Gaddis failed to realize that the massive scale and ambitions of his own novels contradicted their imputed message. The real message of the novels is that literature remains a living tradition, within which the most extravagant victories may still be won, provided one steers clear of the traps that ensnare the likes of Wyatt and Bast. Bast is done in by an inability to focus on his project and recognize the dangers of his entanglements with J R and Crawley. Wyatt, on the other hand, like Stanley, suffers from the misguided character of his devotion to art. Their reverence for art tempts them into cathedrals whose foundations can no longer be trusted. Pure irreverence is no solution, either, unless one takes Max as one's model. It is an *irreverent reverence* for tradition, as epitomized by Gaddis himself, that alone can clear a space within which real work might still be done. The dialectic nature of this stance is given concrete form in the brief self-portrait of Willie carrying "two books, one titled, *The Destruction of the Philosophers*, the other *The Destruction of the Destruction*" (734).

In no aspect of the novel is this spirit of serious play more apparent than in its allusiveness. The overwhelming density of allusion in the novel perturbed many initial reviewers; one typically petulant critic wrote in the *Hudson Review:* "as we press on through Mr. Gaddis's heavy artillery fire (I counted eight different languages *en route,* and there may well have been more) we begin to suspect that his contempt may extend to all those who know less than he" (Green 55). Specious though such a comment may be, it is perhaps understandable when one encounters a typical catalog of Reverend Gwyon's library: "On the desk before him, piled and spread broadcast about his study, lay Euripides and Saint Teresa of Avila, Denys the Carthusian, Plutarch, Clement of Rome, and the Apocryphal New Testament, copies of *Osservatore Romano* and a tract from the Society for the Prevention of Premature Burial. *De Contemptu Mundi, Historia di tutte l'Heresie, Christ and the Powers of Darkness, De Locis Infestis, Libellus de Terrificationibus Nocturnisque Tumultibus, Malay Magic, Religions de Peuples Noncivilisés, Le Culte de Dionysos en Attique, Philosophumena, Lexikon der Mythologie*" (23). A daunting list. But the conclusion that Gaddis is merely showing off reveals more about the intellectual insecurities of critics than about *The Recognitions.* Allusion in fact serves two distinct functions in the novel. By now, it should be no surprise that these functions are at cross-purposes, nor that I believe this to be a benefit.

On the one hand, Gaddis deeply admired Eliot (Koenig reports that he originally planned to bury a line-by-line parody of *Four Quartets* in *The Recognitions* (67)), and his allusive practice owes much to Eliot's and Pound's modernist collage. A framework of key sources underlies much of the novel. As compiled by Moore, these include *Faust,* Dante, medieval alchemy, and Fraser's *Golden Bough*. As in Pound and Eliot the invocation of these sources serves both to indicate the eternal recurrence of certain aspects of human experience and to demonstrate the debased form that that experience takes in modernity. It is not far at all from Eliot's Marvell parody, "But at my back from time to time I hear/The sound of horns and motors, which shall bring/Sweeney to Mrs. Porter in the spring" (43) to Gaddis's echo of Dante: "He stood numb, surrounded by ice, among the frozen giants of buildings, as though to dare a step would send him head over heels in a night with neither hope of morning to come nor heaven's betrayal of its triumphal presence, in the stars" (699).

But side by side with this nostalgic, reverential function, allusion in *The Recognitions* also has an excessive, comic side. One ought to read the catalog of Gwyon's books not as a challenge, but as something of a joke. A similar jocular spirit animates the Hungarian quotations, which Gaddis picked up from patrons at a Hungarian restaurant. While this excessive display of erudition for humorous purposes might strike one as typically postmodern, it is in fact part of a venerable humanist literary tradition. Reverend Gwyon's library would not be out of place in Rabelais, Montaigne, or Shakespeare, who was not just showing off when he had Holofernes say:

Fauste, precor gelida quando pecus omne sub umbra Ruminat,—and so forth. Ah, good old Mantuan! I may speak of thee as the traveller doth of Venice;

> Venechia, Venechia,
> Chi non te vede, non te pretia.

Old Mantuan, old Mantuan! who understandeth thee not, loves thee not. Ut, re, sol, la, mi, fa. (*Love's Labour's Lost* 4.2.95-100)

J R (1975)

J R is Gaddis's great work. While *The Recognitions* is a virtuoso and deeply intelligent novel, *J R* surpasses it in its rigorously disciplined form, its subtle emotional palette, and its unrelenting diagnosis and critique of the infernal state of contemporary America. Gaddis's later novels, each impressive in its own right, together form an extended coda to *J R*, developing its themes and formal innovations. In this novel Gaddis presciently answers Tom Wolfe's much-heralded call for novelists to return to social documentation. Instead of peddling warmed-over magazine sociology dressed up with typographical tricks, however, Gaddis offers genuine and passionate insight into the nature of power and control in this country. *J R* is also among the most exuberantly inventive works in our literature. Its continuing neglect is a cultural crime.

Unlike *The Recognitions, J R* has no clear central character. The novel tracks several distinct story lines, all linked through overlapping characters, locations, and themes. It takes its title from J R Vansant, a sixth grader living in Massapequa, Long Island. Neglected by his parents, J R attends a typical American middle school, the administrators of which are far more concerned with keeping order and implementing the latest technological and curricular wizardry than with educating their students; as the superintendent observes, "all we've got left to protect here is a system that's set up to promote the meanest possibilities in human nature and make them look good" (463).

J R begins his self-education on a field trip to New York, where his social studies class is buying a share in Diamond Cable, in order to introduce the students to the world of "corporate democracy" (49). Diamond Cable is a subsidiary of the conglomerate Typhon International, which is controlled by the family of J R's teacher, Amy Joubert. During the field trip, J R and a friend visit the bathroom and overhear Joubert's uncle, John Cates, talking to her father, Monty Moncrieff, about a proposed tender of Diamond stock set up to allow Cates a substantial tax write-off. Discovering the children, Cates imparts the secret of leverage, advising them that "the trick's to get other people's money to work for you" (109).

J R takes this lesson to heart. He initiates a stockholder suit against Diamond Cable. By borrowing against the proceeds of his settlement, he buys nine thousand gross of plastic forks from the navy, which he sells to the army at a profit. Buying up discounted bonds, he takes over the dilapidated Eagle Mills. Even though the textile company can't turn a profit, he realizes that its pension fund can serve as collateral for more investments, while pieces of the company can be sold off at a loss and capital investments depreciated at an accelerated rate, yielding substantial tax credits. J R rapidly builds a vast commercial empire, with the reluctant aid of the composer and erstwhile music teacher Edward Bast and an expanding set of dubious agents, none of whom realizes that the voice on the other end of the phone is that of a sixth grader disguised with a ragged handkerchief. At their height, J R's holdings include Ray-X, a toy company diversified into weapons and thermocouples, the women's magazine *Her* (soon redubbed *She)*, integrated chains of nursing and funeral homes, the Nobili pharmaceutical company, and the Alsaka Development Corporation, its name taken from J R's misspelling of Alaska.

The empire's foundations are shaky, though. The lawyer Beamish deplores its "near frenzied emphasis on the letter of the law at the expense of, in fact too frequently in direct defiance of its spirit," with corporate activities "preponderately inspired by such negative considerations as depreciation and depletion allowances, loss carryforwards tax write-offs and similar . . ." (525). Shortly after Bast's disastrous trip to Wisconsin to donate major household appliances to a Native American reservation, unfortunately not yet wired for electricity, during which Bast, in a rented Indian costume, delivers an inflammatory PR statement and touches off a riot, the entire scheme begins to unravel. Federal agents converge on J R Corporation's 96th Street center of operations. Narrowly escaping, Bast and J R share a limousine down Park Avenue, during which J R confides, "I just, always, I mean I always thought this is what it will be like you and, and me riding in this here big limousine down, down this, this here big street . . ." (636). The SEC bars J R and Bast from future involvement with publicly traded companies, but at the novel's end, J R is breathlessly explaining his new plans for entry into public life into an unattended telephone.

Edward Bast's role is not limited to that of J R's representative. The illegitimate son of the composer James Bast, he initially teaches music at J R's school, where he is directing a presentation of Wagner's *Rhinegold*. J R plays the part of Alberich the dwarf in this production, until he absconds with a bag of money standing in for the Rhinegold. Bast soon gives up this job after quoting salacious passages from Mozart's letters over the school television system (though Representative Pecci objects less to Bast's reference to "believing and shitting" than to his mention of "superstitious Italians" (42, 40)). This setback is no tragedy, though, since Bast's teaching job is merely in service of his composing. Initially, like his father, Bast plans to write an opera. Through the course of the novel, this ambition progressively declines, first to an oratorio, then to a suite for small orchestra, and finally to a piece for unaccompanied cello.

Bast's financial activities gradually overwhelm his artistic ambitions, even though these activities rarely pay off as promised. His work for J R, ill-defined and undertaken reluctantly, yields payment only when he cashes in his stock options, a move that leads to his investigation for insider trading. He is also commissioned to write a film score by the idiosyncratic broker Crawley. Bast will provide "zebra music" to back Stamper and Crawley's film of African wildlife, intended to drum up support for stocking American parks with big game. In this endeavor as well, Bast finds getting paid difficult, because Crawley expects him to provide not only a score, but a full recording, the cost of which Bast must bear himself. As a third job, Bast begins monitoring the radio for ASCAP, ensuring that no songs are played without royalties. J R gives him a small transistor radio with an earpiece, and, as Gibbs says, "he composes with that thing playing in his ear all the time" (568).

Bast's frenetic activity eventually puts him in the hospital with double pneumonia, nervous exhaustion, and malnutrition. In the hospital Bast completes his piece for solo cello (using a purple crayon). Bast initially attempts to destroy his composition, feeling that it represents a selfish devotion to an ideal with which he does not even identify. This outburst comes in the wake of his roommate Duncan's death and his learning from the lawyer Coen that his elderly aunts' house has been taken away, his aunts consigned to an Indiana nursing home. But after a confrontation with his cousin and half-sister Stella Angel, in which she confirms that James Bast is his father and informs him that their mother Nellie killed herself, Bast rescues his manuscript from the wastebasket. Leaving with his cousin, who has consolidated her hold on the family player piano business, Bast resolves to live on his own terms: "I've failed enough at other people's things I've done enough other people's damage from now on I'm just going to do my own, from now on I'm going to fail at my own" (718).

Bast is aided in his musical and business endeavors by Jack Gibbs, a fellow teacher, who lends him a key to an apartment on 96th Street in Manhattan. This apartment, the setting for the longest unbroken sections of the novel, emblematizes the novel's descent into chaos. Amid its gushing faucets and unhinged doors, a torrent of characters—including Bast, Gibbs, Tom Eigen, Beamish, the foul-mouthed Rhoda, her musician friend Al, and assorted delivery persons and federal agents—struggles vainly to maintain control, slowly ceding the advantage to the onslaught of mail solicitations, self-help packages, and unrealized intentions. Hidden in the oven is Gibbs's unfinished opus, *Agape Agape,* the density of which may be observed in its opening phrase (following the epigraph: "Please do not shoot the pianist. He is doing his best" (288)): "Posted in a Leadville saloon, this appeal caught the eye of art in its ripe procession of one through the new frontier of the 'eighties where the frail human element still abounded even in the arts as Oscar Wilde alone, observing the mortality in that place is marvelous, passed on unrankled by that phrase doing his best, redolent of chance and the very immanence of human failure that century of progress was consecrated to wiping out once for all" (289).

Gibbs, who initially appears instructing a class on the concept of entropy, renews his commitment to completing this study of art and mechanization through his tenderly observed love affair with Amy Joubert. The affair is consummated some time after the bitterly funny night on which Gibbs and Eigen share recriminations about their failed marriages and Gibbs invents "Split, the Divorce Game." Though Gibbs attempts to finish the book to prove his worthiness to Amy, he finds himself unable to do it; the project, diabolically complex to begin with, cannot be successfully taken up again after a lapse of years. Convinced that he has leukemia, later revealed as a misdiagnosis, Gibbs avoids Amy, who submits to a loveless union with the lawyer Cutler. Gibbs sits for his portrait at the book's close, enjoying an ambiguous freedom after abandoning Amy, *Agape Agape,* and his pseudonymous identity as Grynszpan.

Patrick O'Donnell has noted that the complexity of *J R* is most fundamentally located not at the level of plot, theme, or character, but "in the twinned questions of 'who is speaking?' and 'what is s/he talking about?' " (3). *The Recognitions* demands close attention to the details of its multiple plots, but frequent authorial intervention allows the reader to determine without excessive difficulty the identity of characters and the location of scenes. In *J R,* as though Gaddis generalized from Wyatt's namelessness in the earlier novel, pinning down the specifics of any situation becomes a trying task. This difficulty is signaled from the beginning. The novel announces its grand theme in its first words: "Money . . .? in a voice that rustled" (3), an opening that will be echoed in *Frolic*'s "Justice?—You get justice in the next world, in this world you have the law" (13). But only after several lines can the reader see that this line is spoken by Edward Bast's Aunt Anne in conversation with the lawyer Coen.

This initial scene between Coen and the Bast aunts provides a stylistic and thematic model for the entire book. Their conversation proceeds in associative bursts: the aunts' continual rambling from the focus of his questions frustrates Coen, while his use of technical legal expressions only serves to confuse them further, as when he describes Edward as an infant. During the conversation, such crucial topics as the struggle between commerce and art and the control of corporate operations recurrently rear their heads, while Coen's mishaps (he loses a button and breaks his glasses) anticipate later, larger disasters. Following this scene, the first in a series of narrative transitions effects a cinematic pan from the Bast home to the exterior of Whiteback's bank, where we are introduced immediately to Bast, Joubert, Vogel, and Whiteback. But only after scrupulously attending to a hundred pages or so of initially inscrutable dialogue does the reader begin to comprehend the web of interrelations that thread through the disparate locations of school, corporate headquarters, family home, and artist's studio.

J R foregrounds the inferential work which is the basis of reading. Conventional narrative operates by raising questions which the reader expects the author to resolve in time: Who was the third man carrying Harry Lime's body? Will Henchard be reunited with the wife he sold off? An author creates narrative pleasure by creating and confounding expectations, which can arise only if the reader is inferentially engaged with the story. In *J R,* as in his later novels, Gaddis inscribes this essential mystery of narrative into every moment. Not only is the identity of the mysterious stranger or the nefarious mole in question; so is the identity of every speaker, and the import of his or her words. This puzzling aspect of Gaddis's work, akin to impulses in such writers as Nabokov and Perec, is exemplified in the novel's one-sided telephone calls. Here, for example, is Bast on the phone with J R:

No all right, all right! But listen this list of telephone messages Virginia had waiting for me about all kinds of . . . no that broker Crawley about some drug company with an Italian name and something called Endo whatever it is, somebody named Wiles had been trying to reach me about a string of nursing homes and a lawyer named wait a minute, here it is Beaton who wants to discuss drilling rights on those Alberta and Western right of . . . what? No but listen he's a lawyer and Piscator's a lawyer, let him discuss it with . . . well when he gets back then and you and Piscator can get out there and play to . . . to see who . . .? No, no I haven't been up to the hospital today and I . . . look I don't know if he's still whispering his trade secret to the nurse and I can't sit beside his bed day and night to . . . no I don't have a map right here! and I . . . Well of course the brewery is on a river but I don't know where it is in relation to these Ace mining claims or the Alberta and . . . what? You meant to tell me about what Indian reservation right in between what . . . (381)

The rise and fall of J R Corporation is charted in a series of these one-sided calls. Only an observant reader will understand that Bast here refers to Nobili (the "Italian-named" pharmaceutical company), that J R asks him to visit Mr. Wonder, the brewer, in the hospital, to ensure that he doesn't surrender the secret of his beer (cobalt) to the nurse, and that functionaries of Typhon International (Wiles and Beaton) have begun to take an interest in J R.

While O'Donnell sees these conversations as "radically destabilizing," emblematizing in their fragmentation Baudrillard's notion of the hyperreal, such a reading ignores their very readability. They may be difficult to interpret, but Gaddis takes care to give the reader sufficient information to allow eventual interpretation. The conversations, like the novel as a whole, therefore represent the inverse of the advertising slogans and business jargon that permeate its world, as well as our own. Advertising slogans promise a readability they can never fulfill: "you deserve a break today," on its face a simple, friendly invitation, is in fact the end product of a sophisticated and expensive process, the purpose of which is to engender unlimited desire, a system from within which a "break" is theoretically inconceivable. Business jargon, in a converse process, conceals the most banal and brutal ends under a pseudoscientific and unreadable veneer, as demonstrated in Whiteback's persistent correction of *utilize* for *use,* or in contemporary apologetics for the New Economy. Such practices, I gather, are what Baudrillard gestures at with phrases like "gravity and any fixed point must disappear" (qtd. in O'Donnell 1).

In contrast, Gaddis's novel actually makes good on what it promises. It will deliver its message to its rightful recipient, in return for an investment of time, energy, and intelligence. Its decentered surface to the contrary, the novel even follows a roughly conventional narrative pattern, introducing myriad plot threads over the first hundred pages, bringing them into increasing internal and mutual conflict as J R's company mushrooms from its humble beginnings, culminating in multiple climaxes through the extended section set in the 96th Street apartment, and yielding a denouement during Bast's hospital stay. And if its world demands strenuous effort to interpret, if its gaps must be filled in not through willful readerly fiat but by the patient application of analytic imagination, it resembles in these respects above all others the world in which we dwell. Forcing us to recognize the perils of glib platitudes, whether of certainty or despair, may be Gaddis's supreme achievement.

Like *The Recognitions, J R* is not encyclopedic solely in its investigation of the subject matter of business. It also contains a dazzling array of humorous modes and devices. A brief list of examples encompasses double entendre, scatology, puns, comic characters, and comic confusion: 1) Davidoff explains "he wants a look at what Skinner's got laid out this way Mister Duncan, gal I brought along from Diamond topflight track record in curriculum management in here spreading out this whole textbook line," while Skinner has sex with Miss Flesch in the next room (517). 2) After Nora diCephalis retrieves the penny she had fed to her brother Donny:

—Daddy, I got your penny back. Here . . .
—A rag, I said, don't wipe it on your dress! And look at my sandals! she got past them, rounded the corner and shook the bathroom door. —Dad! Are you in there? A rude sound responded promptly from within. (57)

3) Brisboy the Texan funeral home director tells Bast, "when he was describing the entire package idea on the telephone as vertical integration Mother was simply aghast she thought he meant darkies and whites stacked in layers like a giant Dubos torta" (547). 4) Though Crawley, the obsessive big-game hunter, Vogel the lecherous driver-ed instructor, and Ann diCephalis the artistic virago all

have moments in the spotlight, they are eclipsed by the sublimely incompetent Dave Davidoff; he plans Bast's trip to the Wisconsin reservation: "No most of them never seen one had to have Abercrombie's send out some top archery types to show them how, even had to throw in some topflight canoeists so they'd know which end of the paddle to put in the . . . No it's Brook Yellow Brook not stream, Charley Yellow Brook and his . . . must have seen a first speech draft joke the Boss [J R] came up with about a book called The Yellow Stream by I P Daily thought it might break the ice but . . ." (521). 5) Whiteback tells Amy, "right behind you there Mrs Joubert, some pictures just came in I knew you'd want to see right behind you under those clippings somewhere yes in fact you may want to usel, utilize them on the televised portion of your lesson" (450), unaware that the photos are in fact pornographic pictures which Major Hyde's son has received in the mail.

These examples demonstrate not only the range of humorous incident in the book, but the currents of racism and misogyny that underlie much of the humor. Racial difference gives rise to the running jokes of Bast's mistakenly darkened photo in the Union Falls Weekly Messenger and Davidoff's intentionally darkened photo of the visiting schoolchildren in the Typhon Annual Report; it lies behind the reports of rioting Indians and routed Africans, supplied with toy guns by Ray-X, at the book's close. Sexual humor is omnipresent, from Ann's demand that Dan take her in front of the children for educational purposes to the monstrous Zona Selk's comparison of Ann to Amy/Emily Joubert:

—It's not Emily, I just told you that it's some revolting nurse I said get me some crackers, most disgusting magazine I've ever seen tummy bulge sagging tits laxatives this revolting creature doing yogi tricks in a body stocking here show him this Beaton. There, does that look like Emily?
—Here sir it's, there's a surface resemblance but I believe this is the wife of the parent company's personnel manager the man who's just been lost in, who's taking part in this Teletravel trial apparently he used his influence to get her this position with an aid program to Ind . . .
—Which position show him the top one Beaton show him el hedouli, can you see Emily doing that? Ninny wouldn't lift her leg for the king of . . . (707)

One need not subscribe to a representational Puritanism to find these currents troubling. To be sure, Gaddis's work contains a strong antiracist critique: it is in part the racist attitudes of Zona, Crawley, and Hyde that mark them as thugs and boors. More importantly, both *J R* and *Carpenter's Gothic,* as we shall see, undertake a structural critique of contemporary neocolonialist politics and economics, in which Africans and Native Americans represent only obstacles to the full exploitation of natural resources. This critique is encapsulated in the bitter image conjured by Beaton at *J R*'s close: "those who might attempt to stay on the reservation land would have to carry water some distance on their backs to irrigate the corn" (705). Although Gaddis's writing reflects a more pervasive ambivalence toward women, the crude misogyny of characters like Eigen and Vogel is certainly not depicted charitably. And what separates a comic foil like Ann from a sympathetic character like Rhoda is not sexual appetite; Ann is ridiculous because of her pretensions and cruelty, not because she, like Rhoda, flouts conventionality. Still, by exploiting attitudes for comic effect which he critiques elsewhere, Gaddis creates an uncomfortable excess of meaning. A reader like me who finds the image of the decimated Malawi troops armed with toy guns simultaneously comic, horrible, and ethically questionable is forced to confront his own complicity with the systems whose operation Gaddis chronicles so effectively. Unlike J R, we cannot excuse ourselves by claiming, "see like some of these words I didn't have them yet" (651).

Carpenter's Gothic (1985)

Brief by Gaddis's standards, *Carpenter's Gothic* represents less an extension of *J R* than its distillation. Not only do the novels resemble each other in form and theme; even their main characters share distinct similarities: Elizabeth Booth and Amy Joubert, Paul Booth and Dave Davidoff, McCandless and Gibbs. The largest departure comes in Gaddis's adherence to formal unities of time and place. Strictly conforming to this restriction in letter, while violating it outrageously in spirit, Gaddis focuses attention on the continuities and ruptures between his work and literary tradition.

The story takes place entirely on the property of a Carpenter Gothic house in the Hudson River Valley. The house, owned by the geologist McCandless, is rented by an embittered Vietnam veteran, Paul Booth, and his wife Elizabeth, the heiress to the mining concern Vorakers Consolidated Reserve. Paul, who has previously worked as an intermediary between VCR and corrupt African governments ("Paul the bagman" as Elizabeth's brother Billy calls him), is trying to establish himself as a media consultant. His main client is the Reverend Elton Ude, a Southern fundamentalist preacher hoping to expand his radio ministry in the hospitable climate of the early 1980s. This plan is complicated when Ude accidentally drowns a young boy, Wayne Fickert, and an old man during a baptism in the Pee Dee River.

Paul and Elizabeth's marriage is troubled. A heavy drinker who violently forces his whiskey bottle against the rim of the glass, leaving ubiquitous chips, Paul has left bruises on Elizabeth's shoulder. The rare conversation between them not devoted to Paul's grandiose scheming often focuses on their twin lawsuits, for Liz's physical pain and Paul's loss of consortium, based upon Liz's plane crash four years earlier. Liz retreats from this unhappy situation into an aimless routine of doctor appointments, incomplete projects, and telephone conversations. Her dissatisfaction with her way of life is demonstrated by the lies and exaggerations she tells her friend Edie: "I haven't written a word I haven't even looked at it I've, I've been so busy with, with people here a cancer charity and I'm, I mean I've even started Spanish lessons I just started them, just now when you called, I'd just come back when you called . . ." (35).

The arrival of McCandless alters this dismal domestic scene irreversibly. Upon his arrival at the house to retrieve papers from his locked office, he makes a strong impression upon Elizabeth, who immediately alters her unfinished novel to feature a "man somewhat older, a man with another life already behind him, another woman, even a wife somewhere" (64). And McCandless has several lives and wives already behind him. During a confrontation with his former associate Lester, McCandless reconstructs his singular résumé. He has worked for the CIA in Africa, along with Lester and their station chief Cruikshank, now employed by VCR. While in Africa he carried out geological studies searching for gold near a mission station; Lester and his current employers want McCandless's research notes from these assays. Since his return to the United States, McCandless has written a roman à clef about his African experience, in which the protagonist Frank Kinkead, like Wyatt Gwyon, resolves to live deliberately. He has also written science textbooks. This work led to a confrontation with Rev. Ude's followers in the Southern town of Smackover, in which McCandless defended the theory of evolution against Ude's creation science.

Elizabeth sleeps with McCandless, but for all his worldliness and right intentions, he too disappoints her. Unable to relinquish his pose of amused detachment, a detachment signaled most clearly when he continues to call her "Mrs Booth," he soon ignores her when he finds a more willing student of his apocalyptic theories of history: her brother Billy, a classmate of McCandless's son with a taste for Eastern religion. McCandless entices Billy Vorakers with a diagnosis of the darkening global situation based upon the rise of fundamentalist visions of apocalypse in America and violent instability fueled by neocolonialism in Africa.

This vision meshes perfectly with Paul's activities. Embroiled in a growing atmosphere of violence, epitomized in an encounter with a mugger whom he kills, Paul tries to defend Ude from a welter of charges, ranging from impurities in the water he bottles to liability for the suicide of a boy he counseled. Simultaneously, Paul participates in an intensification of Ude's hysterical rhetoric: "you are witnessing the most satanic and unconstitutional attack on the very fundamentals of American freedom, the dark beginnings of a Marxist dictator state casting the shadow of the powers of darkness over the entire world pray for America" (204).

The scenario which McCandless spins out for Africa comes to pass. Ude, sponsor of a growing African ministry, files a claim for mineral rights to the tract which McCandless had surveyed. McCandless predicts: "Paul thinks he's been using Ude but Ude's been using him and Lester's been using them both because he wrote the scenario, set up that site get a few missionaries killed and then that plane gets shot down" (236); on the plane was Billy Vorakers, in an idealistic attempt to avert war, along with Senator Teakell, an associate of Paul and Ude's. It is difficult to say who ultimately is the beneficiary of these machinations. Although McCandless believes that the powers involved ultimately desire a reestablishment of colonialism, in fact the conflict appears more likely to spark a global conflagration in the service of Ude's millenarian ends, as the headlines in the background of the book's closing make clear: "10K 'Demo' Bomb Off Africa Coast: War News, Pics Page 2"; "Prez: Time to Draw Line Against Evil Empire" (259). While such nightmare scenarios may now seem hyperbolic, at the time the novel was written, fear of nuclear war was an omnipresent fact, a facet of the Age of Reagan often erased in the current revisionism.

McCandless, as Liz discovers, knows that this crisis occurs over a barren tract of land, that his earlier surveys in fact found no gold. His cynicism prevents him from trying to stop the impending conflict; this, coupled with a sense of his responsibility for her brother's death, leaves her deeply disenchanted. Sadly, this disenchantment does not last for long. After meeting McCandless's first wife, not the woman who decorated the house, and discovering that McCandless had spent time in a mental hospital, Liz dies. In a highly ambiguous scene, she apparently faints and strikes her head against the edge of a table. Against the backdrop of Armageddon, Paul leaves for Liz's funeral with her friend Edie, pausing to make a pass at her as their car pulls away.

While *Carpenter's Gothic* is often considered Gaddis's darkest novel—Gaddis himself declared, "I will say that this novel probably contains the least hope of the three" (Abadi-Nagy 75)—it also contains some of Gaddis's most lyrical descriptive writing. Consider the book's opening paragraph:

The bird, a pigeon was it? or a dove (she'd found there were doves here) flew through the air, its colour lost in what light remained. It might have been the wad of rag she'd taken it for at first glance, flung at the smallest of the boys out there wiping mud from his cheek where it hit him, catching it up by a wing to fling it back where one of them now with a broken branch for a bat hit it high over a bough caught and flung back and hit again into a swirl of leaves, into a puddle from rain the night before, a kind of battered shuttlecock moulting in a flurry at each blow, hit into the yellow dead end sign on the corner opposite the house where they'd end up that time of day. (1-2)

In this description of the neighborhood children's casual cruelty, Gaddis lightly weaves patterns of internal rhyme, alliteration, and assonance together with a syntax loosely miming the to-and-fro play of the children to create an elegiac tone, an autumnal music transmuting the banal ugliness of the scene he describes into a kind of poetry. In fact, in "*that time of* day," "*yellow* dead end sign," "swirl of *leaves,*" and "*bough* caught and flung back," the passage echoes a key source underlying much of the imagery of the book: Shakespeare's Sonnet 73:

> That time of year thou mayst in me behold
> When yellow leaves, or none, or few, do hang
> Upon those boughs which shake against the cold,
> Bare ruin'd choirs, where late the sweet birds sang.

Steven Moore reports that Gaddis considered *That Time of Year* as an alternate title for the novel.

Lyrical description of this kind figures in all of Gaddis's writing. Patrick O'Donnell says of the brief narrative transitions in *J R:* "Many of these contain lyrical descriptions of nature in contrast to the entropic remnants of the American junkyard landscape, thus reflecting one of Gaddis's familiar themes: the destruction of 'the primitive' in modern technocratic culture" (13). And Knight argues that the enigmatic beauty of the descriptions of the pond in *A Frolic of His Own* provide a transcendental standard of justice in contrast with the merely human standards present in the main plot of the novel. But in *Carpenter's Gothic* such moments of intense, meditative examination are integrated more systematically into the design of the novel, lending an air of Horatian consolation to the otherwise general pall. This consolation must be fleeting, just as the magic of the dove's resurrection in the first sentence of the novel is immediately tempered by the brutality of the actual situation revealed in the second; it is nevertheless a real presence in the book, ignored only at the peril of falling, like McCandless, into despair.

The novel aims to conquer death in another sense as well. Gaddis explicitly aimed at bequeathing new life to long-defunct literary conventions. The Gothic tradition is invoked most visibly in the scenes from *Jane Eyre* which flicker on Liz Booth's television screen. The world-weary tone of Lester and McCandless as they circle each other in McCandless's living room recalls the spy-ridden entertainments of Graham Greene and John Le Carré. How does Gaddis manage to revivify these conventions without making his book merely a parody of earlier forms? His characteristically oblique narrative method turns out to be suited perfectly to such an endeavor. For example, since interest in the mysterious McCandless has been developed from the opening pages, the moment when he first appears in the flesh, so to speak, could easily devolve into postmodern ironic knowingness; this is as stock a scene as can be. But the moment is defused through the use of minimal description and the characters' halting, banal speech:

—Mrs Booth?
—Is, are you Mister Stumpp?
He just looked at her. His face appeared drained, so did the hand he held out to her, drained of colour that might once have been a heavy tan.
—My name is McCandless, he said, his tone dull as his eyes on her, — you're Mrs Booth?
—Oh! Oh yes come in . . . but her foot held the door till it pushed gently against her, —I didn't . . .
—I won't disturb you, he came in looking past her . . . (59)

A similar combination of understatement and misdirection occurs at the close of the fifth chapter. At first, our expectations appear to be satisfied: a fire has finally engulfed the house, as foreshadowed by *Jane Eyre* and Lester's comments. But in fact the fire is outside; Paul, Elizabeth, and the house are still safe. The fire only masquerades as the expected climax of a traditional Gothic novel, centered upon a private, interior world. We will later have a public conflagration, but one rendered offstage, visible only in the glimpse of a newspaper headline.

This reversal is entirely appropriate for a novel seemingly confined to a single setting in which, however, the plot is driven almost entirely from offstage. Two events that do occur in the house seem fraught with drama. But the first, Liz's fling with McCandless, turns out to be almost entirely inconsequential. Paul does not discover the affair, and it seems unlikely that he takes enough notice of his wife ever to suspect much of anything. And, as noted before, McCandless remains too set in his ways, too sure in his interpretation of self and others, to be changed by his encounter with Liz; as a result, she is only disappointed. The second event, Liz's death, remains fundamentally ambiguous. Much critical ink has been spilled speculating on the cause of that death. Some writers have suggested that Paul has arranged to have Liz killed, signaled by the open door noticed immediately before her death and Paul's suspicious conduct afterward, while others insist that Liz succumbed to her health problems, perhaps compounded by McCandless's heavy smoking. Though Gaddis attempted to settle the question in a brief aside in *A Frolic of His Own,* in which Christina Lutz declares that Liz died of a heart attack (335), this seems to me a rare instance of his giving in to an authorial temptation he often railed against, that of chasing after a book to explain it. Like the question of McCandless's credibility, punctured by his wife's intimations of mental illness, Liz's death retains an obscurity that seems paradoxically fitting in this most straightforwardly plotted of Gaddis's books.

A Frolic of His Own (1994)

With a deserved reputation as his most accessible book, *A Frolic of His Own* foregrounds Gaddis's comedic and parodic skills. It does meditate upon the question of justice, especially in the play-within-the-novel, *Once in Antietam,* and its protagonist Oscar Crease, like many Gaddis characters before him, grapples with an emotionally tangled father-son relationship. For the most part, though, Gaddis's turn to the law allows him ample material for the construction of exquisite chaos. This playful satire of American litigiousness and commercialism lacks the bitter edge of his earlier work.

Oscar Crease is the scion of a notable American family. His grandfather, Thomas Crease, served on the Supreme Court with Oliver Wendell Holmes. His father, also named Thomas, is a judge on the Virginia Federal District Court, nominated to serve on the U.S. Court of Appeals. Oscar, despite continual desire and occasional effort, has not lived up to this grand lineage. A community college history professor, he wrote a play in his youth intended to commemorate his family's history. This play, *Once in Antietam,* centers upon an unusual incident in Justice Crease's life. During the Civil War, Thomas Crease was subject to competing claims from both sides. Though he fought for the Confederacy at the Battle of Ball's Bluff, receiving a scar on his cheek when he fell from a horse, he also became eligible for Union conscription when he took command of a family mining operation in Pennsylvania. To discharge these competing obligations, Crease obtained substitutes on both sides. These substitutes met on the field of battle at Antietam and died at one another's hands.

Although Oscar's Civil War play, like Gaddis's original, has never been produced, the story appears to have made it into public view nonetheless. *The Blood in the Red White and Blue,* a movie directed by the notorious Constantine Kiester (formerly Jonathan Livingston Siegel, formerly Jonathan Livingston) and starring among others Robert Bredford, shares many plot points with Oscar's play, though the movie is also spiced with obligatory quantities of sex and gore. Oscar sues Kiester for copyright infringement. The progress of this action provides the book's main plot. Oscar's brother-in-law, Harry Lutz, an attorney with the white-shoe firm of Swyne and Dour, refers him to another attorney, Harold Basie. Basie initially expresses skepticism about the case, particularly after Oscar cannot find the rejection letter from his original submission of the play to Kiester, under the guise of Livingston. But Basie admires Oscar's underdog spirit and presses on with the case. Kiester's studio retains Swyne and Dour. Jerry Madhar Pai, an associate with the firm, conducts a deposition of Oscar, at which he establishes Oscar's indebtedness to Plato, as well as similarities between *Once in Antietam* and O'Neill's *Mourning Becomes Electra.* After Oscar rejects a settlement offer of $200,000, because the settlement would barely cover his legal costs, the movie studio is granted summary judgment; the judge relies on the theory that, under New York law, a plaintiff in an action for unfair competition must establish that his or her work is novel, which Oscar, indebted to earlier authors, cannot do. Basie recommends an appeal to the Second Circuit, a forum likely to overturn a lower judge. Though Oscar's hopes look bleak when Basie disappears one step ahead of the revelation that his law degree is fraudulent, Basie's theory prevails. Judge Bone of the Circuit Court finds that the relevant New York law is preempted by federal law, so that novelty is not the only governing standard. His decision is guided by a brief submitted covertly by his old colleague, Judge Crease. Crease's law clerk later confides to Otto that the judge's decision was driven not by paternal solicitude, but by love for the law. Oscar is initially awarded all profits from the film. This award is later reduced to one-fifth of the net profits; when the movie's creative accountants declare that it netted an $18 million loss, Oscar is finally given an unspecified amount smaller than the $200,000 settlement offer.

Crease v. Erebus et al. is by no means the sole lawsuit in the novel. The book is replete with legal proceedings, including *Fickert v. Ude* (carried over from *Carpenter's Gothic*), *Episcopal v. Pepsi-Cola,* or "Pop and Glow," the mammoth trademark-infringement case which eventually consumes Harry Lutz, the O'Neill estate's action against Oscar for copyright infringement, Oscar's girlfriend Lily's divorce proceedings, and Oscar's suit against the historical society where the Crease family papers have been deposited. Of these many lawsuits, the two most notable are *Szyrk v. Village of Tatamount* and *Ace Fidelity Insurance v. Sosumi. Szyrk,* the case that Judge Crease is hearing at the book's outset, revolves around a dog trapped in a outdoor steel sculpture. Szyrk, the sculpture's creator, sues the town initially to enjoin it from altering the structure in order to free the dog. (The incident recalls the child trapped in one of Schepperman's statues in *J R.)* In granting Szyrk his injunction, Judge Crease inflames local sentiment against himself. The demagogic Senator Bilk panders to this public outrage by blocking the Judge's accession to the higher court. The genesis of *Ace Fidelity v. Sosumi* occurs when Oscar accidentally runs himself over: the starter on his Sosumi doesn't work, so he hot-wires it while standing in front of it. The case threatens to spin out of control, as an insurance company representative explains to Oscar: "Our legal department sought out the person you bought it from who had joined the Navy and so proceeded against the dealer from whom he'd purchased it new and the dealer then sued the wholesaler who has brought suit against the manufacturer who in turn is suing the assembler of the defective component parts . . ." (476). With Lily's assistance, Oscar obtains a settlement that will cover his medical bills.

While Oscar commands some sympathy in his struggle to prevail against the Goliaths of Hollywood, he is too caught up in his lawsuits to react sympathetically when tragedy strikes several characters around him. Lily's brother Bobby is killed in a Porsche accident. Harry Lutz, who has already suffered a car accident as a result of exhaustion, dies of unspecified causes. Oscar's inability to regard Harry's death except through the lens of his own legal travails is particularly blameworthy given Harry's regard for Oscar. Harry, who turned to corporate law only after frustrated beginnings as a novelist and public interest attorney, tells his wife Christina (Oscar's half-sister) that "he really admired what [Oscar] tried to do because he'd tried it himself that's what he used to say, about failing at something worth doing because there was nothing worse for a man than failing at something that wasn't worth doing in the first place" (461). Finally, while Oscar is stricken by Judge Crease's death at the age of ninety-seven, this death affects him primarily because of his unfulfilled need to prove himself to his father. The novel closes with the three survivors, Oscar, Lily, and Christina, regressing into a chaotic and childish state, merely breaking even on their long-awaited settlements and inheritances, while around them ring out insistently the trochaic rhythms of the schoolroom classic "The Song of Hiawatha."

The novel, in which the interpretive process of common law plays so central a role, itself gives rise to a wealth of interpretive issues. One might begin by investigating the several genres of text folded into the larger narrative: Oscar's play, the deposition, the legal opinions. There is the issue of class and ethnicity, underlined in various characters' reactions to the African-American lawyer Basie and the Indian lawyer Madher Pai. Knight organizes a stimulating discussion around the differing concepts of justice espoused by several of the leading characters. And the Darwinian imagery of the nature programs Oscar incessantly watches could fruitfully be connected with the dog-eat-dog legal world which drains Harry Lutz's life away. While all these issues invite fuller consideration, my discussion of the novel will take its starting point from a more pointed and seemingly narrower question, a fitting method for a novel in which the figure of Socrates looms so largely: Why does Gaddis recapitulate the story line of *Once in Antietam* so often?

We are initially given the story of the play in its original form, Oscar's manuscript. About a third of the novel's first hundred and fifty pages is given over to direct quotation of the play, as Oscar contrives to have Lily and his students read it to him. While we are thrust into the prologue of the play in medias res, a characteristic Gaddis technique, by the end of this section we have been introduced to virtually all the play's major characters (though we never see Thomas's wife Giulielma) and learned the outlines of Thomas's story. The play is discussed next in Oscar's deposition, during which Madhar Pai and Oscar agree that Kane is a figure for Socrates. In the course of this line of questioning, several new, briefer passages from the play are quoted, including Bagby's parodic retelling of the story of Gyges. After his case is initially dismissed, Oscar is surprised to find Madhar Pai accompanying Christina's friend Trish on a visit to the Crease estate. Madhar Pai and Oscar discuss the play further during this visit. The lawyer subtly reminds us of the roles of the various characters, while engaging in a racialist reinterpretation of the play. Soon afterward, Judge Bone's decision, overturning the lower court's dismissal, is quoted in full. The first half of this case contains a detailed retelling of the story of the play, complete with the third act we have not yet seen, along with a comparison of the play to the film *The Blood in the Red White and Blue*. When Oscar, Harry, Lily, and Christina watch the film on televison, a narrative commentary provides our final encounter with this by now familiar story.

Gaddis's use of the play provides one more example of the omnipresent technique of repetition which we saw at work earlier in *The Recognitions*. But the recapitulations of the play differ in two respects from these earlier repetitions. There is a genuine article at the origin of this series of repetitions: the text of Oscar's play. And in each encounter with the play, a new dimension of its meaning is revealed; we are really given not repetitions, but reinterpretations. Some of these reinterpretations are more successful than others. For instance, Jerry Madhar Pai reveals the layers of allusion in the play in his deposition of Oscar, conclusively demonstrating its lack of novelty. In his later interpretation, Madhar Pai suggests that Kane is Jewish, because he is a peddler, and that the play anticipates contemporary strife between African Americans and Jews. This interpretation seems capricious, revealing more about the reader than the play, and perhaps confirming Harry's judgment that Madhar Pai is clever but narrow.

Through this process of successive interpretation, the novel comes to resemble the institution which is its central concern: the law. It is appropriate, then, that Judge Bone's legal opinion takes up a question left open in our earlier encounters with *Once in Antietam:* How does the play end? The play's last act seems an object of oddly general disregard. Oscar doesn't ask his students to read it, Madhar Pai has not read it, and the filmmakers have not used it. In a striking parallel, neither Oscar nor Harry are quite sure how the film ended after watching it on television. Bone briefly describes the endings of both the play and the film. While we learn that much of the last act is a replica of Plato's *Crito,* the final scene is described vaguely as "claw[ing] for the heights of Greek tragedy." (352). The description of the film's ending, no less vague, is nevertheless extremely suggestive: "The rest of the picture seeks simply to lend dramatic credibility to Randal's eventual self destruction with his discovery of certain letters drawn by defendants from the public domain" (354). This description bears little resemblance to the end of the televised film, but it closely resembles the end of *A Frolic of His Own*. Oscar's final retreat into the world of childhood is triggered by his discovery of certain old family letters. He learns from these letters that his interpretation of his family's history is largely false. *Once in Antietam* itself is revealed as just one more step in the series of provisional, fallible interpretations.

Of course, the discovery of the letters on its own cannot make the play a failure. It is Oscar's intention in writing the play that makes him vulnerable to this final blow. He writes the play in order to lay claim to his family's history and prove himself to his father. Artistic considerations are entirely secondary, as is indicated by Oscar's lack of apparent interest in writing anything beyond his single play. As a result, he is held hostage to the essential contingency of human life: like his play, Oscar's relationship to his father never attains closure, particularly given Judge Crease's instructions that he have no funeral. Oscar, in the end, can only retreat into a world of his own creation, because he lacks that essential quality of his creator: the tenacity to persevere, and finally to succeed, at something worth doing.

American fiction itself has seemed at times during the past two decades to suffer from the same crippling lack of self-confidence or its counterpart, a blustery posturing, that assails Gaddis's failed artists. In recent years, though, work by writers including, though by no means limited to, Colson Whitehead, Joy Williams, David Foster Wallace, and Don DeLillo has demonstrated a renewed commitment to fiction of ambitious scale, experimental form, and deeply serious ethical and political content. Predicting the future, aesthetic or otherwise, is a charlatan's game; countless contingencies conspire to veil the art of tomorrow. But one can at least hope that trends detectable in contemporary writing will continue to make two things clear: in the twentieth century the experimental strain has been the most vital in American fiction, and few of its practitioners have written with the vigor, courage, and mastery of William Gaddis.

WORKS CITED

Abadi-Nagy, Zoltan. "The Art of Fiction CI: William Gaddis." *Paris Review* 105 (1987): 54-89.
Eliot, T. S. "The Waste Land." *The Complete Poems and Plays: 1909-1950*. New York: Harcourt, 1971. 37-55.
The Gaddis Annotations Project. Ed. Victoria Harding. 16 February 2001 <http://www.gaddisannotations.net>.
Gaddis, William. *Carpenter's Gothic*. New York: Penguin, 1985.
——. *A Frolic of His Own*. New York: Scribner, 1995.
——. *J R*. New York: Penguin, 1993.
——. *The Recognitions*. New York: Penguin, 1993.
——. "The Rush for Second Place." *Harpers* April 1981: 31-39.
Green, Jack. *Fire the Bastards!* Normal, IL: Dalkey Archive, 1992.
Gussow, Mel. "William Gaddis, 75, Innovative Author of Complex, Damanding Novels, Is Dead." *New York Times* 17 December 1998: C22.
Johnston, John. *Carnival of Repetition: Gaddis's "The Recognitions" and Postmodern Theory*. Philadelphia: U of Pennsylvania P, 1990.

Knight, Christopher J. *Hints and Guesses: William Gaddis's Fiction of Longing*. Madison: U of Wisconsin P, 1997.

Koenig, David. "The Writing of *The Recognitions*." In *Recognition of William Gaddis*. Ed. John Kuehl and Steven Moore. Syracuse: Syracuse UP, 1984. 20-31.

Koenig, Peter William. " 'Splinters from the Yew Tree': A Critical Study of William Gaddis's *The Recognitions.*" Diss. New York U, 1970.

Kuehl, John, and Steven Moore, eds. *In Recognition of William Gaddis*. Syracuse: Syracuse UP, 1984.

———. "An Interview with William Gaddis." *Review of Contemporary Fiction* 2.2 (1982): 4-6.

Leverence, John. "Gaddis Anagnorisis." In *Recognition of William Gaddis*. Ed. John Kuehl and Steven Moore. Syracuse: Syracuse UP, 1984. 32-45.

Moore, Steven. *A Reader's Guide to William Gaddis's "The Recognitions."* Lincoln: U of Nebraska P, 1982.

———. *William Gaddis*. Boston: Twayne, 1989.

O'Donnell, Patrick. "His Master's Voice: On William Gaddis's *J R.*" *Postmodern Culture* 1.2 (1991): 26 paragraphs.

Shakespeare, William. *The Complete Works of Shakespeare*. Ed. Hardin Craig and David Bevington. Rev. ed. Glenview: Scott, Foresman, 1973.

Smith, Dinitia. "Gaddis in the Details." *New York* 3 January 1994: 34-40.

Weisenburger, Steven. "Paper Currencies: Reading William Gaddis." *In Recognition of William Gaddis*. Ed. John Kuehl and Steven Moore. Syracuse: Syracuse UP, 1984. 147-61.

A William Gaddis Checklist

The Recognitions. New York: Harcourt, Brace, 1955; New York: Penguin, 1993.

J R. New York: Knopf, 1975; New York: Penguin, 1993.

Carpenter's Gothic. New York: Viking, 1985; New York: Penguin, 1986.

A Frolic of His Own. New York: Poseidon, 1994; New York: Scribner, 1995.

William Gaddis
Photograph by Miriam Berkley

Mary Caponegro

Robert L. McLaughlin

In his review of *The Star Café and Other Stories* Steven Moore places the author, Mary Caponegro, with those writers "who prefer to play the ventriloquist, deploying a variety of voices and styles so that their collections more closely resemble an anthology by various hands. This is more daring commercially and aesthetically; commercially, because the writer refrains from creating a recognizable and marketable style, and aesthetically, because the writer must start from square one with each story, like a musician learning to play a new instrument for every composition." For me, it is this formal and stylistic versatility, the surprise and, yes, the wonderful weirdness, that I find in each new work, that is the hallmark—and the challenge and the delight—of Caponegro's work.

For Caponegro, stylistic virtuosity is a manifestation of a worldview and an aesthetic. The world is a complex place, ever moving, ever changing, ever resisting our attempts to pin it down. In fact there are dangers in our attempts to pin it down; we risk not only distorting the way we know the world but also imprisoning ourselves in a static, stunted relation to the social world. Caponegro asks us to be alarmed about "political conservatism/repression on the one hand, extreme forms of political correctness on the other" ("Impressions" 27). Both would limit the ways in which the world can be known and experienced; both would restrict the discourse through which the world can be imagined. The purpose of fiction is to resist these impulses, "to push limits, boundaries, of narrative, of reality" ("Impressions" 26). Fiction, that is, innovative, envelope-pushing fiction, helps its readers develop ways of perceiving, understanding, and relating to a complicated world in flux. Caponegro counts herself among those who are "devoted to the expansion and dissemination of imagination" ("Impressions" 27). One sees that, for her, the imagination is not a luxury or an indulgence, but a vital tool for negotiating reality.

Many of Caponegro's technical experiments will be discussed in detail later in this essay, but we can get a sense of her stylistic variety by looking at two stories, one of her earliest and one of her most recent. "Tales from the Next Village" is a series of ten brief narratives, written in the style of eighteenth-century Chinese folktales. This stylistic dislocation allows the author both to emphasize the narrational aspects of the narratives (that is, the pretense that these tales have been heard and then retold to us, à la *The Arabian Nights)* and to introduce a magic realism into the presentation of this foreign world. The stories, focusing, for example, on a man who wants to buy silk from the mermaids and is instead lured into drowning, a widow who was allergic to her husband's sperm, but who in grief throws her legs open to the rain in which her husband's spirit lives, a woman who rebels against her husband by turning into a tree, a wife who calmly accepts the introduction of her husband's mistress into the house, are written in a simple yet exquisite prose style. Unconnected narratively, they share an exploration of the nature and consequences of desire and how they change as personal and social contexts change. Caponegro wrote these tales at the suggestion of John Hawkes, one of her mentors, who wanted to prove to her that fiction could do anything poetry could. Indeed, the precision of the language and the use of the fantastic image as metaphor linking emotion and meaning can be found in much of her later work.

"Epilogue of the Progeny, or Whoever Is Never Born with the Most Toys Wins," the final story in Caponegro's latest book, *The Complexities of Intimacy,* is an example of a juxtaposition technique wherein two very different ideas are treated in terms of one another. Here, the two ideas are the cruising culture, in which men and women engage in a dance of seduction, seeking one another out, maybe for something long-term, but more likely a one-night stand, and parenthood: the result is a through-the-looking-glass world where children, from infants to adolescents, sit in bars and in parks, letting themselves be approached by adult couples loaded down with toys or pets. When they choose a couple, they go off to their home to be their child for maybe a night, rarely longer than a few weeks, and then back to the bars and parks. The defamiliarization this juxtaposition creates allows the story to explore the degradation of personal relationships in a society where desire is channeled through the discourses of commercialism and where identity is determined not by who you are but by what you own. The story ends on Christmas morning, with the children, amid their presents, jealous of the baby Jesus, both implicated in, but somehow apart from the commercialization of the season and secure in an identity-providing narrative they themselves never achieve.

If one had to identify the elements common to Caponegro's technique, they would probably be the ones we see in these two stories: a careful, beautiful prose style; a fantastic surrealism; and possibilities for meaning created by setting distinct ideas, voices, and styles into dialogue. These stories also show us the ongoing purpose of Caponegro's writing: her innovative technique, far from seeking to sever the representational link between life and art, ever tries to capture and articulate the complexities of being human in the contemporary world.

Caponegro's refusal to stand still as a writer has caused some confusion in the critical reception of her work. Unlike Moore, most reviewers, even when praising the fiction, have wanted to find ways to categorize it and thus have not always done it justice. Mary Banas, for example, after telling us that the stories in *The Star Café* "aim to shake up our intellectual universe" (one gets the impression this is not a positive thing for Ms. Banas), applies fairly obvious feminist "messages" to the stories (obsessive love, anorexia), which is, to my mind, a very limiting approach. Richard Eder, in a long, thoughtful review of *The Star Café,* places Caponegro in a cultural trend exemplified by the work of David Lynch, Peter Greenaway, and Madonna, makers of works that have brilliant style and execution but that "reveal nothing," that offer "sensation without experience" (3). He then seems to contradict himself by applying an overlay of feminist interpretation to the stories and finding meaning in them after all. Again, in seeking to categorize, he has oversimplified and distorted the work. Similarly, critics and scholars frequently have wanted to see Caponegro's work as representing Italian-American experience. For example, an essay on Caponegro's sojourn in Rome, by Blossom S. Kirschenbaum, appeared in the journal *Italian Americana*. While this approach to the work may be rewarding, it is also limiting. Caponegro's is an extremely rich fiction, which should not be bounded by the reader's preconceptions of feminism, identity politics, or theories of postmodernism.

Mary Caponegro was born on 21 November 1956 in Brooklyn, New York. She was raised Roman Catholic and educated for twelve years in Catholic schools, the long-term aftereffects of which can occasionally be discerned in her fiction. In the mid-seventies she attended Bard College in the Hudson Valley, where she came under the influence of the mentors who would encourage and shape her as a writer. One was poet and small-press publisher George Quasha, who was instrumental in giving her the courage she needed to start writing. Caponegro remembers that he "helped me understand about adventurousness on the page and in the imagination" (Letter). Another mentor was William Gaddis, fortuitously at Bard during one of his brief teaching stints. Caponegro recalls his presence, "this wonderful larger-than-life novelist" (Letter), the chance to study with whom pushed her toward being a fiction writer. The third and probably most important mentor was poet and fiction writer Robert Kelly. He guided her undergraduate writing, suggested books to read and entire areas to study, and, in general urged her, in her writing, continually to question the status quo. Given these early influences, it should be no surprise that Caponegro turned into the writer she's become or that she considers her own teaching such an important part of her career. She recently wrote to me about her Bard experience:

As teachers I do believe that we are indeed "modeling" through our behavior, and the relationship a teacher has to his/her writing and to the world and to the world of writing has a huge impact on a student or aspiring writer. The value of art, for instance. That this vocation was a worthy one. And that I was worthy to do it. Those basic things I had to be persuaded of, and when my work was too inchoate to be valid in any objective sense, I—because of who knows what, a quality of sincerity?—was accepted as if I were already an accomplished artist at Bard. . . . I guess there's no more conscious influence on this earth than that of a teacher whose job is to influence.

In the early eighties Caponegro earned her Master's in the fiction writing program at Brown University, where, still blessed with brilliant mentors, she studied with John Hawkes and Robert Coover, among others. She credits Hawkes with helping her learn how to build cause-and-effect, the narrative line, in her work and also with encouraging her to mine sexuality as a subject for her fiction. Coover's influence is most obvious in her formal experiments. Caponegro notes that one early story, "Analysis of the Vessel and Its Contents," is particularly Cooveresque. Both men introduced her to fiction writing as a profession, in fact, a big business.

Shortly after completing her Master's, Caponegro was invited by C. D. Wright and Forrest Gander of Lost Roads Publishers to submit some of her work for a book in their "Lost Roads Series." The result was *Tales from the Next Village,* a collection of seven stories, published in 1985. Around this time, too, she became one of the core group of writers around whom Bradford Morrow built his journal *Conjunctions*. That publishing relationship has continued to the present; Caponegro considers *Conjunctions* her periodical home, "The place where I belong." In 1990 Scribner's published *The Star Café and Other Stories,* which was treated, despite the earlier volume, as a debut collection. The next year, Caponegro was awarded the Rome Prize Fellowship in Literature, which funded a year's residence at the American Academy and Institute of Arts and Letters in Rome. This first of many trips to Italy provided her with the time to connect with her Italian roots, to learn the language, and, at the Academy, to collaborate with other artists, once again seeking

ways to expand what her art can do. It also served as the inspiration
for the series of fictions that would be collected as *Five Doubts* and
published by Marsilio in 1998. Her newest collection, *The Complexities of Intimacy,* containing stories written over the same period of
time she was working on the Italian stories, is being published this
fall by Coffee House Press.

Since earning her Master's, Caponegro has also been a dedicated
teacher, primarily at Hobart and William Smith College, in Geneva,
New York, and in the M.F.A. program at Syracuse University.
Thinking of the good fortune she had with her teachers, she remembers "the gifts that can never be repaid except by imitation—which
is why a good deal of my life's energy has been for almost twenty
years devoted to my own students" (Letter). Given her own aesthetic principles and the commercialized, conglomeratized state of
the publishing industry, she thinks it is important for the future of
imaginative fiction that someone teach "young aspiring writers to
write *against* the marketplace's limitations" ("Impressions" 26).
Bringing her career to something of a full circle, Caponegro has recently been named to the first Richard B. Fisher Family Professor-
ship in Literature and Writing at Bard College, where she will be
able to give to new generations of students the guidance and inspiration she herself received there.

Tales from the Next Village

Caponegro's first collection, *Tales from the Next Village,* contains
two pieces, the title story and "The Star Café," which will open her
first commercially published volume, *The Star Café,* five years later.
The other five pieces in *Tales* show Caponegro developing her style
and technique and treating themes that will continue to fascinate
her. These include issues of identity, the constricting and liberatory
possibilities for art, especially narrative, and the tension between
the need to depend on and the desire to flee the family.

The first story, "Monday," is narrated in something of a fairy-tale
style by a woman with an unsettled identity (she is nameless and
throughout refers to herself as "we"). The reader follows her
through a series of housewifely errands—visiting the cobbler, the
tailor, the grocer—which seem to overwhelm her. She accepts the
implied conventions of her society that tell her she is responsible
for these and other chores, but she is also insecure about her ability
to accomplish them; as it turns out, this is a well-founded insecu-
rity, as each errand is a failure, and instead of accomplishing
chores, she ends up with more to do and little idea of how to do
them. Her role of victim to societal expectations is made most clear

when, to indulge herself, she buys a single rose, something beautiful to admire amid her chores. However, she immediately loses control of the rose as the florist, the grocer, and eventually her husband
see it and create their own stories about it and what it signifies
about her. None of these stories is true, but because men create
them, they have the power of truth which the woman can't contradict.

"The Vessel and Its Contents" begins with a narrator giving a rigorously objective description of a woman and two men rowing on a
lake, plus another man, possibly in distress. The narrator then sub-
merges herself into the consciousness of each of the three main
characters in turn to explore the subjectivity of their relationship.
The story takes on a garden-of-the-forking-paths structure as, at
several points of crisis (e.g., one of the men jumps into the lake to
rescue the apparently drowning man in distress), the narrator gives
us multiple possible outcomes (e.g., the second man also jumps in to
the rescue; the man and woman sail away, abandoning their friend;
the victim turns out to be a tree branch, etc.). As the story jump cuts
from focalization to focalization and possible narrative to possible
narrative, the characters and the situation seem increasingly the
product of the woman's creative imagination. In one section the
men in the water wonder, "Where is the woman, who was the muse,
as it were, of this whole project, who incited this rescue mission
with her poetic imaginings and then the dangerous repercussions of
those imaginings? Who will take responsibility for that reckless creativity?" (26). In another section the woman, "having just seen the
tree she feels responsible for making into a man, thinks, 'Did I really do that? Do I have such powers of evasion that instead of exer-
cising the will to excise said men from my life, I had to create such
elaborate artifice? I should recognize my power' " (19-20). Where the
narrator of "Monday" was the victim of narratives, the woman here
is empowered by her creative imagination.

A similar empowerment is seen in "Deformity," a precursor to
"Materia Prima" in *The Star Café*. Here a young girl resists her parents' efforts to socialize her into the perfect young woman first by
imitating the physical deformities of the misfits she sees at the cir-
cus and then by transforming herself into a variety of animals:

> Several times a day Mother pleaded that Josie emerge, then threat-
> ened when instead of her young lady she saw a creature of some other
> sort.
> "Time to go to gymnastics," and a rabbit would bound from the draper-
> ies.
> "The French tutor will be here soon," and a parrot on the mantle would
> mimic, "Comment allez vous?"

"Are they mechanical, do you suppose," Mother asked Father.

"It was your idea she take those acting lessons," Father said.

And no sooner had both turned to see a cat stepping across the plastic keys of the spinet, creating not uninteresting dissonances, when it leapt from the bench to floor and away. Not an hour later Mother could be heard to say, "Come out of that clever dog suit, Josephine," but nonetheless she lay newspapers on the kitchen floor. (81)

This reckless creativity will frequently be celebrated in Caponegro's work.

These ideas about identity, the creative imagination, and art come together in the collection's final story, "Heart as Nails." It is narrated by a young woman who, on the one hand, wants very much to escape her family and achieve independence and, on the other hand, constantly betrays her fascination with and dependence on her sister. As in the previous stories, this narrator recognizes the importance of art for establishing an autonomous identity. She writes,

I am convinced that one knows everything in the back of one's mind, but needs objects to crystallize the knowledge, to draw it into focus, almost as if to reorder the very molecules of oneself into the object's own arrangement, giving perspective and retrospective both.

Art is perhaps the best example of this alignment: the artist cannot know what he has done, or even what he is capable of doing, until the product confronts him. It's a kind of benign inside-outness of things, that the knowledge would seem to come flooding back to the mind at the same moment it is in fact pouring into the thing. Then we have a shiny badge to wear upon our thoughts, and engraved upon it the very words we had always been saying. (84)

The difference here is the narrator's emphasis on art as finished object, product, as opposed to the ongoing creative imagination we see in "The Vessel and Its Contents" and "Deformity." The narrator here is suspicious of art as process, as she suggests in her complaint about language: "it is a dreadful reduction, which is the result of being trapped in this system of code-words where every attempt at articulation only touches the surface. How often the system fails, breaks down, causing language to trivialize, to make a travesty of the very thought it is trying to convey" (95). She contrasts the limitations of language to having her back scratched by her sister, whose impossibly long nails—her hobby and her passion—necessitate a gentle approach: "But when my sister would scratch my back, it was different. By barely touching the surface, she heightened response; she elicited sensation as deep as her gesture was soft" (95). The narrator misses the point. Indeed, it isn't until her sister cuts off the nails and sends them to her after an argument that the narrator appreciates them. Alive, growing, they were her sister's eccentricity. Clipped off, dead, they are an art object, to be preserved and cherished, to be displayed in just the right way. She finds the perfect box in which to keep them and then resists the temptation to share them with others. She concludes, "Some things, some very special things, are meant to be contained. Containment is the whole of their existence" (107). The narrator ends contained and constrained too. She never achieves the independence and autonomy she sought at the beginning of the story; her continued fascination with what was a part of her sister and her superficial relationship with everyone else in her life indicate that in misrecognizing the power of art and language she has trapped herself.

The Star Café and Other Stories

"The Star Café" is perhaps Caponegro's most well-known story. Surreal in its form, it focuses on Carol, a timid and lonely woman, as she goes through what seems to be a life-altering experience. Disturbed in her apartment one evening by a mysterious noise, Carol discovers its source in a café on the ground floor of her building, which, for some unexplained reason, she had never before entered. She is so relieved that the noise has come from an innocent blender for making daiquiris that she opens up in a flood of conversation with the conventionally handsome café owner and she is soon in bed with him, enjoying the most satisfying sex of her life. She awakens to find herself in a completely mirrored room: "The way school buses have mirrors to cover every possible vantage, this room, from her position on the bed, allowed her to see her body from every angle" (27). The café owner returns and reinitiates sex, during which Carol is shocked to discover that, while she can see herself in the multiple mirrors, she cannot see her partner. This shock throws Carol into confusion about the reality of the moment, her relation to the café owner, and her socially received knowledge of right and wrong, but also brings into focus for her a disjunction she has always felt which has resulted in her feeling not at home in her own body. Later, after finding her way out of the mirrored room and back into the café, Carol fights with the café owner not so much over the nature of what has just happened as over their inability to communicate at all. She huffs into an "androgynous" rest room (42), where, aroused by her own image in the mirror, she masturbates without guilt and, apparently, unself-consciously. She leaves the rest room determined to go exploring.

The story's form serves as a metaphor for Carol's progress in two ways. First, just as the narrator is both inside and outside Carol (the narrative distance between the narrator and Carol goes from very great, as she describes Carol seemingly objectively, to completely merged, as she speaks through Carol's voice), Carol begins the story both inside and outside her body. Put simply, she has never felt at home in her body, and her sense of identity has consequently suffered. This point is established at the very beginning of the story, where we see that Carol "knew so little about this building she lived in" (24). The placement of a light switch at only the bottom of the stairs and there being windows only on the tree-shaded western side of the building are design decisions that confuse her, but rather than actively criticize them, she seems to defer to the architect's expertise, even if she doesn't understand it. This parallels her confusion about her body and its connection to her sense of identity, as the narrator makes clear when Carol is in the mirrored room: "On some level she knew she was an intuitive person, but she hadn't learned to trust herself, too cautious, as if there were a very strong force at work inside her all the time that wasn't allowed to come to expression, like all that sun missing her house, all this foliage in her head, that was so pretty and interesting and alive, but how much it got in the way" (38). As we will see, Carol's head is filled with socially transmitted ideas about right and wrong, proper and improper behavior, and even rules of etiquette that, because they are unexamined, are like the foliage that gets in the way. Just as Carol has to find her own way out of the mirrored room, she also has to learn to navigate her body and her sense of self on her own.

The second way that the story's form mirrors Carol's progress is in its pattern of tension and resolution. Of course, this pattern is fundamental to narrative: conflict introduces tension which the course of events then seeks to resolve. But here, Carol as a character feels the pattern more immediately than is common in fiction: the tension she feels because of the mysterious noise is relieved in her stream of talk when she meets the café owner; the tension of sexual intercourse is relieved in her orgasms; the tension caused by her needing to urinate is relieved in urination. Interestingly, much of the narrative tension originates in Carol's body, and how she deals with this tension, how it is released or relieved, says much about her progress in coming to terms with her own body. At one particularly important moment, in the mirrored room, after their half-unreflected intercourse, as she watches the café owner dress, Carol has a spontaneous and unexpected orgasm: "out of nowhere her body had produced this gratuitous release to no accumulated tension, in an instant of incredible intensity that left her completely drained, as if she'd been building up to it for some time. She'd often wished she could speed up that process but this was a most undesirable other extreme, this joyless, arbitrary orgasm; it was in no way satisfying. If anything, scary. This strange ventriloquism made her furious" (33-34). This incident contributes to Carol's growing realization that she is not in control of her body. Just after this, when Carol has an urgent need to go to the bathroom, the only help the café owner offers is to lead her to two urinals, concealed in an alcove of the mirrored room. As she tries to figure out how "to put feminine function into masculine form" (36), she repeatedly asks for the man's help, but they both eventually see that there's nothing he can do. Carol contrives a way to use the urinal, but "relief was thwarted by the awkwardness of posture" (37). The compromised release of tension here suggests the extent to which Carol's bodily needs are dependent on and must adapt themselves to an implied male authority. But her observation that the urinal "vaguely resembled a baptismal font" (37) prepares us for a possible rebirth of her character, a transformation via image and art by which Carol resolves the tension in her sense of identity, body, and sexuality.

The first two sections of the story—covering Carol's entrance into the café and her experiences in the mirrored room—establish the problems in her sense of identity and bring them to a crisis. We see from the very beginning that Carol is fragmented, lacking a coherent sense of self. In the story's first sentence, when Carol hears the noise, we're told "she'd actually been half undressing for bed and half searching for the book she had intended to read in bed, but after she heard the noise she was only a third involved with each of these tasks and a third involved in trying to figure out where the noise had come from" (23). As we have seen, her noncritical acceptance of architectural expertise indicates a general deference to authority. In her initial encounter with the café owner, she feels that "she was acting out a role that came very naturally, almost as if she'd rehearsed it" (26). This tendency to act a role in relation to others suggests both the critical distancing connected to her disjunction between self and body and a passivity which leads her to respond to others' initiatives, to play the role that the situation and the others around her demand. In acting situation-appropriate roles, Carol leaves herself open to be acted upon by others and thus avoids the need to act, in the sense of taking action.

Carol's crisis comes in the mirrored room, where the various characteristics that keep her from being an independent, coherent person are exaggerated to their illogical extremes. Here her fragmented identity is made, if not literal, then certainly visual, as Carol sees multiple versions of herself, from every angle, in the room's many mirrors. Her fascination quickly turns to fear, as there are far too many Carols for her to identify with. Any possible sense of self that might come through identification with a reflected image is lost by the apparently infinite dispersion of images. We're told, "It reminded her of fancy New York stores in which it is difficult to find one's way because the different departments are separated by walls of mirrors" (27). Connected with this, her seeing herself but not her partner in the many mirrors leads her to begin to question her dependence on the café owner and, perhaps, men in general. She thinks, "what had seemed the most natural thing in the world suddenly de-naturalized and was transformed into the most awkward" (29). This defamiliarization of what seems natural—a man and woman engaged in sex—provides Carol the opportunity to reconsider the power relations between men and women, especially her deferral to and dependence on men.

Throughout this section, Carol is almost embarrassingly dependent on the café owner and not just for her sexual pleasure. When he comes into the mirrored room, she assumes he's there "to rescue her" (27), but he initiates sex with her instead. After he's finished, she begs him not to go: "Don't leave me alone. I'm afraid to be alone here" (32). She asks for his help both to find a bathroom and then, when he offers the urinals, to urinate. She also wants his help to get out of the room, but all he tells her is "If you want to leave . . . all you have to do is figure it out" (35). Carol's dependence on the café owner seems absurd, because he never provides her the help she needs. More important, it points out the sense in which, throughout this scene, Carol has been acted upon by the café owner—in his startling and unilateral initiation of sex and his oblivious continuation of the act long past Carol's receptiveness and pleasure—to the point that her passivity moves toward a complete surrender of agency. The exclamation mark to all this comes when the man somehow generates the spontaneous orgasm in Carol from across the room.

Connected with this debilitating dependence on men is a reliance on the authority of received wisdom, much like Carol's deferral to the expertise of the architect in his peculiar design for the building. When she first sees herself but not her lover in the mirrors of the room, Carol "felt humiliated and horrified, and guilty too, though she couldn't have said why" (28). Her reactions to this and to her entire encounter with the café owner are influenced by received knowledge of morality, of social strictures (what her mother told her) and even of etiquette (wondering how to end the sex act, "she wanted to say, 'Excuse me, do you think you'll be through soon?' as if to someone at a pay phone" (30)). It's not that any of these influences are bad, but Carol accepts them too uncritically. Although her situation has resulted more from the café owner's choices and actions than her own, she feels guilt and repeatedly concludes that she is being punished somehow for her transgressions. But this socially conditioned self-castigation is complicated by the feeling that her conditioning might have worked in ways other than those intended and that the experience in the mirrored room has been positive for her. Carol thinks,

> He elicited from her a quality of her own femaleness that she'd never before experienced on that physical plane—a response she realized might be hopelessly bound up in the conditioning of role, but was nonetheless immensely powerful. It was getting clear again, with the distance, with his going, the power of the sensation that had made her respond in a way she never had: totally. She'd come outside herself to meet him through the medium of body, through the act of letting him inside her, and yet never felt so fully in her body, in her self, as when she had. (33)

At the end of this section, Carol sums up her dilemma:

> She cursed her intuition, because she'd never had stayed with him if she'd weighed, considered, evaluated. On the other hand, she'd never do anything if she always weighed, considered, evaluated; that was precisely what kept her from doing any number of things, things she felt a genuine desire to do, but couldn't get over this habit or obsession of getting stuck, nothing resolving itself. She felt the irony of the whole thing as deeply, as physically, as a metallic taste in her mouth: that the only time she'd ever felt not removed from her body, when will and act had meshed, was with him; it had felt so right, but clearly had been wrong, as wrong as anything could be. (38)

The basis of her evaluations of her actions is the social conditioning—including the conditioning that has taught her to be dependent on and play roles in relation to men—that she seems to have accepted so uncritically. Her intuition arises from herself, from her personal way of making sense of her world, a way which is stunted because she has so little confidence in herself and, really, no coherent sense of self around which this sense-making can organize. In drawing her attention to this dilemma, the mirrored room has upset Carol's previous sense of self and offered a path to devising a new one. The first clue comes after the café owner has finally finished the sex act, when Carol's shock and feelings of victimization fade in her consideration of his body: "at this moment she wasn't so much aroused by the sight of him naked as interested in his body aesthetically" (32). During this consideration, she realizes that for the first time she'd felt fully in her body. She uses here the aesthetic as a way of giving meaning to her experiences. The second clue comes after Carol has finished at the urinal, when she resolves "to try to create some sense, even a contrived one, of order, in this most peculiar, relentless universe" (37). Finally, the café owner had told Carol that she needed to discover the way out of the room herself—just as she needs to negotiate her body as home—and, evidently, she does.

Back in the café, Carol's situation and her identity are unsettled. She no longer knows how to relate to the café owner. The performative aspect of her relationship with him, into which she had fallen quite naturally before, is confused now: "She had no idea what role she was playing" (39). Her attempts to question the café owner about what has just occurred between them are frustrated by constant miscommunication. (When she asks if he was there, meaning the room, he thinks she's referring to the travel posters on the walls and tells her about being in Greece.) Most interestingly, where earlier she had been glad to receive his comforting words and gestures, now she angrily rejects them, demands answers to her questions, and confidently challenges his knowledge of the building (she needs a rest room again). Indeed, her bodily tension—the need to urinate—parallels the conflict between the two, a conflict that's resolved in Carol's standing up for herself, in effect declaring her independence, and the café owner telling her, "We're through" (42).

During this exchange, Carol receives the first intimation of the power of the aesthetic to provide a contingent order and meaning to the world. In perusing the travel posters, she thinks about Ancient Greece: "That was the world of myth, of gods and goddesses, of honor and heroism, justice, revenge. That was a much larger world than her own, she felt, that company of furies and sirens in which choice was fate, and fate was really everything, but no matter what brutality caused by what whim of some god's arbitrary favoritism, reliable rosy-fingered dawn was always waiting in the wings to make it all into poetry. She was enamored of that civilization which was a celebration of the splendor of form" (40). This inspires her to think of the evening's experiences in the form of art: "she could envision her own story painted across some urn, the woman whose lover wasn't there, in little scenes that reminded her of the travel poster, except that they weren't photographed and weren't in boxes, little red figures depicted on the urn: Carol in her apartment, then going downstairs, then in the bar, Carol in bed, then in the mirrored room, Carol looking in the mirrors, him there, him not there, but Carol crouching in the urinal was really too squalid for the likes of any Grecian urn" (41).

Carol's asserting of herself and her beginning to think of her experiences in terms of art prepare for the final stage of her transformation. The androgynous rest room is mirrored on the walls, floor, and ceiling, but, interestingly, Carol sees only one reflection of herself this time, and in watching her reflection, she considers herself aesthetically, much as she had considered the café owner back in the mirrored room. We're told, "she found the entire image attractive" and "Her flesh seemed firmer than she remembered, more muscle tone" (43-44). Although she initially thinks of this image as another woman, as she admires the image, watches it dance, becomes aroused, and begins masturbating, she internalizes it and identifies with it: "She was so tensed and excited that her vision was blurred; she'd lost the mirror's reflection, but it was firmly fixed in her mind; she dwelled on all the postures, the confronting gaze, the beauty, the sensuality of that body" (45). The aesthetic view here provides a way for Carol to feel at home in her body; it offers a means of making order and meaning, knowledge that is necessarily subjective and contingent but all the more valuable for being personal. Carol leaves the rest room, naked and unashamed, drawn to the travel posters, unconcerned about the café owner—"she wouldn't let him keep her from exploring" (45). She has achieved a coherent sense of her own identity, around which she can now proceed to organize a world.

Similar themes are treated in a very different style in the collection's next story, "Materia Prima." Caponegro considers this her most accessible story, in that its coming-of-age narrative will be familiar to readers; indeed, after its initial publication, it was awarded the General Electric Foundation Award for Younger Writers. Here, we follow a young girl, Clara, through childhood and adolescence as she seeks to establish an identity for herself independent of her parents and family. The complexity of the problem of identity is indicated by the story's complex structure, in which discrete sections, each narrated by a distinct voice, suggest both the fragmented nature of identity and the power of dialogic interaction to create meaning. Among the different sections are those narrated by an apparently mature Clara, looking back on her childhood; journal-like sections narrated by young Clara; letters to Clara from her cousin Laura; passages from textbooks, reflecting Clara's interest in natural science, especially birds, and, later, the myth of the Phoenix; an unnamed omniscient narrator who takes over the narrative late in the story; and a concluding playlike section, in which Clara's mother speaks while stage directions suggest that Clara is turning into a Phoenix. The reader's work in connecting these fragments and constructing an interpretation of the story parallels Clara's work in trying to stitch together a coherent and autonomous sense of self.

Clara's two voices rarely connect or overlap—the events and ideas that concern the younger Clara are rarely remarked upon by older Clara, and vice versa; one might be tempted to think they are two separate characters—but they work together to develop Clara's struggle for identity. Younger Clara, because of her age, is in many ways alienated from the world of her parents: she doesn't understand that world, and even when her parents explain things to her, she doesn't understand the explanations. She says that she is scared by the elevators in her family's apartment building, "but papa said it is safe it works by cables. I don't know who cables are but they are less scary than thinking it goes all by itself up and down in the air" (50). Younger Clara is so disconnected from her world that she frequently has to perform roles so as to conceal the extent to which she feels lost. When her father tells her that her mother has had a miscarriage, "I don't ever tell him the things I feel but he looks at me funny and says I know you are sad about this Clara which means it would be wrong not to feel sad" (60). Later, when her grandmother dies, she tells us, "I can't feel happy for more than two years" (62).

But while Clara is confused by the grown-up world, she also resists becoming a part of it. Older Clara tells us her parents' concern: "I was not, to their mind, becoming 'socialized' . . ." (63), and indeed, probably unconsciously, younger Clara rebels against the socialization process. There are many ways in which younger Clara does not want to grow up, as when she wants to keep sleeping with her parents or wants to ride in a shopping cart like a baby. As she nears puberty, her desire to stay a child becomes a crisis. She fears her body becoming like those of the adolescent counselors she sees in the showers at camp, and she breaks off her friendship with her slightly older cousin, Laura, when Laura gets a boyfriend, wears makeup, and generally begins acting like a grown-up. Most dramatically, while at boarding school, she stops going to meals, trying to stay small physically and ending her menstruation. Even the style here suggests Clara's need to stay young: although she ages, her writing style—few capital letters or multisyllabic words, many run-on sentences—remains childlike. The play sequence at the end connects the desire to stay a child with the socialization process. Her mother, while trying to train Clara in traditional women's chores, like cooking, knitting, and sweeping, carries the adolescent girl like a baby and reflects nostalgically on her pregnancy, even wishing that Clara could crawl back into her womb (a recurring image in Caponegro's work). What young Clara has perhaps on some level realized and feared is that growing older and being socialized—especially being socialized as a woman—marks a loss of individuality in the taking on of a societally approved role to play. Thus Clara stresses that Laura, who has embraced growing older and her socialization, is wearing makeup, like a performer.

Older Clara, in looking back at these years, is not so much concerned with these issues as she is with epistemology, especially how knowledge is validated, the nature of memory, and the potential of the creative imagination. She remembers gatherings during which family history was the main topic of conversation, and she is still bitter that her attempts to join in, "to reactivate the past" (49), were always rebuffed because she was too young to have participated in or known the event or person in question: "Only one's parents can steal past and present irrevocably in one dismissive blow" (50). In retaliation older Clara decides to develop her own expertise, natural science, especially birds. This knowledge, which the adults in her family lack, gives her an authority they cannot challenge:

during its initial stages, the project lent me the validity I sorely needed; for if I presented my mother with information about mating habits, gestation period and respiratory structures of bird, fish or insect, she would more than likely say, "Isn't that interesting Clara," rather than challenge me on the subject, quibbling over the technicalities of sound repetition in bird vocalization, or debating whether double circulation is a feature ascribed to mammal or fish. She had no investment in that information; thus it did not constitute a threat. (57)

Clara goes from one extreme to the other: upset that her subjective imaginings of the past aren't granted validity by others, she gains mastery by learning specialized knowledge from books—passages from which are scattered throughout the story—but a knowledge that is absorbed from an outside authority and then repeated can't really be considered a knowledge of her own.

The tension between these two different kinds of knowledge is resolved as a result of her parents deciding Clara is unhealthily obsessed with her research and taking away her books. At first, older Clara writes, "I was genuinely distraught, felt I no longer had identity" (67). Desperate for a substitute discipline to master, she begins studying literature and myth, mostly because of their references to birds. But she discovers that this is in many ways a different kind of knowledge: "This language was much harder to decode than that of fact: what I was accustomed to. But I became engrossed, immersing myself. . . . As my new passion was not on the surface, subversive, it was as good as invisible, and thus truly inviolate; affording me rebellion in the guise of acquiescence" (67-68). This kind of knowledge is based in something outside herself but also involves something inside her—her creative imagination.

Through this study, older Clara is able to declare her autonomy and her individuality. She sums up her final position:

All relationships, be they past, present or future—my grandmother passed away; my cousin, once the closest human to my heart; my parents, who might have in some different circumstance been close to me, available; and the potential peers, communication with whom was destined to be unrealized—were reduced to alienation. Irreconcilable alienation. Only in reading and in dream did I find solace. And the more the imagery of literature yielded to my labors, the richer my dreams became, sometimes themselves the equivalent of poem or myth. These realms, exclusively, held hope: a glimpse of liberation. (73)

In the story's concluding section, as the dramatic form becomes dominant, her mother seeks to socialize Clara to traditional women's work, while stage directions and another, nameless narrator describe Clara's Phoenix-like transformation. In contrast to the sweeping, cooking, and knitting the mother tries to teach her, Clara's "different and singular task," we're told, is "pouring forth sound into air, in articulate, rapturous flame" (80). The narrator explains, "What the child is becoming, however, is one whose very existence is memory: no longer Clara, no longer mere girl, but a medium for eternity. And what destiny could more completely, more perfectly meld Parmenides' stasis with Heraclitus' fire, than to be, through transforming flame, the worm-turned-bird and bird-turned-worm who stitches all of time together?" (81). As Phoenix—read artist—Clara has the ability to tie the past, here connected with memory, history, received knowledge, stasis, together with the present, connected with creative imagination, potential and possibility, subjective knowledge, motion, to create a future. The narrator sums up Clara's lesson: "To see instead the flow from past to present into what has yet to be is to be less deceived: to see there is a continuum which cannot be, except artificially, arrested" (86). "The Star Café" ended with Carol determined not to let the café owner keep her from exploring; here, we're told, "Now there is no stopping the girl's creation, her perpetuation: secret to unceasing song" (87).

These two stories' ideas about art and identity are developed in a different way in the collection's final piece, the novella-length "Sebastian." The story follows the title character, from whose point of view the story is narrated, through several simple, yet increasingly surreal events. On his way to the airport to catch a flight for a business trip, Sebastian stops for gas only to find the service station unattended; to kill the time until someone returns, he goes to pick up some dry cleaning, only to find that that store too is closed, a sign on the door announcing "BACK IN FIFTENE" (94). Killing more time provides him the opportunity to reflect on, well, time, American culture (he's British), his childhood, and, mostly, his relationship with Sarah, his fiancée, who, beyond their sexual chemistry, is in many ways his opposite. In wandering, Sebastian stumbles across Sarah's studio, which he's helping to pay for but which he's never visited. He finds a gallery—in which much of the art seems based on him or his saint namesake or inspired by his relationship with Sarah—complete with gift shop, staffed by a Sarah wannabe, and, behind the scenes, dozens of employees helping Sarah in creating paintings, sculptures, multimedia arts, stained glass, mobiles, weaving, etc.

The contrast between Sebastian and Sarah develops out of a basic conflict between stasis and motion, illustrated in the studio, where his desire to be still and have a conversation about their relationship and her art is frustrated by her continuous movement from room to room and project to project. Sebastian wants an orderly, organized existence; thus he seeks ways to ground himself in what too often (too often for him) seems a scattered, chaotic world. He looks for social status and a sense of identity in his possessions—Jaguar, Rolex watch, Mont Blanc pen—as if the quality of the tools by which he transports himself, marks the hour, and expresses himself can help keep motion, time, and language under control. Language, indeed, should be taken seriously: he is precise in his language use and is critical of others who misuse language (as in the dry cleaner's sign) or degrade it; he also feels anxiety when he finds his ideas eluding his language. Like T. S. Eliot, he believes in aesthetic standards, because art—real art—provides a way to see order in the world. He thinks, "This is what art should do: offer clarity and tranquility, a kind of order, rather than the opposite" (153). For him, art accomplishes this by freezing the motion of the world. As he says in one of his remembered arguments with Sarah, "Perhaps I require in my life certain immutable standards, in contrast to your own credo, 'what is is always changing'" (135). He subscribes to Aristotelian analysis, especially the philosopher's analysis of time, which concludes that "time is not movement" (131). But this desire to ground himself in the world and for the world to be grounded too contributes to a lifelong fear: that the world will stop spinning. Grounding requires gravity, and gravity depends on the earth moving; the stasis implied in his sense of order is made possible by a larger movement of which he is forever suspicious:

Stasis less precarious, while motion, it seems, must inevitably sometimes cease, even if only transformed to another kind, of motion. Things can be severed, interrupted, done away with; can they not? Bodies that breathe one day cease to be, all their elaborate motion of fluid and blood disrupted; the processing, healing, exchanging no more. Some piece from inside, for example, might break off—just as earth from sun—and block an essential passageway, or some normal cell distort itself. So who is to say what potential friction might one day accost the earth: some unbidden celestial body or particle in irregular orbit? (119)

Sarah, on the other hand, embraces the world's and life's fundamental motion, that motion that Sebastian would seek to deny. For her, all is in flux, constantly changing, and, to Sebastian, it seems that she is too: she "would appear to fluctuate between nubility and ripeness—a cycle that must be his perception, but he could swear objective—perhaps depending on her mood. She has such powers, he believes, just as she changes hair color or style on whim" (125). This protean quality influences her thinking on language and art. For Sarah, language is something to be played with, for an ever-changing world requires an ever-changing language. This is best seen in her variations on Sebastian's name: S. B., S o' B, Sebastard, Seebee, C. B., Sweet Bee, Starburst, Sea Bass, Sagebrush, and so on. Similarly, art's value is in the process of creation, not the finished product. She explains, "my art, my creativity, isn't some fossilized entity on the walls of a museum or between the covers of a book. It's fluid, active. Orgasmic" (134). In this sense her art reflects the changing world in time. Far from seeking to stop time, she embraces its change. In her rendition of the Annunciation, the Virgin says, "I would not be so presumptuous . . . as to place my finger in some page to save a place, for it is already clear to me there is never any going back to that moment. Life has already changed; has it not, Angel?" (156). Where for Sebastian, art is something that imposes order on the world to defend us from its chaos, for Sarah, there are no clear distinctions between art and the world: "I mix up my life with my art; I can't help it. It's the way I make sense of things, the way I make sense of the world" (172).

We see most clearly here that the art that Carol, of "The Star Café," and Clara, of "Materia Prima," need—to help them to break from family and social ties and expectations, to reconcile their bodies and sense of self, and to negotiate their way through the world—is a postmodern art, not a nostalgic longing for the failed aesthetic order of modernism. Sebastian is aptly named after the saint famously pierced by so many arrows, because he desires to be fixed, to be, like Eliot's Prufrock, "pinned and wriggling on the wall" (Eliot 5). The art that Sarah espouses is internally generated by a subjective, creative imagination; it provides the means for continual self-re-creation; it offers a means to relate contingently to the never-stopping flow of the world.

Five Doubts

Five Doubts, Caponegro's next collection of stories, arises from her time spent in Italy, primarily a year-long residency at the American Academy in Rome in 1991-1992. The stories here, like those in *The Star Café,* are connected thematically and stylistically, but are also connected by a single inspirational technique: each story launches itself from an image or text from Italian history, culture, and art: "Il Libro dell'Arte (or The Apprentice's Mistress)" is inspired by Cennino d'Andrea Cennini's *Il Libro dell'Arte;* "The Spectacle" by a mosaic depicting a tiger being captured, her attention distracted by a mirrored sphere, from the "Great Hunting Room" of Piazza Armerina in Sicily; "Tombola" by a Neapolitan Tombolone game board; "An Etruscan Catechism" by a Tarquinian tomb painting of a bull running toward two men having sex in a field; and "Doubt Uncertainty Possibility Desire" by a detail from Andrea del Verrochio's *Baptism of Christ,* two angels on the Savior's right, one of them thought to have been painted by Leonardo da Vinci. The stories in *Five Doubts* explore many of the same ideas we found in *The Star Café,* especially issues surrounding epistemology and art, but here the form is even more experimental, making even less use of the conventions of narrative. Instead of surreal narratives centered more or less around an individual human consciousness, the stories in *Five Doubts* seem more aware of themselves as texts, more precisely, as constructed of texts.

"Il Libro dell'Arte (or The Apprentice's Mistress)" functions as a transition between *The Star Café* and the new volume. It is the first of the collection's responses to the volume's epigraph, from the writings of Leonardo da Vinci:

When you wish to see whether the general effect of your picture corresponds with that of the object represented after nature take a mirror and set it so that it reflects the actual thing, and then compare the reflection with your picture, and consider carefully whether the subject of the two images is in conformity with both, studying especially the mirror. The mirror ought to be taken as a guide—that is, the flat mirror—for within its surface substances have many points of resemblance to a picture; namely, that you see the picture made upon one plane showing things which appear in relief, and the mirror upon one plane does the same. The picture is one single surface, and the mirror is the same.

The picture is intangible, inasmuch as what appears round and detached cannot be enclosed within the hand, and the mirror is the same. . . . [It] is certain that if you but know well how to compose your picture it will also seem a natural thing seen in a great mirror. (3)

The story then begins with what seems to be a description of a Renaissance painting of an abundant rustic scene:

> wide variety of trees: almond, fig and olive; lindens, poplars, willows, wal-
> nut, maple, chestnut, peach and pear. Birds perch on the branches; closer
> scrutiny reveals how mixed their breed as well: doves and geese, hens and
> . . . vultures; it hardly seems a recipe for harmony; chickens, rabbits, white
> rather than black hogs, minivers, a pond of fish. There is not sufficient
> order to imply breeding, farming, harvesting or gardening; the land, how-
> ever, is not idle. An axe lies on the ground.
>   And then a house: a rustic one, perhaps a barn, some structure that
> appears to have been partially burned down. . . . (5)

At this point the story complicates the two-dimensional, mirror-up-
to-nature model of art da Vinci espoused, first by introducing an
observer—an unnamed person seeing, taking in, and trying to make
sense of the scene—and then, as the observer peers into the door-
way of the previously described house, a third dimension. Next, as
the observer turned second-person narrator notices that "the air is
redolent of garlic, most pleasant of its smells" and realizes that he is
hungry (6), senses other than sight are added. Finally, as we are
told, "You have heard of this house" (6), and some of the rumors
about the house's inhabitants are recounted, contextual knowledge
becomes part of the scene. Established here at the very beginning
are issues that will concern the rest of the book: the role of the inter-
preter in the meaning of art; art's relation to nature; art's function
within a larger sociocultural context.

The scene depicted is the studio of Lorenzo, an apprentice to
Cennino Cennini. The observer is probably Cennini himself, come to
see his pupil, though he never announces himself. Instead, he follows Lorenzo's assistant, Giovanna, as she explains her various duties in helping her master prepare the materials for his art and laments that he, having pledged celibacy for the six years of his
apprenticeship, is indifferent to her love for him. Her monologue
alternates with other narrative modes: the never-completed letters
Lorenzo writes to Cennini; conversations the observer imagines
taking place between the represented human figures in the studio;
the book of art Giovanna writes, first as Lorenzo's assistant, then,
at the end of the story, after she has displaced her master, as
Cennini's apprentice. The result is a meditation on the means of
making art contrasted with ways of being human.

In a sense, the barn and barnyard here remind us of Sarah's studio in "Sebastian": seemingly chaotic, with a variety of animals
roaming the place and art, all kinds of art, in progress everywhere.
At first, it seems to be a similar celebration of art as process. But
unlike Sarah, Lorenzo is clearly not in control of his art; everything

is in process and nothing nears completion, but, rather, entropically falls apart. His desire for absolute perfection, in his art, in his writing, in his apprenticeship, leads to stasis, for two interconnected reasons. First, since his art can never perfectly capture nature, it is never finished; he strives toward nothing less than perfection and thus goes nowhere. Second, his notion of perfection in nature implies a motionless, static, essentially dead nature. A world that is constantly moving and changing—like the world of nature in the studio—can never be captured perfectly in art or language, as Lorenzo should learn when he tries to make a plaster cast of a living bird and fish. It is a disaster, of course, as he writes to his master, "I could not keep them still. . . . I thought, O foolish creatures, how can it be that you protest an opportunity for immortality?" (12). Giovanna sums up these problems when she complains that Lorenzo never finishes his letters to Cennini,

"he claims they are incomplete, and I say, should you not then finish one so as to free your mind to start another? (poco a poco finché tutto è aposto?) instead of juggling many works in progress, as we are required by circumstance to do in this our workshop, with our formulae and artifacts? Conversely, with your words, I've counseled him, you might move in a more reasonable, expedient manner, yes—be spared the overwhelmedness that one can't help but feel when confronted with . . ." —she gestures theatrically with her graceful golden-downed forearm, toward the entire contents of the workshop to indicate what words cannot translate. (9)

While following her master's instructions, Giovanna spends much of the story questioning the uses to which they put the animals and natural objects that fill the studio. Everything there—the animals, eggs, nuts, fruits, liquids—is meant either to make the materials of art, the pigments, glues, parchment, brushes, oil, wood panels, gesso, or to serve as models of the proper colors and shapes to which the art should aspire. Giovanna repeatedly apologizes to the observer that she has no food to offer him, despite the apparent abundance around them. She also laments that just as nature's bounty is not used as it seems intended, Lorenzo's repression of his body's sexual needs is likewise unnatural. She says, "What we see as nourishment or sustenance, moreover succulence, what we take between our lips to put against our tongue and suck or crack between our teeth to rend from tough exterior an oily, savory essence meant to please the palate, is, in these quarters, something meant to serve the eye, which focuses all other senses, toward a far greater glory. In sum, my master sacrifices life to make all manner of work to please the eye, for others' eyes to gaze upon, and thus to obtain a love through indirection" (17). Giovanna thinks Lorenzo is oblivious to her comparatively mundane sexual desires, but the observer and the reader can see from his blushes at her sexual references, his sudden urges to relieve himself as he spreads plaster on her body, and his nervous incompetence at his tasks when she is too near that he is as unable to cope with his sexual desire as he is the protean world around him. Near the end of the story, Giovanna concludes,

"And in the manual I, Giovanna, aim, if ever time permits, to write, I will include what master's manual omits—questions such as this: if the body is creative, should not the artist who inhabits it be in equal measure creative, exploiting all resources, nothing wasted; nothing overlooked? I feel that I can say to you, a stranger, more straightforwardly than I can to my retiring master: why piss and spit be privileged over other liquids? And why saliva in one's palm but not skin's other surfaces? And if man's body be the model of all beauty, and thus each man inherently correct in form, why not make that truth available to all concerned, at least to Giovanna, earnest eager diligent apprentice, who seeks to learn all that she can in as expedient a manner as possible?" (32-33)

She seems to argue that it is better to use eggs, fruits, and nuts for food and better to make human love than to make art about divine love. Far from perfectly representing nature, Lorenzo's art seems a willful perversion of it, raising intriguing questions about both art's ability to represent the world and the potential damage that can be done in the effort to represent the world.

Similar questions about the relation between nature and art and between art and entertainment are foregrounded in the next story in the collection, "The Spectacle." This story is set in the ancient Roman Coliseum, during a grotesque entertainment for the emperor and thousands of others, and is divided into brief sections—called "acts" to stress the performative element—which alternate in focalization between the nameless human spectators and the captive animals who are doing the performing. This narrative technique allows us to see the perversity of the entertainment both from the point of view of an observer, describing, for example, how the elephant is made to kneel by means of javelins thrust between each toe ("You think he has such thick skin he cannot even feel" (46)), and the point of view of the animals as sentient beings: "I had not meant to swallow this strange projectile, that forced its way into my mouth, and chokes me now, while the only mobile part is gripped with his other hand, strangled by his fist" (43). The ostensible purpose of the entertainment is the titillation aroused by the exhibition of exotic animals, a display of nature, but the exhibition is so contrived—as in the hobbling of the elephant or in the chaining together of the panther and the bull, who would otherwise flee each other—as to distort the natural.

That holding a mirror up to nature, far from accurately reproducing it, distorts it, is made most clear near the end of the story, when the narrator imagines a tiger whispering in his tamer's ear the story of how she was captured, the story behind the mosaic that inspires this piece:

As you trapped me do you recall the crystal ball you tossed upon the ground to furnish my diminutive reflection, so all that was maternal and protective in me thought I saw an embryo of my own flesh and blood, thought my cub lay trapped yet in my reach, so every instinct bid me lick to heal the poor abandoned newborn. But while my tongue made contact with the surprise of cold smooth surface I anticipated would be warm and yielding and familiar, you surprised me in much grander style. You closed in on me and I had no defenses. You kicked away your trick, your crystal ball and made me march. (51)

The mirror evokes an instinctive response in the tiger, only to use that response against her.

The story's final section further complicates the distinctions implied in the spectacle, distinctions between the "real" world and the art world, between performance and spectator, and between animal and human. Here, the Coliseum is flooded so that horses and bulls can pull boats around in an extravagant faux-armada. What appears to be a shepherd piloting the largest boat turns out to be a lion, standing upright and wearing a cloak. The narrator, now separated from the focalization of the animals and the spectators, says, "Is it a trick of light? The Mediterranean sun dances on the sudden liquid skin of the arena. Gaze well, ladies and gentlemen. Gaze until the sun makes you squint to see beyond the surface shimmer. What you fix your gaze upon with indefatigable fascination is itself a kind of mirror. The oval frame contains a portrait you have painted. But there's no need to sign a portrait titled 'Self' " (52). The spectacle, far from holding a mirror up to nature, holds it up to its audience, asking which is more beastlike, the animals who are forced to perform or the spectators, whose cruelty and desire to be thrilled fuel the performance. This is an art that substitutes shallow emotional charges for ideas, that simplifies and distorts nature rather than face the complex problems implicit in any attempt to represent the world, and that deadens instead of enlightening and enlivening its audience. How much is lost here is suggested through the story's section titles—"What Is a Human"; "What Is Identity"; "What Is Intimacy"; "What Is Memory"; "What Is Eros"—questions implied in but ignored by the spectacle, but which should be explored in every work of art.

The next two stories, "Tombola" and "An Etruscan Catechism," further develop these ideas about how art seeks to represent nature and the audience's role in the realization of the work of art. "Tombola," like "Materia Prima," puts different kinds of texts into dialogue. Each of its thirty-three sections has two parts. The first is created stories inspired by and combining the cartoonish images on the Tombola game board, such images as a hunchback, a woman lifting her dress, a priest saying mass, three soldiers, a cannon, etc. The second is found material from contemporary Italian magazines that Caponegro has chosen and translated; these passages deal with such topics as the Mafia, contemporary Italian religious practices, ideas about the family, and changing notions of women's roles. The form and the style here demonstrate the fecundity of the creative imagination, but also place that imagination firmly within a sociocultural context. Further, they demonstrate the active participation of the reader in the creation of meaning, as he or she must make connections among the characters and situations in the created passages as well as connections between the created passages and the found material. As in "Materia Prima" the reader is given the responsibility of stitching the parts together into a meaningful whole.

As its title suggests, "An Etruscan Catechism" is presented as a series of questions and answers. But here, the usual format of a catechism, a religious authority asking questions of a member to test his or her mastery of the religion's dogma, is reversed as the questions are asked of the Etruscan priest, the haruspex. Moreover, the questions move from being informational to expressing doubt about and challenging the haruspex's dogma. The haruspex claims infallibility, though he admits that his mediation between the gods and people is based in interpretation of certain signs. The questioner, using the picture of the bull and the men having sex in a field as an example, argues for the multiple interpretation of signs—multiple, contradictory but equally valid interpretations can co-exist. The haruspex reveals his shaken faith as he moans, "Your questions, your questions, I am suddenly weary of so many questions!" (87). From his point of view, the questions represent doubt about the totalized worldview he accepts unquestioningly; from the questioner's point of view, they represent the indeterminacy of meaning and the creative possibilities of interpretation.

Many of these ideas and also a look back at *The Star Café* are incorporated into the collection's long, final piece, "Doubt Uncertainty Possibility Desire." Carrying even further the formal experiments of "Materia Prima" and "Tombola," this story is composed almost entirely of cut up, found material. As Caponegro explains in an author's note—unfortunately, inadvertently left out of many copies of *Five Doubts*—the story is a collage of material from a variety of sources, including: *The Notebooks of Leonardo da Vinci; Leonardo da Vinci on the Human Body,* by Charles D. O'Malley and J. B. de C. M. Saunders (1952); *Medicine's New Visions,* by Howard Sochurek (1988); *Dimensions of Cancer,* by Charles E. Kupchella (1987); *Breast Cancer,* by Rose Kushner (1975); *Cancer Risks and Prevention,* edited by M. P. Vassey and Muir Gray (1985); *Virtual Reality,* by Ken Pimentel and Kevin Teixeira (1995); *Managing Computer Viruses,* by Eric Louw and Neil Duffy (1992); *Inventing AIDS,* by Cindy Patton (1990); *The Social Context of AIDS,* edited by Joan Huber and Beth E. Schneider (1992); and articles from the *New York Times* (*Five Doubts* 138). Interspersed among the passages from these sources are passages created by Caponegro in the voice of Salai. Salai is a young boy apprenticed to da Vinci, but his real relationship to the artist is ambiguous: he is helper, model, son, possibly lover; but most important, he is the voice of doubt haunting Leonardo. He says at one point, "We both know it is our destiny that we be strangely linked, like breath to flame, like hand to kite. Your destiny is to be always seeking flight, and mine: to pull you down to earth, to make you roll in dirt, or worse. This game depends on your participation. You remain eternally enamored of possibility, and I, at every moment, your desire's doubt" (109).

This conflict between Leonardo and Salai, or, more abstractly, between desire and doubt, provides a general structure for the arrangement of the various passages. Far from being randomly or haphazardly arranged, the passages are in fact carefully ordered in two ways. First, adjacent passages will often treat the same topic across time and discipline or will often be centered around the same image, as in one section that links a passage in which a woman tells of her hand discovering a lump in her breast with one explaining how a computer translates a gloved hand into a computer-generated virtual hand with another describing rubber gloves protecting medical personnel from exposure to AIDS (114-15). These passages are related dialogically, either implicitly, as above, or explicitly, as when da Vinci's speculations on measuring the intestine are connected to contemporary accounts of using barium to film the intestines, and Salai complains about Leonardo's spending "hours diagramming all that nature in her wisdom hides inside" (113-14).

On a larger scale, the story is ordered around a chronological progression in the depicting of the human body. This is established in one of the passages: "Man has progressed from cave painting to canvas to camera and now to machine vision" (108). Leonardo, as Salai reminds us, has made a transition from painting "saints and angels" (117), divine perfection in human form, to experimenting so as to reach a perfect understanding of the body. We see the offspring of da Vinci's science in contemporary accounts of new technology with which the body, inside and out, may be seen and examined and illnesses diagnosed: PET scanners "watch" brain cells (99); ultrasound makes pictures of fetuses or tumors (99); a mammogram's "color enhanced image" reveals malignant cancer in a woman's breast (101); sound waves map blood flow (106); radioactive gas makes a picture of the lungs (107); and so on. Technology has advanced to the point that computers can go beyond depicting the body to actually absorbing it, as with the virtual hand: "You're actually inside the computer because you can see your hand in there" (115). One wonders if computers are replacing people, having become so human as to be threatened by viruses of their own.

This idea about the blurring of the line between human being and machine is developed more fully in the story's concern about the control scientific discourse has over our understanding of the human body. As the story continues, we see that Leonardo's search for perfect knowledge of the body is complicated, if not made impossible, by that knowledge being always situated in a social and ideological discourse. For example, one passage from the *New York Times* reads, "Responding to the arrests Sunday of more than one hundred people protesting his statements on homosexuality, AIDS and abortion, John Cardinal O'Connor said yesterday that his approach could be changed only 'over my dead body' . . ." (124). This and other passages make clear that the understanding, diagnosis, and treatment of illnesses like AIDS and breast cancer occur in an ideologically charged context and that layers of patriarchal, heterosexist, and conservative Christian discourse surround the body, affecting the way it is spoken about and known. The attempt to control the body by means of these and other discourses is founded in the belief in science's ability—Leonardo's quest—to know the body perfectly. As one passage says, "rarely do we question the ability of science to know" (130). Moreover, "Although science is often not specifically referenced, the common assumption underlying debates on public policy or the voicing of personal views about safer sex, is that science can, ultimately, answer any troubling questions" (130). This certainty "filter[s] out into the social and imaginary world" (131) and is the unspoken assumption behind social, ideological, and religious judgments about the body. Thus knowledge about the body is changeable and subjective, in that it is meaning imposed on the body by social discourses, but is perceived as objective, because it is supposedly based in science: "it is the logic of science that anchors the power relations which determine whose knowledge counts as 'real,' as 'objective' " (131).

The story, then, suggests that claiming one's body as one's own is a more challenging task than Carol, apparently triumphant at the end of "The Star Café," realizes. Part of the challenge is the paucity of available discourses with which to claim the body. One passage near the end reads, "This was a situation in which any kind of speech recognizable as operating within the discourse of unitary or of network power was captured by science, the media, the politicians" (133). A possible answer is suggested in what appears to be the continuation of this passage, later on the same page: "The only remaining form of speaking was that which fell between the legitimated discourses, something approaching the discourse of art, but an art of the body in resistance" (133). Interestingly, a story which began with da Vinci turning from art to science for more perfect knowledge of the human body now suggests returning the body to art to save it from the implications of his search. The story doesn't go on to explore what "an art of the body in resistance" might be, but it does offer itself, in a way its form underscores, as an example of how art can function in a contemporary society in which most available discourses are absorbed into the officially defined power structures. The author's notes tells us, "The title 'Doubt Uncertainty Possibility Desire,' derives from the Italian subjunctive mood, the Congiuntivo, which is used to express hypothetical conditions and convey expressions of emotion, doubt, and uncertainty" (138). The Congiuntivo serves as a model for art here: it offers doubt to subvert assertions of certainty; it offers subjunctive possibilities the discourses of science and ideology would deny. The mood is represented in the central tension of the story: Leonardo desiring and pursuing perfection in form and knowledge; Salai introducing doubt and uncertainty to keep forever available the possibilities that resist the totalizing closure of perfection.

The Complexities of Intimacy

Stylistically, *The Complexities of Intimacy,* Caponegro's most recent collection, seems closer to *The Star Café* than to *Five Doubts*. In fact, the material in the two more recent books was written over the same period of time: Caponegro began *The Complexities of Intimacy* stories before her initial trip to Italy and the experiences that inspired *Five Doubts;* she then returned to those stories after coming back to America, to get briefly away from the fermenting Italian material, and then she would alternate between the two collections. Thus, while the stories in the two books are quite different in form, their thematic concerns overlap. But where *Five Doubts* extends and complicates ideas about art introduced in Caponegro's earlier work, *The Complexities of Intimacy* seems more focused on developing ideas about the family, more specifically, the desire for individuality versus the sense of identity dependent on family relationships. The family here, though, is rendered as a darker, more poignant, and more complicated set of relationships than in the earlier works. This book uses the erotic as a metaphor, projecting it onto different surfaces, displacing it so as to defamiliarize family relationships.

The narrator of the first story, "The Daughter's Lamentation," has fallen victim to the fear of the narrator of "Heart as Nails": she has failed to escape her family. While her sisters have long ago moved into their own lives and her mother has died, she has remained at home, a decaying house on the shore of one of the Finger Lakes in western New York, to care for her aging father. Where in earlier stories, Caponegro's characters pursuing identity through independence had to resist the stasis-seeking influence of those around them and place their faith in less secure, contingent ways of knowing the world, here the roles are reversed. The narrator's father, an architect, has spent his life (and great chunks of his family's lives too) studying the great buildings of the world and the spectacular sights of nature, striving impossibly to capture the dynamic flux of nature in his work, without distorting it by imposing artificial structures on it. In old age he obsessively observes the lake, seeking to know it, to experience it, without any kind of mediation. As the narrator tells us, he "now desires to be so intimate with nature that no static can interfere, not even the impressions of another, his daughter."[1] The result of his philosophy can be seen in the house:

The house . . . is another matter, conforming to no law with which I am acquainted: a kind of wood box slightly askew; not saltbox, neither hat nor shoe, a leaning tower without a Pisa's dignity, haphazard, squat, and deep within, a strange conglomerate of spaces extending from cellar to attic, each appearing infinite, made separate instead of connected by series of steps, altogether unfinished yet cramped. He would finish the basement, he always said, so I and my sisters could play, and also the attic, to use as his study, but we were as family too transient to allow feasibility of any long-term project—still less likely now to be considered by he who communes incessantly with Infinity.

In a sense, this all may remind us of Sarah's "what is is always changing" credo from "Sebastian," but here, the father's denial of structure has resulted in deleterious effects on his family, especially the narrator. Denying structure in his family, much as in his architecture, the father has reversed, transgressed, or made meaningless family roles and relations: in his old age, the narrative present, he has become the child and his daughter the parent; more significantly, in the past he sexually abused his daughter.

As a result of this abuse, which was covered up by the family doctor and ignored by her mother, the narrator is dislocated psychologically and in space—thus her inability to navigate the maze of their house, similar to Carol's confusion in the mirrored room in "The Star Café." Like Carol, too, the narrator seeks an order, "even a contrived one" (*Star Café* 37), to provide stability and meaning. Far from finding her father's structurelessness potentially liberatory, the things that appeal to him—the house, modern paintings—strike her as "unfinished; in fact unbegun." In contrast to her father, she seeks a structure to impose on the world, going so far as to find a structure to make motion motionless (also Sebastian's obsession). We see this in her preoccupation with her early interest in ballet:

. . . I entertained the fantasy of ballet as vocation (though now it seems absurd), enacting over and over on a stage the most stylized of romances—ironic that a sequence of steps and positions take nearly a lifetime to prepare and yield at best a stilted corporeal narrative—one is always leaping up from or into the arms of a man whose sex is trapped in a stocking, like the squeezed face of a thief: to make one pair of mobile mannequins, layered in gauze to render us weightless, lighter than air as we rise (in defiance of gravity), invisible buildings described by our bodies, rarely remaining for more than a moment.

She apparently wants to transform the protean motion of her life into stasis: finished narrative; genderless inanimateness; human architecture. But even as she yearns for these things, she recognizes their failure. She ends her story, "How shall I bear to maintain this curious house, which of course it will be my legacy to inherit? I will dance as if in ritual atonement or bereavement—I who must atone for others' sins, I whose grief precedes this one—I'll dance before the setting sun to keep illusion of equilibrium as I nightly drown." What seemed to be solutions for the characters in *The Star Café* are here turned upside down: immersion into the motion of the ever-changing world is selfish and hurtful; application of a contingent order to the world is useless. The narrator seems destined never to navigate her way out of the house nor to negotiate a relationship with the social world around her nor to articulate a sense of identity.

The next story, "The Mother's Mirror," presents a similarly disheartening view of the entanglements of family. The narrator here, whose voice and use of the identity-dispersing first-person plural to refer to herself recall the narrator of the early story "Monday," practices self-sacrifice—sacrificing her needs, desires, and comfort to her family—to the point of self-effacement. This is carried to the extreme of trying to deny her need to urinate because her children monopolize the bathroom. She says,

Not only are our physiological functions hindered by these rituals; pragmatic matters of the house are left on hold as well. We would like to start the laundry, so his sweatshirt and her ragged dungarees will be available on demand. We would like to let the dishwasher initiate its cycle, now that we have cleared away all traces of the repast we spent the afternoon preparing. Ingeniously we have fit all the vessels into the wire racks of the appliance: the pots and pans and flatware, even the tiny plate on which we put our own supper—the full-sized dinner plate that completes the Blue Danube pattern china set was accidentally broken recently—his girlfriend is our guess, but we are not so small, so petty, as to mention it, make issue of it—and we would not want to ask any other family member to make the sacrifice of crowding food onto such a diminutive surface. Still we are tentative about pressing the oval silver button that starts the cycle, lest we alter the consistency of our husband's bath—known to last over an hour—or perhaps the children's showers are now in progress: those pre-trysting rituals during which the steam rises and disseminates to fog not only the bathroom mirror, but all the windows of the house, as if our family resided in the humidity of the tropics rather than the temperate climate of a northeastern suburb of the United States.

Finally, she timidly enters the bathroom, only to find a weirdly ideal gathering of her family engaged, together, in bathroom activities that seem "both ordinary and exalted." She thinks herself a part of this magical scene, but after observing in delight the others, she sees her own face in the mirror, wrinkled, puffy, cold, old. She has become so lost in her service to the family, letting that service define her as a person, that she never develops an individual identity but also is not really a member of the family.

Similar themes are explored more hopefully in "The Father's Blessing," narrated by a comically obtuse priest, Father Faraday, devoted to the mystery of time's arrow. He thinks to serve a newly wedded couple by offering to perform Last Rites, a reminder even amid the joy of a marriage of the one-way direction of time, ending in death. He returns that night to their bed, while they are having sex, with the local undertaker, to measure them for their coffins. Several months later, as the bride is giving birth, Father Faraday shows her a Polaroid of a stillborn baby. He is not discouraged by the couple's horrified rejections, as he knows that "Moments of the truth are all we can bear." This commitment to the movement toward death at the expense of moments of life (marriage, conception, birth) is grounded in an inability (like Sebastian's) to deal with the vitality of an ever-changing world. The priest laments at one point, "our world fluctuates before us daily; appearances ever-unreliable indices of truth." But the certainty of the movement toward death is undercut for him by two events near the end of the story. Through a keyhole, he observes the bride, her husband and just-born child gone to the hospital, invite her mother to join her on a journey into her own womb. He overhears her explanation in a muffled voice:

"In the excruciating and terribly lonely pain of labor, when all of me was opened up, I felt almost delirious, and yet very . . . present, painfully connected to what was happening, and in between contractions I just decided I should be able to inhabit that space myself, in a soothing way; a therapeutic way, I guess you could call it. Shouldn't the haven we give others be available for us too? Doesn't it seem right to you mamma? Anyway, suddenly I was in a place I'd never known, but that I wanted to come back to, and when I saw you now, I knew I had to bring you with me. I'm very glad you agreed to come."

The bride goes on to say, "My first journey in this world was through a room just like this, that you guided me through. Then somehow we grew estranged from one another." This return to the womb—which in "Materia Prima" was seen as a desire to stop change and an attempt to keep Clara from developing as an individual—is here a blow against one-way time and a return to a close relationship between mother and child. After the two return to the bedroom ("The bride seemed to turn inside out"), time is reversed again as first the mother, then Father Faraday, entering the room stealthily to offer his help, suck the milk from the bride's swollen breasts, the literal and symbolic parents becoming babies again. This reversal of time shakes the priest's beliefs: "Here the undertaker had no place, it seemed. And my own truths seemed disturbingly incomplete." Unable to bring himself to leave the room, he begins composing his next homily with what seems to be a new sense of service, but one which he can't articulate clearly—just as he can't find the perfect words to address (and relate himself to) his congregation—apparently more willing to accommodate his sense of service to the changing circumstances of a changing world.

"The Son's Burden," the novella-length, penultimate piece, pursues the collection's interest in identity, family, and art and looks back at both *The Star Café* and *Five Doubts*. Unusual for a Caponegro story, "The Son's Burden" has a specific historical setting: Chicago; New Year's Eve, 1933. The Smalldridge family is gathered in their home for an annual ritual: son Tom's presentation of an invention, one which will, unlike the previous years', succeed, make his fortune, and establish him among the great American in-

ventors. This is his father's goal for him, a goal to which his older
sister, Eleanor, is apparently sympathetic, and to which his mother,
in her upstairs room, ever playing her harp, is not. This year's gathering is complicated by the presence of Cecilia, Tom's fiancée,
though he has yet to give her a ring. He hopes, this evening, either
to receive as a gift from Eleanor the ring left over from her aborted
engagement to a doctor or to borrow from his father the money to
buy one. Tom sums up the significance of the evening for him and
his sister: "how to transcend this Smalldridge 'new' year ritual and
all it connotes, to achieve what is ideally, truly, our destiny—unless
rising be not in our future, and destiny already in our midst, not in
the least inscrutable. And if destiny be already at our feet, it seems
reasonable to suppose that no matter how vigorously or frequently
we might pick them up, they will yield us no motion other than run-
ning-in-place; thus stasis remains our legacy: the proverbial animal
chasing its tail—somehow less nobly tragic than Sisyphus and his
trusty appendage." This early in the story, Caponegro has already
introduced her familiar themes of the need for an identity independent of the family and protean flux versus stasis.

The father, Hubert Smalldridge, is a devotee of creation in the
form of technological invention, and he has lived to pass this devotion on to his children. A railroad conductor (he never removes his
conductor's cap), out of work because of the Depression, he has filled
his house impossibly full with eccentric inventions and his
children's heads with the history of invention and inventors. His
faith in invention is akin to a faith in human progress, a technological evolution, the goal of which is an ideal society. He says at one
point of inventors, "Our job is to remember that everything these
fine men made took society one notch further toward perfection."
For him, these men "furthered civilization." He wants his children,
especially his son, to participate in this progress for the monetary
success it offers, for the fulfillment of the American Dream it promises, and for the glory of being part of the movement of history.

His goal, however, is complicated by several problems. First, he
tries to turn his children into inventors by making them, from a
very young age—they have been home schooled—master the history of inventors and inventions. Tom explains one early lesson:

For example, as recreation to pass the hours during journeys and rainy
days of our youth, my sister and I were permitted to play (as carefree as
we were to be in all our lives), a common children's game. "I packed my
trunk and in it I put" was the reprise, and this game's goal was the accrual
of the entire alphabet in objects—rendered only verbally, of course, with
players alternating letters. The Smalldridge version deviated from the
standard game in this respect: the alphabetized contents of our verbal

baggage were confined to one category—inventions. It began innocently enough, but evolved over time, under Father's tutelage, into a version far more stringent, whereby we were enjoined to exhaust the alphabet repeatedly until no invention was left unuttered. I'd volley with my sister: abacus, brake, cogwheel, digging stick. . . .

As the siblings grow older, they are forced to memorize not only inventions' names but also their inventors, their inventors' biographies, their development, even their patent numbers! Indeed, part of the New Year ritual is a series of pop quizzes, wherein the father barks out an invention and expects Tom to recite from memory all relevant and some irrelevant information about it. The father seems not to realize—as Clara finally realized in "Materia Prima"— that the mastery of received knowledge is not the same as, or even a precursor to, creation. The second complication in the father's goal is implied in the above: in becoming a tough schoolmaster to his children, he has in many ways stopped being a father to them. We see him through Tom's eyes as a crude, ill-mannered bully, trying to have his way through shouts and insults, demanding the respect owed to a father while offering none of the love expected from a father. The third complication is in the basis of his enterprise, the faith in technological and social progress. Tom, in explaining the annual ritual, wonders about this certainty in progress: Can one see evolution only in retrospect? In the midst of history or his life, how can he tell if he is progressing or spinning his wheels? Later, he wonders about the end of technological progress, the perfect society his father sees. If all human accomplishments are moving step by step toward this end, does the achievement of this goal imply an end of motion, some kind of apocalypse? Thinking of Roman roads, he fantasizes, "Why then, could not the roads stand up again, lift off the ground to roam the earth as celestial bodies, a Stonehenge in flight, and leave in their wake the debris of stone and bronze and iron age: pottery shards, bronze pumps, water wheels, sails, arrows in orbit through bows, levers, wedges, pulleys and screws, aqueducts, all aflame around a shell of steel that itself surrounds a wrought-iron core, reheated until the whole thing ignites and the universe explodes—you lose the whole shebang, pal—BOOM, so much for your order, Father, try to rein it all in and it explodes in your face." Tom further connects the apocalypse toward which time's arrow points to an incident in which Thomas Edison, after whom he was named, accidentally blew up a baggage car on a moving train:

And what if the trunk we children packed were indeed capacious enough to house all the world's progress in one alphabetical unfolding, and this fantastic trunk had been in the special secret corner of the baggage car on the Port Huron-Detroit line train, which exploded because Edison was so driven—or unscrupulous—or rambunctious—as to perform his chemical experiments on the job!

I packed my trunk and in it I put the Butcher, the Baker, the Candlestick-maker, did I say two *b*'s make an *a*? Why not make it three, go BOOM! Whoops, let's start over: *a* is for Armour, *h* is for Hammond, throw in Pullman, quick, add Swift and swiftly light the candlestick to create a conflagration more dramatic than Chicago's legendary fire—and please do not let even one invention, phoenix-like, rise again, let them all be reduced to ash, so that dust they shall remain.

Tom's mother is in many ways the opposite of his father; in fact when the mother narrates the story of their courtship, how such an unlikely pair got together, it seems an elaborate joke. Where the father worships technological invention, the mother thinks, as she explains, "an invention is something in no more than two or three parts that was written by Bach!" She associates creation with artistic creation, more specifically music. She is a harpist and devotes herself almost exclusively to her playing. She only infrequently comes downstairs to join the family gathering, though Tom imagines he can discern her supportive influence in her choices of music, wafting down from above. For Tom, the mother's music is the pathway to all other art, as he has learned to explore painting, sculpture, and literature by these other art forms' depiction of harps. While on the one hand, Tom seems torn between his parents' separate and opposite notions of creation, on the other, the mother shares with the father some of the same problems. She plays on the harp, but she does not compose for it. Thus, while her devotion to art is real, rather than create art, she re-presents others' artistic creations. Though not as obsessively as the father, she is fascinated with past accomplishments of harpists, composers, and conductors (not train conductors). But, again, mastery of the past is not the same as creation. More important, her absorption into her music has, for years, drawn her away from the family. From the father's and Eleanor's comments, and even from hints dropped by Tom, it seems that the mother neglected her children in favor of her harp while they were in the womb, while they were infants, and ever since. Eleanor has, in bitterness, rejected her mother, adopting as her own her father's positions on creation and his loathing of his wife. Tom, as we shall see, has tried to find ways to reconcile his parents' divergent personalities, interests, and beliefs and tries to find a way to return, like the daughter in "The Father's Blessing," to a symbiotic, womblike relationship with his mother.

Eleanor, Tom's ally in trying to please their father and the father's ally in attacking her mother, introduces another notion of creation into the family mix. Her interest, beyond the history of invention which was imposed on her by her father, is the study of biological oddities, the abnormalities the human body is capable of producing. Tom calls this her study of "the furthest outposts of the body." She makes Cecilia sick with her lists of weird bodily formations: anal tags, the double epiglottis, the womb with two orifices, the double uterus, duplex bladders, and so on. For her, these are ad hoc, spontaneous creations of the body. She expounds on her beliefs:

> "The body is indeed full of wonder, full of portent," Sister carries on. "We tend to single out mechanical inventions for admiration, while the body's innate creativity is ignored, or worse yet, shunned." No one has the power to stop Eleanor.
> "Why, mysterious things indeed emanate from the body, things which can themselves merit the status of creature: the dermoid cyst, for example, unbidden extension of cerebral vesicle, eye, hair, molar tooth. In what category does it belong? The body's mascot? Neither conventional excrescence nor an offspring, something far more wondrous; it makes us shudder. To bear a child is commonplace in comparison, wouldn't you agree, Miss Crittenden?" (Cecilia's lips part but no sound emerges.)

Eleanor's notion of creation is distinct from her father's and mother's in that, while she can study its history, there is no implied progress or evolution from one incident to another and in that it is creation separated from conscious intention.

Cecilia, the outsider, does not offer a position on creation, but her presence is nevertheless important. She is a social worker in a settlement house, someone interested less in an abstract, future society, perfect through technology, than in alleviating current human suffering. She clearly does not fit in this gathering, but she is a reminder of the social context in which all creation occurs. She tries desperately, but unsuccessfully, to connect the Smalldridges' conversations to the immediate social and cultural context, making reference to such figures as Frank Lloyd Wright and Mussolini.

Tom spends the story, as he seems to have spent much of his life, trying to negotiate a position among all these relationships. His annual inventions are designed to merge and reconcile his parents' opposite positions and interests. His presentations, in the discourse of a salesman's pitch, periodically interrupt the story. Thus we learn he has presented the harp headboard, the harpists' page-turning fan, the harp crib, the harp bed, the harp hammock, and this year's invention, the combination teething ring/tuning device. At one point Tom tells us, "It is fitting that the story of Orpheus and Eurydice was adapted by Gluck and Handel for instrumentation that includes the harp, for in my private musicology, I am Orpheus reconstituted, unable *not* to turn and look back, despite the dire consequences." It's clear that each of his inventions constitutes a looking back. Each is an attempt to erase the neglect he felt from his mother in favor of her harp, neglect that he refuses to acknowledge consciously, but that he admits with each new invention. Their aggregate purpose is to make it possible to be a good, loving, involved mother and a dedicated harpist at the same time. As Tom says, explaining the teething ring/tuning device, "only when the string has gone lax need the infant's teething be interrupted. And thus he can feel a part of the instrument's maintenance, sharing in his mother's whole existence. He is not threatened or bereft, because he is continuous with his mother's instrument."

The father's annual, vituperative rejection of the proffered invention is based not just in its connection to the mother and her despised instrument, but also in its implied challenge to his faith in progress and perfection. Far from aiding in the inevitable progress of social evolution, Tom's inventions reverse time's arrow, looking back, trying to recover for Tom himself what seems to have been lost. Thus he tries ineffectively to prove to his father that the neat forward path of history he imagines never really existed. He points out that in the lives of the great inventors are "a host of incongruities" and that "Edison's life was not a straight path to success." Not surprisingly, these kinds of arguments make little headway against the father's intransigence.

Then, at the story's climax, Eleanor offers a different kind of argument, an example of creation meant to substitute for Tom's rejected invention. In Tom's description,

She throws herself at Father's knees, entreating him, then casts herself face-down across the fringed, overstuffed ottoman called the Pouf, hoisting her skirt up to her waist, too rapidly this time for anybody's intervention. Does my sister invite a beating, making herself a scapegoat for me? How can I allow it? And then I see the truth, for she lowers her undergarments to reveal between her buttocks, an approximately five-inch length of cartilaginous protuberance—awe-inspiring really, in the manner of a meteor shower or eclipse or some celestial display visible only several times a century. Her tail must have been sequestered for more than 30 years. . . .

Earlier, when Eleanor had been reciting her mental collection of biological oddities, Tom had explained, "these individuals of medical lore might be said to have a physiology in reverse, a beauty so rich, so conceptual, if you will, as to be beyond our present aesthetic." Seen this way, Eleanor's tail serves as the only genuine creation to come out of the Smalldridge house and thus calls into question many of the household's preoccupations. As a biological anomaly, it challenges the construction of the historic continuum, creation—art or invention—moving inexorably forward, evolving step by step. As an accidental creation—that is, one not the product of conscious intention—it challenges the presentation of the creator—artist or inventor—as an individual genius. Rather, as an artifact, an art object, it startles, upsetting accepted, predictable ways of thinking about art, history, progress, the body, and offering a multitude of new potential worldviews. Like the proposed art of the body in resistance at the end of "Doubt Uncertainty Possibility Desire," it, at least for a moment, unsettles the old and makes possible the new.

This epiphany, however, does not lead to the possibly hopeful endings of "The Star Café," "Materia Prima," or even the muted hope of "Doubt Uncertainty Possibility Desire." Instead, in his coda Tom despairs: "We are ill and woefully weary. Dawn is nowhere at hand and there is so much history yet to be accounted for. Already we are nauseated, and the nebulous climax toward which we climb has yet to show its countenance." Tom seems to have rejected his vision of the apocalyptic end of his father's faith in progress, the inevitable target of time's arrow. His language here is entropic, implying a world running down, exhausting itself while New Year's midnight, society perfected, or the final BOOM loom ahead in the distance, but are never reached. Not desiring to go forward into progress or back into his mother's womb, he now embraces the entropic moment, wishing to dissolve into the undifferentiated dark.

In her body of work Mary Caponegro has done her several mentors proud. Her fictions have expanded the possibilities for what fiction can do, and they have offered her readers pictures of the complex world, offered them new ways to see and new ways to be. It's hard to predict what she will give us next (she's hinted to me that she's starting to explore what more mimetic fiction may have to offer, as she puts it, "letting my avant-garde guard down" (Letter)), but if her past work is any indication, it will be surprising, entertaining, intelligent, and beautiful.

NOTES
[1] I am quoting from the typescript of *The Complexities of Intimacy*. After revision, these quotations may appear slightly differently in the published version, to be released by Coffee House Press this fall.

WORKS CITED

Banas, Mary. Rev. of *The Star Café and Other Stories,* by Mary Caponegro. *Booklist* 15 May 1990: 1777.

Caponegro, Mary. *The Complexities of Intimacy.* Ts., 2001.

——. *Five Doubts.* New York: Marsilio, 1998.

——. "Impressions of a Paranoid Optimist." *Review of Contemporary Fiction* 16.1 (Spring 1996): 23-27.

——. Letter to the author. 15 May 2001.

——. *The Star Café and Other Stories.* 1990. New York: Norton, 1991.

——. *Tales from the Next Village.* Providence: Lost Roads, 1985.

Eder, Richard. "This Is Not a Book Review." Rev. of *The Star Café and Other Stories,* by Mary Caponegro. *Los Angeles Times* 1 July 1990: 3, 9.

Eliot, T. S. "The Love Song of J. Alfred Prufrock." *The Complete Poems and Plays: 1909-1950.* New York: Harcourt, 1971. 3-7.

Kirschenbaum, Blossom S. "Mary Caponegro: Prize-Winning American Writer in Rome." *Italian Americana* 13.1 (1995): 24-31.

Moore, Steven. "Visions and Voices." Rev. of *The Star Café and Other Stories,* by Mary Caponegro. *Washington Post* 23 August 1990: D3.

Mary Caponegro
Photograph by Marco Jorge

A Mary Caponegro Checklist

Fiction Collections

Tales from the Next Village. Providence: Lost Roads, 1985.
The Star Café and Other Stories. New York: Scribner, 1990; New York: Norton, 1991.
Five Doubts. New York: Marsilio, 1998.
The Complexities of Intimacy. Minneapolis: Coffee House, 2001.

Recent Uncollected Fiction

"Ashes Ashes We All Fall Down." *Conjunctions* 34 (Spring 2000): 12-24.
"Odradrek, or The Cares of a Family Woman." *Sulfur* Spring 2000: 48-49.
"Synthesia." *États-Unis: Formes Récentes de l'Imagination Littéraire* 29 (December 2000): 257-60.
"Because I Could Not Stop for Death." *A Convergence of Birds: Original Fiction and Poetry Inspired by the Work of Joseph Cornell.* Ed. Jonathan Safran Foer. New York: Distributed Art Publishers, 2001. 156-78.

Margery Latimer

Joy Castro

American modernist Margery Latimer (1899-1932) is remembered
today only as the first wife of Harlem Renaissance author Jean
Toomer, the lover of leftist poet Kenneth Fearing, or the close friend
of Georgia O'Keeffe, yet her early death cut short the promise of an
extremely successful literary career comparable to that of many
canonized modernists. Reviewers of the period compared Latimer's
two novels and two volumes of short fiction to the work of Katherine
Mansfield, D. H. Lawrence, Gertrude Stein, and James Joyce; indeed, she published in many of the same venues. Her oeuvre blends
an experimental modernist aesthetic with her own brand of feminist and leftist critique, urging our renewed interest.

Modernist to the core, Latimer was brilliant, innovative, passionate, revolutionary, and self-conscious in the best sense of the word.
Her genius is for transmitting a certain immediacy of experience—
transcendent moments, small epiphanies—by means of the carefully rendered physical detail. Veering from sensuous lyricism to
clever, biting satire, her prose employs striking metaphors—a
woman's vengeful glee surfaces "like an actual shawled body rising
from mud, smoothly dripping" (*Nellie Bloom* 24)—and experimental
narrative techniques (such as a melding of first-, second-, and third-
person narration in a single story) to jolt and engage the reader.
Her work explores issues central to the modernist movement, such
as the role of the artist in society, the breakdown of social verities,
the liberation of sexuality from Victorian mores, and the sometimes
thrilling, sometimes alienating impact of technology and urban existence.

While such stories as "City" and "Confession" (1929) illuminate
the excesses, idealism, and loneliness of urban bohemians—
Latimer was herself a habitué of the wild all-night parties of Greenwich Village in the 1920s—most of her work uses the experimental
language and narrative structures of the avant-garde to render rural small-town life in middle America. Like her modernist contemporaries T. S. Eliot, F. Scott Fitzgerald, and Ernest Hemingway,
Latimer hailed from the heartland, and her fiction turns repeatedly
to the Midwest, particularly to small rural communities, both inter-
rogating their provincialism—she has been called a feminist
Sherwood Anderson—and commemorating their simplicity and

natural beauty. In Fitzgerald's worldview, the Midwest is the place from which one escapes by whatever means necessary, as Jimmy Gatz does to become Jay Gatsby, and the American small town is where one returns when one has failed, as does Dick Diver at the end of *Tender is the Night* (1934). Between Sherwood Anderson's *Winesburg, Ohio* (1919) and Sinclair Lewis's *Main Street* (1920), small-town Midwestern America had been revealed as a petri dish of dysfunction, philistinism, and banality, yet as the focus of American life shifted toward urban centers, Anderson and others also sounded an elegiac note of affection and grief in their portraits of these rural remnants of America's history. Latimer did so as well: in an essay published shortly after her death, poet Horace Gregory recalls her as a "country girl" who criticized Proust's "drawing rooms and desiccated people" and preferred instead "an open field in spring, where brown-skinned farmer boys tend slowly-moving cattle" (2). But Latimer also brought to her depictions of village life a critical feminist sensibility that illuminated the prevalence of child abuse, sexual exploitation, religious and social hypocrisy, marital inequality, and the sexual repression expected of women. Without essentializing Woman as Nature, her work connects the colonized female consciousness with the destruction of nature as small towns expanded and modernized.

In the American tradition of Walt Whitman and the modernist tradition of James Joyce, Latimer reclaims the body as a site for epiphanic spiritual experience. But in Latimer's case, it is primarily the female body that is reclaimed. The pleasures and pains of women's sexuality are explored throughout her work, from an overwhelming and transcendent experience of pregnancy in "The Family" (1929), to a devastating abortion in the novel *This Is My Body* (1930), to a young girl's awakening sexuality in "The Little Girls" (1932). Particularly compelling are her fictional critiques of traditional marriage and family structures, which she analyzes in light of the changing status and freedoms of women.

Works such as *We Are Incredible* (1928), "Possession" (1929), and "Guardian Angel" (1932), which fictionalize Latimer's intense and lengthy mentorship by the older writer Zona Gale, delineate the passionate complexities of women's relationships with each other. Indeed, the eroticized language with which Latimer describes these relationships and the violent breaks that end them strongly suggest the presence of what Patricia Juliana Smith has labeled "lesbian panic" in her analysis of British women's fiction of the modernist period: the "disruptive action or reaction that occurs when a character—or, conceivably an author—is either unable or unwilling to confront or reveal her own lesbianism or lesbian desire" (2). In the face of such desire, Smith argues, characters are either restored to institutional heterosexuality or annihilated, as happens in *We Are Incredible.*

With its focus on the body and its exploration of clearly autobiographical material, Latimer's work resists the new critical representation of modernism that views texts as independent art objects suspended in ahistorical space, complete unto themselves, for she relentlessly ties her writing back to her own lived experience and to others' perceptions of her body in the world. Ravishingly lovely, Latimer was remarked everywhere for her statuesque beauty and her blaze of red-gold hair. Journalist Blanche Matthias, recalling the first time she met Latimer, describes her as "a glorious looking young woman. Her red-gold curly hair was like a halo as the sun coming through the windows touched it" (1). In "Margery Latimer— Wisconsin's Newest Writer," an interviewer's physical description focuses on Latimer's hair as well: "Tall, red-haired, very much alive and vigorous, still under thirty, Margery impresses one with her vitality. She often wears her thick hair so that it falls to her shoulders" (Buss 15). By giving many of her protagonists physical characteristics similar to her own, Latimer deliberately links her texts to her embodied self—herself as perceived by those who knew her, herself as presented to the public by journalists. The events of her novel *This Is My Body* follow the contours of her own life so closely that scholar Robert Ryley refers to it unproblematically as a roman à clef (ix). Latimer's work thus deliberately questions that strain of modernism that leans toward impersonality, toward the separation of the art object from its larger sociohistorical context. She diverges, too, from the classical impersonality of much Anglo-American modernist writing, from the austerity that ignored personal emotion and experience called for by Eliot, Pound, and others. Instead, Latimer's concern is expressionistic, focusing on subjective emotional, intellectual, and aesthetic responses. Thus she contributes to that strand of modernism that revisits and extends the romantics' investigation into consciousness, the self, and intensified experience.

Two of Latimer's major themes, the role of art and the role of women, merge in *This Is My Body* and in stories such as "The Family" and "Guardian Angel," which explore the relation of the female artist to sexuality, domesticity, and mysticism. In rebellion against nineteenth-century prohibitive attitudes toward the body and female freedom, Latimer labored to express women's physicality, sensuality, and spirituality, while insisting on women's intellectual and creative capabilities, thus anticipating the work of later feminist writers and theorists. In a striking number of Latimer's texts, we find a portrait of the artist as a young woman, struggling to forge both a self and an art. In an era in which many ambitious women eschewed romance and family life altogether, artistic talent often meant an either-or choice for women. Latimer sought, in her fiction as in her life, to combine both kinds of experience, and her work explores the ramifications of sexuality and family life for the female artist, elucidating the difficulties of being a woman of genius in a prefeminist age. Yet this is not her only concern. From varying vantage points, Latimer's work protests the rigidity of gender roles, the institution of marriage, the accepted child-raising practices of her day, the disparities between economic classes and among ethnic groups—"Confession," for example, self-consciously satirizes the first-person narrator's white privilege, anticipating recent critical inquiries into the construction of whiteness—and the terrible costs women paid for being sexually alive.

Born on 6 February 1899 in Portage, Wisconsin, a town of about 3,000 at the time, Margery Bodine Latimer was the younger of two daughters of Clark Watt Latimer, a traveling sales representative, and Laura Augusta Bodine. Genteel but not affluent, the Latimers scrimped to maintain their middle-class status in the community.

In 1917 Latimer published one of her short stories in the local paper, and it caught the eye of her neighbor Zona Gale (1874-1938), by all accounts a remarkable woman. A liberal activist and suffragist profoundly alive with ideas, Gale had earned two college degrees before the turn of the century and demonstrated a serious commitment to work in her successful career as a journalist, fiction writer, and playwright who would be the first woman to win the Pulitzer Prize for drama. Not only did she live alone (until the age of fifty-four) and like it, but she instructed other ambitious women to do likewise. She was a long-time close friend of both Jane Addams and Charlotte Perkins Gilman, and Mark Twain and Frank Lloyd Wright numbered among the admirers of her work. Gale invited Latimer to tea and, impressed by such talent in one so young, deemed her "one of the most exquisite centres of intuitive experience imaginable" (Derleth 172). Gale would become Latimer's mentor and confidante for the next fourteen years, supporting and controlling her in an intense relationship that both women would explore in their fiction.

Latimer entered Wooster College in Ohio in the fall of 1918; lonely and homesick, she returned home after a semester. In the autumn of 1919 she entered the University of Wisconsin-Madison, but her restless intellect made her impatient with the focus on sports and sororities. In 1921 Latimer moved to New York City, where she attended playwriting workshops at Columbia University, volunteered at the Henry Street Settlement House, and held a short-lived position writing fashion copy for the mass-circulation magazine *Woman's Home Companion*. At Columbia, she met Blanche Matthias, the wealthy and lovely Chicago art critic, journalist, and poet, with whom she developed a lasting friendship; a recent biography of Georgia O'Keeffe suggests that Latimer and Matthias may have been lovers as well (Eisler 341).

The material circumstances of Latimer's life were not luxurious. In 1922, for example, Latimer's father, to support a family of four, earned only a little over $1,000, roughly the equivalent of $10,000 in today's terms (Loughridge 218). Conscious of her protégée's difficult financial situation, Gale instituted the Zona Gale Scholarship at the University of Wisconsin that year. Its generous terms were tailor-made for Latimer, who returned to Madison as its first recipient. While there, she served on the editorial board of the university's literary magazine, to which she also contributed several striking early pieces. In 1923 she left college permanently to focus on her writing career.

Raised in Portage, Latimer had extensive personal knowledge of rural small towns and placed most of her fiction in such settings. Yet after her sporadic early education, she based her literary life in New York City and specifically in Greenwich Village. Her first home there, a meeting place for other young writers and artists, was commemorated by Horace Gregory in his first volume of poetry, *Chelsea Rooming House* (1930), and she later shared a Staten Island apartment with the dazzlingly talented leftist poet Kenneth Fearing, whose own work is currently enjoying a revival of scholarly interest. Fearing and Latimer, who had met in Madison in 1923—he followed her to Manhattan—carried on a tumultuous romantic relationship until 1928, an affair marred by Fearing's penchant for borrowing money and sleeping with other women. Latimer's "Two in Love," "Wind," "City," and *This Is My Body* include clearly recognizable Fearing figures.

In Manhattan, Latimer constructed an active social life. She formed a close friendship with Meridel Le Sueur, the labor activist and feminist writer, who later claimed that Latimer's prose had influenced all her own writing; Le Sueur had also been a protégée of Zona Gale, and both she and Latimer labored in their writing to express women's physicality and sensuality in rebellion against Gale's prohibitive attitude toward the body. Latimer also befriended such artists and writers as Georgia O'Keeffe, Lewis Mumford, Anita Loos, Louis Zukofsky, Blanche and Alfred Knopf, Carl and Irita Van Doren, and Walt Kuhn, the painter who helped organize the New York Armory Show of 1913. Known as a great beauty wherever she went, Latimer was a favorite at the extravagant mixed-race parties of writer and jazz critic Carl Van Vechten and his wife Fania Marinoff. Poet Carl Rakosi, who knew her at the University of Wisconsin-Madison and in Manhattan, recalls her striking physical presence: "She wore no make-up, no high heels, no frills of any kind and only the most plain dresses. Her walk was unselfconscious, very straight and direct, without being masculine. What struck one immediately was her radiant presence. Blake would have described her as a cloud of gold" (qtd. in Loughridge 217).

Throughout the 1920s, Latimer published stories in a variety of journals, from mainstream publications such as *Scribner's,* the *Century,* and the *Bookman* to avant-garde literary reviews such as *Pagany* and *transition,* the groundbreaking Parisian journal that published Joyce, Stein, and Hemingway. She reviewed fiction for various periodicals, including the *New York Herald* and the *New York World*. Her remarkable short essay on experimental writing, "The New Freedom," which anticipates Virginia Woolf's ideas in *A Room of One's Own,* appeared in the *Reviewer* in 1924. In 1928 her novel *We Are Incredible* received mixed but admiring reviews, while her first collection of short fiction, *Nellie Bloom and Other Stories,* met with excellent notices the following year. A second novel, *This Is My Body,* appeared in 1930 and was both praised and damned for its experimentalism.

In New York, Latimer supported herself with clerical jobs while continuing to write. In 1983, in his *Collected Prose,* dedicated to "Margery Latimer Dearest Friend of My Youth," Rakosi recalled her financial situation: "In those days young women were not expected to support themselves, and I assumed therefore that when she lived away from home, she was on an allowance the way Kenneth [Fearing] and I were. I was shocked to learn from her biographer that there was no money for this at home and that she had to depend for her subsistence on . . . an occasional publisher's advance or book review, for which the usual fee then was five dollars" (95). While her experimentalism drew her toward the modernist project, the economic circumstances of her life kept her close to class struggle, and her fiction contains an aggressive blend of modernist technique and material detail, positioning Latimer as a leftist feminist intellectual who rode the crests of multiple movements during the 1920s and early thirties.

Latimer, whose work often depicts moments of transcendent awareness, had been interested in the Gurdjieff spiritual movement since 1924, attending lectures on Georgei Gurdjieff's philosophy in New York and discussing her literary work with Katherine Mansfield's editor, A. R. Orage, then the movement's American leader. In 1931 Latimer's interest came to fruition when she helped the new leader, Jean Toomer, organize a communal retreat for Gurdjieff students near her hometown. Known as the "Portage Experiment," the retreat was sensationalized in the press as a haven for radicals.

Her turbulent romance with Fearing over, Latimer was drawn to the brilliant, handsome, and charismatic Toomer, whose book *Cane* (1923) is widely regarded as a harbinger of the Harlem Renaissance. In October 1931 Latimer and Toomer were married in Portage, but they soon became the objects of a nationwide antimiscegenation scandal: Toomer, who claimed some African ancestry, was accused of trying to mongrelize America, and Latimer, who could trace her Anglo-American heritage back to Puritan poet Anne Bradstreet, was seen as a traitor to white racial purity.

When *Time* magazine reported the marriage in March 1932, for example, it placed the article under the general heading "RACES." Titled "Just Americans," the piece opens with these inflammatory lines: "No Negro can legally marry a white woman in any Southern State. But Wisconsin does not mind, nor California," referring, respectively, to the states where Latimer and Toomer had married and temporarily settled. The other item under "RACES" concerns a young Apache's murder of a white woman with whom he'd had sex; *Time*'s page layout juxtaposes a photograph of Latimer and Toomer with one of the Native American (an "undersized Redskin buck") in his jail cell. Rather than marking Latimer and Toomer's marriage as a meeting of two literary minds—rather than reporting it, for instance, in the "BOOKS" or "PEOPLE" section—*Time* sensationalized the relationship as one of racial and sexual transgression, which is how it was widely viewed. While Latimer and Toomer found support in the artists' community of Carmel, where they mingled with the Lincoln Steffens-Robinson Jeffers circle, Latimer's parents, who received threats and hate mail, had to leave their Portage home until the scandal abated.

When Latimer learned she was pregnant, she and Toomer returned to Chicago to be near Latimer's mother for the birth. Just ten months after her marriage, Latimer died in childbirth on 16 August 1932, after delivering a healthy daughter. She was thirty-three.

Latimer's final collection of short fiction, *Guardian Angel and Other Stories,* was published posthumously in 1932 to great acclaim; the title story had been previously published in *Scribner's* as a finalist in its $5,000 story competition. Reviews of *Guardian Angel* compared Latimer to Mansfield and Lawrence and mourned the loss to American literature incurred by her early death.

The feminist project of reviving women's writing led to a renewed interest in Latimer's work, and in 1984 the Feminist Press issued a reprint entitled *Guardian Angel and Other Stories,* which drew stories from both earlier collections. The volume includes three afterwords: a useful biographical essay, a warm tribute by Le Sueur, and a critical appraisal by former Modern Language Association president Louis Kampf. An edition of the original *Guardian Angel* is also in print from Books for Libraries Press; it includes four additional stories. The remaining twelve stories from *Nellie Bloom* and both of Latimer's novels remain out of print and difficult to obtain.

Little critical work has been done on Latimer. Though her accomplishments rival those of her modernist contemporaries, her brief output, early death, and buried reputation have obscured her achievements.

During her own time, however, Latimer was clearly regarded as an active architect of the new writing, as is evident from the journals, anthologies, and presses whose editors chose to feature her work. While several of her stories appeared in mainstream literary publications such as the *Century,* the *Bookman,* and *Scribner's,* a consideration of the avant-garde journals that published her work reveals that influential progressive editors ranked her work with that of the period's leading modernists. Latimer's short story "Grotesque," for instance, originally appeared in 1927 in the revolutionary, experimental journal *transition* together with Stein's "As a Wife Has a Cow" and an installment in the serial publication of Joyce's *Work in Progress,* which would later become *Finnegans Wake.* Founded by Eugene Jolas and Elliot Paul as "a linguistic and creative bridge between the countries of the Western World," *transition* provoked controversy in 1929 with Jolas's famous "Manifesto: The Revolution of the Word," which damned the plain reader. Hemingway's "Hills Like White Elephants" first appeared within the pages of *transition,* and its covers were designed by such artists as Picasso, Miro, Kandinsky, Duchamp, and Man Ray. During its run between the world wars, the journal featured the work of writers such as Katherine Anne Porter, Laura Riding, Dylan Thomas, André Breton, Franz Kafka, and Samuel Beckett.

Pagany, another journal that chose Latimer's fiction, was one of the most important literary magazines of the Depression. Launched by Richard Johns in consultation with William Carlos Williams, *Pagany* showcased the work of Stein, Ezra Pound, H. D., John Dos Passos, e. e. cummings, Mary Butts, and Tess Slesinger during its brief run between 1929 and 1932. Two of Latimer's stories, "Monday Morning" and "The Little Girls," first appeared in its pages. The original venue for Latimer's story "Picnic Day" was the socialist journal *New Masses,* the first to publish Richard Wright. Along with journalism, fiction, and poetry by socialist writers like Mike Gold, *New Masses* published Hemingway, Dos Passos, Muriel Rukeyser, Dorothy Parker, Theodore Dreiser, Thomas Wolfe, and Langston Hughes.

Editors of little magazines were not the only ones to perceive the importance of Latimer's work. In 1927, when editors Van Wyck Brooks, Alfred Kreymborg, Lewis Mumford, and Paul Rosenfeld assembled the anthology *The American Caravan: A Yearbook of American Literature*—dedicated to Alfred Stieglitz as "a yearbook conducted by literary men in the interests of a growing American literature"—they included Latimer's story "Penance" in conjunction with pieces by Hemingway, Stein, Dos Passos, Louise Bogan, Robert Penn Warren, Hart Crane, Eugene O'Neill, and William Carlos Williams. A later volume in the series, *The New Caravan,* includes Latimer's posthumously collected "Letters to Georgia O'Keeffe" alongside the work of such writers as Anderson, Wright, Toomer, and Wallace Stevens.

Latimer's books found homes with presses similarly dedicated to advancing the new writing. New York editor Harrison Smith formed the publishing house of Cape and Smith in order to print avant-garde works, such as Faulkner's *The Sound and the Fury* in 1929; the following year, he added Latimer's novel *This Is My Body* to their list. When Smith left to form a subsequent publishing partnership with Robert Haas, Faulkner and Latimer were two of the authors he took with him. Smith and Haas published both Faulkner's *Light in August* and Latimer's collection *Guardian Angel and Other Stories* in 1932; Latimer's title story had appeared previously in *Scribner's* alongside Faulkner's "Spotted Horses." Smith, like many editors of the period, recognized Latimer's work as congruent in both content and style with the aims of modernism.

Latimer was certainly involved in reading the new writers, for her correspondence (now housed in collections at Yale's Beinecke Rare Book and Manuscript Library and the University of Wisconsin Memorial Library in Madison) indicates a broad and deep familiarity with contemporary literature and the modernist corpus. In letters to friends, Latimer discusses Pirandello, Henry James, Joyce, Proust, Dostoyevski, and Gide. She recommends Lawrence, Steffens, Jeffers, Somerset Maugham, and her contemporaries Hemingway and Wolfe, though her most enthusiastic recommendations are reserved for the work of other women writers: Mansfield, whose work she most passionately admired, Stein, Sigrid Undset, Virginia Woolf, Kay Boyle, and Rebecca West. Her correspondence casually compares the treatment of sexuality and the body in *Ulysses* to that in *Lady Chatterley's Lover,* takes Willa Cather to task for her lack of innovation ("just that old, old thing over again but beautifully built") and comments wryly on Mansfield's published letters: "Not nearly as good as the journal though. Mr. Husband must have left a lot out." Her avid reading of the lives of writers and artists included Margaret Anderson's *My Thirty Years' War: An Autobiography* (1930), which details Anderson's establishment of the modernist literary journal the *Little Review,* her publication of *Ulysses,* and her various attempts, in Latimer's admiring description, to "live hazardously." One letter includes a witty sketch of Edna St. Vincent Millay in the evening gown she'd worn to a reading. In all, Latimer's correspondence suggests her active engagement in the exuberant modernist milieu of New York in the twenties and early thirties.

Latimer was also on the radar screen of other important writers of the modernist period. In a letter written from Vienna in 1933, H. D.'s partner Bryher laments the fact that she cannot find "the early Margery Latimer book" (Friedman). Bryher may have been referring to Latimer's first novel *We Are Incredible,* reviewed by Katherine Anne Porter and praised by Upton Sinclair; according to poet Genevieve Taggard, *We Are Incredible* surpassed the work of Katherine Mansfield.

Reviews of Latimer's fiction were extremely positive—a review of *Nellie Bloom and Other Stories* in the *New York Herald Tribune,* for instance, argued that Latimer had outdone both Mansfield and Sherwood Anderson—yet many critics were troubled by the experimental elements of her work (Haxton 3). While the *New York Times Book Review* acknowledges "the excellent craftsmanship which is the outstanding feature of her work," the general critical response focused on Latimer's unconventional choice of form (*Guardian Angel* 6). For instance, Gertrude Diamant in the *New York World* chides that it is "precisely because Miss Latimer can write with ruthless objectivity that it is wasteful for her to compromise her genuine power with the attempt to be modernistic," throwing out the baby with the ideological bathwater in an implicit criticism of the modernist project as a whole. Diamant was not troubled by any artistic failure on Latimer's part but rather by her experimentalism.

Similarly, the anonymous critic in the *Saturday Review of Literature* gives and removes praise in the same gesture: "Miss Latimer gives liberal evidence of her proficiency in that compressed fiction form wherein plot and cumulative dramatic tension are not called into play," as if to say that, while she may be good at it, it's not worth doing (*Nellie Bloom* 42). A *New York Times Book Review* critic, discussing Latimer's 1930 novel *This Is My Body,* censures it for being "intensely subjective" and continues: "by [Latimer's] very immersion in the colors and sensations of life, she sacrifices much of the feeling of reality for which the book apparently strives" ("Hungry" 9). Again, it seems to be Latimer's experimentation, which privileges "immersion in the colors and sensations of life" over straightforward traditional realism, that draws critical fire. Reviewer Edwin Seaver objects to the same text on the basis of its disruption of genre: "Miss Latimer's book, it seems to me, is rather to be taken as an autobiographic fragment than as a novel," a critique easily leveled against such modernist classics as *A Portrait of the Artist as a Young Man*. The talent is there, the critics agreed, but what on earth is she doing with it?

Mainstream reviewers who complain in 1930 that Latimer writes "in the manner of James Joyce," or that her characters "go a little Gertrude Stein occasionally and fling fantastic chains of words about," see these resemblances as flaws ("Hungry" 9, Wakefield 10). While Joyce, Stein, and other experimental writers eventually won widespread approval—Faulkner's seventeen books were not even in print when critics revived his reputation after World War II—Latimer's work was already out of the public eye by the time this recuperation occurred.

Latimer's feminism was another factor that made the critical reception of her work problematic. Her decision to focus on the seldom discussed experiences of girls and women drew belittling attacks from critics, who questioned whether such material was relevant to readers and rebuked Latimer on the grounds of what might now well qualify as gender bias. *We Are Incredible,* for example, "rockets into the hysterical with a thin, unsupported shriek," according to the *New York Evening Post.* Today such complaints can be read in light of the reviewer's potential sexism or reevaluated in light of recent work by feminist critics, such as Gabrielle Dane, who limn hysterical rhetoric as a form of feminist protest against sexual abuse or violation. Latimer's second novel, for instance, describes a young woman's coming-of-age: sexual pressure from boyfriends, an episode of sexual harassment by an older professor, a lover (the Fearing figure) who lives off her meager earnings yet prefers the company of prostitutes, and an illegal and traumatizing abortion. Compounding the protagonist's difficulties, her ambitions and confidence are met at every turn by a dismissal grounded solely in gender. When a male poet asks her, "What are you planning to do with your beautiful body?" she replies, "Be a great writer." His response is telling: " 'Yah,' he cried in disgust. 'That is for homely women. You have that child' " (169). Hysterical rhetoric, Dane argues, is not merely a fitting but the only response available to women in a society that routinely silences their experience and reduces them to their sexual and procreative capacities.

As a chronicle of a young woman artist's maturation, *This Is My Body* represents a significant contribution to the tradition of women's coming-of-age writing, for it stands as one of the only female-authored *Künstlerromane* of the period. In her scholarly study *A Portrait of the Artist as a Young Woman,* Linda Huf reminds us that "Jane Austen, the Brontës, George Eliot, Virginia Woolf, Edith Wharton, Katherine Anne Porter, and Flannery O'Connor never wrote a portrait-of-the-author novel" (1-2), and Patricia Meyer Spacks wonders in *The Female Imagination* if there exists a novel that can function as "the female equivalent of *A Portrait of the Artist as a Young Man*" (200). Fearful of recrimination for narcissism and egotism, female authors "have frequently balked at portraying themselves in literature as would-be writers," Huf notes, but Latimer audaciously does just that (1).

Compounding the difficulties of writing a female *kunstlerroman,* moreover, was the fact that critics were likely to misread such a narrative. The reviewer at the *New York Times,* for instance, seems baffled by the trajectory of *This Is My Body:* "It would be almost unfair to the book to accept it, in the common sense of the phrase, as telling a story. Miss Latimer has taken ten years of a girl's life—the ten years which include late adolescence, college, first love, the eager investigation of latent powers, the fumbling for a start at life, and the final emergence into maturity. Of these ten years she has woven a highly colored tapestry" ("Hungry" 9). The passage's first sentence seems contradicted by what follows, giving rise to questions as to what might constitute a legitimate story. Clearly the anonymous reviewer's criteria for meaningful plotlines did not include the experience of girls and women: a young woman comes of age, sexually and emotionally, and becomes a successful artist against substantial odds, and yet the narrative does not count as "a story." One wonders in what "sense of the phrase" it would be fair to call it such. But Eleanor Wakefield of *New York World* concurs: "Plot there is none in the conventional sense." Latimer does experiment with traditional narrative structure, but not so radically that cohesive development is difficult to perceive. The pique of critics seems to issue from the fact that a novelist would consider "ten years of a girl's life" worthy of exploration at all. Blinkered by standard (male) narrative patterns of development, few critics comprehended Latimer's accomplishment.

Although reviewers in the *New York Times Book Review* and the *Saturday Review of Literature* remarked upon the book's "almost hypnotic sense of power," its display of "fine and genuine talent," "sensitive observation and emotional keenness," "standard of serious excellence," and "cultivation of an individual prose style," they and other critics took the protagonist Megan Foster severely to task (9, 1073). "Miss Latimer's heroine," argues F. L. Robbins in the *Outlook,* "is an hysterical, egocentric girl whose talk is all of the 'realities' of life, but who has not learned the reality of her own insignificance," and the novel is dismissed in the *New Republic* as the "entirely subjective story of a frenzied adolescent" (148, 227). The *Saturday Review of Literature* concurs that Megan "exhausts one's sympathy and exceeds one's patience a hundred times over," while the *Bookman* labels her "definitely neurotic" (1073, 216). M. C. Dawson moans in the *Nation* that it is "without doubt the most exasperating book I have ever read," while seeing it as nonetheless "a novel of rare and permanent value," and Edwin Seaver of the *New York Evening Post* decries "its annoying honesty" (552, 10).

Her posthumously published collection of fiction, *Guardian Angel and Other Stories,* met with immediate critical success when it appeared in 1932. Even so, the *Saturday Review* characterizes Latimer's talent as "original" but "circumscribed" due to its continued dwelling upon "so slight a theme" as "feminine adolescence: its terrors, its joys, its hesitancies" (179). Critics' preconceived notions as to whose stories were important—and whose were not—had a powerful impact on Latimer's reception in the public sphere.

Latimer's sharp critiques of the traditional nuclear family also proved problematic for reviewers. *We Are Incredible* was widely praised for its originality and style, yet critics of the period were quick to leap to the defense of home and family when they encountered the Frys, a small-town family that today's readers would quickly describe as dysfunctional. The response of the *Milwaukee Journal*'s critic is typical: "Unnecessarily emphasized, it would seem, are the constant bickerings between husband and wife, the squalling of untidy and ill behaved children, the ugliness of small town gossip, the dullness of small town existence" (17). Yet despite the critical doubt, Latimer's emphasis on family dysfunction in *We Are Incredible* is hardly unnecessary. Readers today, for instance, would note with interest the reviewer's criticism of "untidy and ill behaved children" that omits mention of the physical and emotional abuse of the youngest daughter, a gentle and dreamy four-year-old who is repeatedly slapped, shoved, humiliated, and threatened with parental abandonment, and whose mother's disregard of doctor's orders culminates in the child's death. The objectionable "small town gossip" includes a story of an adolescent girl who has been sexually used by so many of the town's citizens—including her own uncle, a churchgoing man—that no one person can be settled upon

as the father of her child; she is sent away to work on a farm until
the child is born and will then be sent to the city until the scandal
blows over. The shame is figured as hers and her mother's (for not
controlling her), not the men's. Rex Fry sleeps with his secretary;
his wife Myrtle threatens suicide but continues to wash the supper
dishes. Hardly unnecessary, Latimer's biting analysis of the family
and of small-town America—"meager lawns and screaming children who tottered after dogs who would not play"—forms an indispensable backdrop, the cramped context in which her characters
are forced to make choices (129).

Recent feminist work on the period enables us to situate
Latimer's work and recognize its significant contribution to
reconfigurations of literary history. She has much in common, for
instance, with the women writers publishing between 1892 and
1929 whom Elizabeth Ammons, in *Conflicting Stories: American
Women Writers at the Turn into the Twentieth Century,* sees as
"united by gender, historical context, and self-definition" (4). Like
the seventeen writers Ammons analyzes, Latimer exhibits "an
emerging, shared, and often defiant confidence in the abilities and
rights of women" as well as sharing these writers' "avowed ambition, with few exceptions, to be artists. . . . in the modern high-cul-
ture sense of the term in the west, makers of new, challenging, and
typically idiosyncratic forms" (4-5). Like these writers, Latimer
demonstrates in her work a focus on radical experimentation, spot-
lights the role of the woman artist in society, and displays her interest in gender and racial social structures, what Ammons calls "issues of power: the will to break silence by exposing the connection
among institutionalized violence, the sexual exploitation of women,
and female muteness" (4-5).

Latimer's work also contributes to the recent redefinitions and
expansions of the modernist canon prompted by the realization
that, as Elaine Showalter notes, "the post-war literary movement
that we have come to call the Lost Generation was in fact a community of men" (104). The publication of Latimer's first book coincides
with what Bonnie Kime Scott sees in *The Women of 1928* as a pivotal moment in modernism, and Latimer's work pursues issues,
such as a radical critique of the conventional family structure, that
are common to the women modernists Scott anthologizes in her
groundbreaking 1990 volume *The Gender of Modernism.* With H. D.,
Mansfield, Stein, Woolf, and the lesser known writers in the collection, Latimer's texts "write the erotics of the female body" and explore female creativity, anticipating much recent French feminist
theory (Scott 13-15). Latimer's insistent foregrounding of the
subjectivities of traditionally sidelined female characters, too,

works to deconstruct received narrative structures. By repeatedly placing marginal characters at the center of her fiction, Latimer allies her work with that of Jean Rhys, Djuna Barnes, and other modernist forerunners of postmodern and postcolonial strategies (Hite 25).

Margery Latimer, then, was firmly ensconced in the project of high modernism, publishing in the same venues as Joyce, Stein, Hemingway, Faulkner, and other canonical modernists. Analysis of the mainstream critics of the period reveals that they rejected precisely those aspects of her work—its experimentation with language, focus on subjectivity, and disruption of traditional narrative structures—which we have come to see as defining characteristics of modernism. While with time the experimentation of modernist works came to be seen as acceptable, even laudable, by critics and the wider reading public, Latimer's reputation was already lost by the time this reevaluation occurred. Due to her brief output, early death, and buried reputation, her work was never reevaluated with the critical hindsight that benefited other modernist writers.

Moreover, Latimer's focus on female experience dovetailed with her trenchant critiques of traditional family and social roles to form significant ideological stumbling blocks for many critics of the twenties and thirties. As Scott and others have convincingly demonstrated, a disproportionate number of modernist women who, like Latimer, were actively publishing work that pursued such themes were winnowed away during the initial period of canon formation. Inadequately understood in her own time, Latimer would not live long enough to see the development of a body of criticism that would explain and appreciate her work.

We Are Incredible

Latimer's longest treatment of her conflicted relationship with Zona Gale, the 1928 novel *We Are Incredible,* addresses two competing paradigms of womanhood available to young women in the early years of the twentieth century: the domestic wife-and-mother and the sexually pure intellectual-artist. In *We Are Incredible* Latimer caricatures a thinly veiled Gale in the character of Hester Linden, a beautiful older woman who seduces her young admirers (both male and female) with an antiseptic spirituality and urges them away from the life of the body. Her controlling rejection of sexuality results in the demise of two of her young protégés, Stephen Mitchell and Dora Weck, whose forbidden attraction to one another ends in their mysterious deaths.

The text bears a telling resemblance to Gale's own 1920 best-selling novel *Miss Lulu Bett* (which, when adapted for the stage in 1921, won Gale the Pulitzer), as if Latimer were deliberately re-working Gale's plot. The situations are strikingly similar, yet the traditional nuclear family, depicted as benignly vapid in *Miss Lulu Bett,* becomes openly destructive in Latimer's novel: Latimer's Mr. Fry, the pontificating husband, is also a callous philanderer; his wife is desperately frustrated and lonely, yet helplessly, bitterly urges marriage and motherhood on all women; and their youngest daughter, Deva, "the only delicate member" of the family, dies from parental neglect (7). The romance that ends successfully in Gale's book, with marriage for Lulu Bett and Neil Cornish, ends with death for Latimer's protagonists.

We Are Incredible, which unfolds across a nine-day span, employs a third-person narrator whose limited omniscience dips into the psyches of each of the three main characters, and the tripartite structure of the book serves to emphasize the centrality of their roles as focalizers—the sections are entitled "Stephen Mitchell," the man who views ironically his old enthrallment by Hester; "Dora Weck," the young woman who is currently enthralled; and "Hester Linden," the Gale figure. In her use of third person, Latimer relinquishes the openly subjective stance of much of her short fiction in favor of one that explores a combination of detachment and empathy, leaving room for irony and critique.

While the dire effects of the Gale character serve as the focus of most contemporary reviews of the book, far more of Latimer's actual text is devoted to descriptions of the Fry family, whose function as backdrop to the main plot threatens to displace it. Stephen Mitchell boards with the Frys; Dora Weck is Mrs. Fry's younger, unmarried sister, a financial burden the Frys are pressed to assume upon the death of her mother. Eager to rid themselves of Dora, Myrtle and Rex Fry urge her to marry Joe Teeter, a local boy who has done well in his family's creamery business. Simple, genuine, and eminently acceptable as husband material, Joe nonetheless fails to interest Dora, who, influenced by Hester Linden, longs for someone more complicated, more worldly—someone more like Stephen Mitchell. Since the choices that Dora must make have everything to do with available paradigms of sexual relationships and womanhood, the development of the Frys' family situation, seen by reviewers as excessive and negative, can be read as a development of the home-and-family option for women and therefore as an elaboration of the issues at the heart of the novel.

In *We Are Incredible* Latimer develops characters who represent both available paradigms for women, yet neither role is featured as a compelling option for the young Dora—whose hair, we are quick to learn, is "a blaze of copper," marking her as an autobiographical Latimer figure (5). The life of the mind is represented by cool, manipulative Hester, "a virgin, a woman years older . . . who was so fastidious she was sterile, so exquisite that she was cruel." Described as "masked, evasive, . . . an arid old maid," Hester derides the sexual impulses of her young friends as "tiresome," "silly and vulgar," and they, in turn, express their ties to her as "bondage" (4, 36).

In contrast to Hester, Dora's older married sister, Myrtle Fry, stands as a figure for fecund womanhood under patriarchy, she "whose most intense psychic and physical energies," in Adrienne Rich's words, "are directed towards men" (219). Myrtle plays the role of the "mother-woman," as Kate Chopin phrases it in *The Awakening,* a representative of "women who idolized their children, worshiped their husbands, and esteemed it a privilege to efface themselves as individuals and grow wings as ministering angels" (181). Myrtle, however, is a blighted caricature of such angelic self-effacement. Marred by her complete social and economic dependence on her husband, she is pathetic, and—seen from Stephen Mitchell's point of view—revoltingly fleshy, a corpulent chatterbox, a "warm, coarse" product of her own "automatic fertility" (10). What beauty and character she once possessed have been obliterated by the changes wrought upon her body by motherhood: "Her clear blue eyes, her mouth, a delicate downward curve, seemed like irrelevant details in the masses of rolling flesh" (11). When her husband eyes his typist, she demands his respect by threatening to leave him, but to no great effect:

"But you know what I can do, Rex Fry, and don't you ever forget it, either. Sometime you'll come home and I'll be gone."
"Aw, Myrtle."
"Well, I will." She could barely speak and stopped, her eyes filling with tears. "And—and I'll be in the canal." (57)

The only power Myrtle perceives herself as wielding in her marriage is the power of self-annihilation; her options, as she sees them, are little different from those of Chopin's Edna Pontellier. But her intermittent plays for power are futile; the desired response is not forthcoming from her husband, who instead ignores her:

"Don't think for one minute, Rex Fry, that you can treat me the way you do because you can't. You'll come home some night from that fine typewriter of yours and find me gone—you just wait!"
As Rex lighted his cigar Mitchell noticed that Myrtle, instead of falling

into a faint, had begun to pick up the dishes listlessly. Suddenly she discovered a rhubarb stain on the cloth and began examining the condition, then, of her best napkins. (57-58)

Though Stephen Mitchell expects hysterics, Myrtle turns to her domestic duties, for the Fry family cannot afford the sort of domestic help Hester Linden takes for granted. Fainting fits, Myrtle discerns, are the luxury of leisured women, not of those solely responsible for the daily management of children and a household—a household that takes in boarders, at that. However she might protest, her life is entirely defined by domestic responsibilities and the burdens of class, and she knows it.

Hester Linden and Myrtle Fry represent the historical paradigms of womanhood between which Dora, the young Latimer figure on the verge of adulthood, must choose. Searching for a story, a life for herself, Dora sees the two older women as the only available role models. Both are inadequate: "She couldn't marry Joe or Mitchell, even, or any other man. They would touch her and she would wither and grow hideous like Myrtle and all the others but if she kept beyond their touch like Hester she would stay beautiful and young and they would worship her. There was no place in the world for her" (119). There is indeed no place for Dora in the world of the novel, no place for any woman who would combine both independence and sexuality. It is male "touch," heterosexuality and its consequence of childbearing, which in Dora's mind produces the physical changes she fears. Following Hester's example, Dora has the option of keeping herself "beyond [men's] touch" and thus keeping them in her thrall, but while this option works for the mysteriously wealthy Hester, it breaks down for penniless Dora, who is reliant on her sister's husband for support. Following in Hester's footsteps does not appear to be feasible for Dora. Yet to reject men is also unthinkable, due to their complete social and economic power: after a brief experimental stint as Hester's maid, Dora, without education or a profession, "fear[s] taking care of herself, even the thought of work and loneliness filled her with terror" (118). Neither Hester nor Myrtle suffices to offer her a vision of retained selfhood combined with active sexuality.

When Dora attempts to overcome this dichotomy, claiming for herself the right to sexuality without the institution of marriage, the text reveals that there is indeed "no place in the world" for her: the novel ends with her death. She goes "into the garden" with Stephen Mitchell in romantic rebellion against Hester's sexual prohibitions; Hester witnesses their sexual liaison from her window, and their bodies are found the next morning (276-77). Dora's death is specifically sexualized in a figure of lost virginity—"there was blood on her dress," cries Hester's maid (281).

Yet the actual cause of death remains obscure within the text, as if the very transgression of social and sexual boundaries has resulted in the characters' spontaneous demise. The "hands that had brought them death" are "white and still" at Mitchell's sides, we are told, but the fact that the couple is found entwined leaves room for ambiguity as to whether the hands in question are Stephen's, Dora's, or both (283). Additional ambiguity arises from the fact that, since no cause of death is defined and no murder weapon mentioned, readers cannot know if the "hands that had brought them death" are meant literally (Stephen could have used his hands alone to kill Dora by strangling her, but he could not have successfully strangled himself) or if the very fact of touch, sexual contact, represented synecdochically by "hands," has killed them.

In its violence and ambiguity, the closure of *We Are Incredible* anticipates similar endings in the novels of Latimer's female contemporaries, novels which, like hers, attempt to address the social strictures surrounding women's sexuality and domestic roles. Nella Larsen, for instance, deliberately leaves the ending of *Passing* (1929) unresolved: Was it murder, suicide, an accident, or some slippery combination thereof? The closing of Ellen Glasgow's 1932 *The Sheltered Life* was so ambiguous in its initial edition that a new version, clarifying Eva Birdsong's murder of her philandering husband, was issued. Rather than a failure of authorial skill, this lack of explicitness may more fruitfully be read as a direct attempt to confuse issues of culpability. Obscuring the locus of blame raises questions about all the characters involved, diffusing responsibility throughout the sexual and cultural dynamic.

In Dora's case, moreover, death is freighted with additional significance, for it returns her to the lost mother. Mrs. Weck has died prior to the action of the novel, crucially affecting Dora's development; as Myrtle tells Mitchell, "She always has had a good strong constitution, but since Mama died she hasn't been the same girl" (60). Like motherless Rachel Vinrace in Woolf's *The Voyage Out* (1915), like motherless Anna Morgan in Jean Rhys's original version of *Voyage in the Dark* (1934), Dora dies as the culmination of her social and sexual coming-of-age; her subsequent dissolution in death functions to reunite her with the dead mother. While figured as the heroine's failure to adopt her gender role, such deaths also serve to return her at a symbolic level to the long-lost maternal, the realm of the semiotic, characterized by pre-Oedipal fluidity, mutuality, and lack of differentiation. Woolf, Rhys, and Latimer, in response to the period's impossibly contradictory conditions for women, reject for their protagonists the institution of heterosexuality.

In *We Are Incredible* marriage is figured as wholly negative, and Hester Linden's austere aesthetic, the only alternative to conventional domesticity, is destructive and dissatisfying. But when Stephen and Dora attempt to overthrow both codes, attempting love and sexuality without institutional endorsement, they meet with a bloody end, suggesting that those who try to make a life in the interstices between systems cannot survive.

Nellie Bloom and Other Stories

When Latimer's first volume of short fiction, the richly diverse collection *Nellie Bloom and Other Stories,* appeared in 1929, it met with immediate critical acclaim. Dedicated to Kenneth Fearing, the collection contains sixteen stories, several of which had been previously published in venues such as the *Century, New Masses,* and *transition.* "Possession" fictionalizes the relationship of Latimer and Gale from the Latimer figure's first-person point of view. "City" wittily chronicles a woman's fledgling attempts to be a writer in New York: "I began to wonder seriously how one asked for a job. I practiced by myself. I was myself asking and I was an editor answering. But they were all very nice to me and encouraging" (85). "Confession" links the frenetic self-indulgence of urban and international bohemians with their childhoods of domestic abuse and political trauma. Key stories in the collection include the title work, "Nellie Bloom," "Mr. and Mrs. Arnold," which examines a day in the life of an older married couple, and "The Family," a novella that offers Latimer's first serious portrait of the artist as a young woman.

In "Nellie Bloom" Latimer focuses on the attempt of a younger woman to gain self-understanding by exploring the experience of a woman from a preceding generation. The unnamed first-person narrator, a young woman, has undergone a personal emotional trauma which remains undefined. Returning to her family home, she becomes intrigued with the story of a woman who had died of a broken heart in her small hometown many years before. In "Nellie Bloom" Latimer reworks the "Poor Joanna" episode in Sarah Orne Jewett's *The Country of the Pointed Firs* (1896). Jewett's old Mrs. Todd and Mrs. Fosdick tell the young female narrator about Joanna Todd, who, "crossed in love," retreats alone to an island, where she spends the rest of her days in solitude (61). Latimer's Nellie Bloom is similarly betrayed by her fiancé, and the young female narrator investigates Nellie's story much as Jewett's narrator voyages to Joanna's island herself. Other similarities between the texts suggest Latimer's deliberate patterning of her own fiction upon Jewett's. Yet Latimer's text is more frank about erotic desire and anger, and Latimer also sets the tale in a Midwestern small town, where there are no island refuges; Nellie must face daily the town's persistent curiosity and the continued presence of the man who betrayed her.

As the narrator imagines the varied events of Nellie's life, her empathetic connection—which Latimer figures as intimately linked to bodily experience—quickly deepens: "Then it was summer and I was Nellie walking home from school in a slim white dress. Dark curls warmed my shoulders and the strapped books were heavy in my warm, tired hands. For an instant I could feel the scraping of a garter and a little ache in my flesh where it rubbed the skin" (5). The narrator learns from Mrs. Alverson, a neighbor in her eighties, that Nellie's heartbreak arises from her betrayal by her best friend, Bird, and her fiancé, Dorr, who fall in love and decide to marry when Nellie is briefly out of town. When Nellie first finds out about the betrayal, her breakdown is represented as a death: "They took her into the spare room and she lay like a corpse, her hair covering the pillow, her face blank and dead white" (10). The imagery recalls tableaux in fairy tales like "Snow White" and "Sleeping Beauty," with the beautiful maiden arranged on her deathbed, waiting for the prince to come and kiss her back to life. But in Latimer's alternate version, the prince (now happily married to someone else) never comes.

Nellie's sense of betrayal, like the narrator's identification with her, is depicted as physically overwhelming: "Nellie's blood turned to pain and burned those arms that had held Dorr, burned the breasts that he had kissed and the white neck where the vague little curl lay, rushed like a burning storm through the long limbs under stiff silk" (9-10). Her pain and desire are here figured as profoundly embodied, profoundly physical, but neither emotion can be safely displayed to the community. While the whole town wonders what will happen, Dorr and his new bride set up housekeeping. Nellie puts a brave face on things, making several attempts to forgive and befriend them again, but she privately struggles with obsessive fantasies of revenge. Latimer represents Nellie's effort to "love" Dorr and his wife as a struggle between the acceptable utterance and the unacceptable feeling: "she sat helpless, struggling occasionally to say, 'I love them,' while her mouth pulled down with scorn and loathing. . . . Finally she sat down on the floor and pressed her head into the bed, whispering to it, 'I love them—I love them,' but all through her and about her were little spirals of laughter, fine and bright as coiled wires" (24-25). The discord between what she actually feels and what she is supposed to feel threatens Nellie with madness.

The resulting relationship among the three characters is understandably somewhat strained, yet it continues for five years, polite on the surface, while Nellie privately agonizes to Grandma Sweeney, the older woman who cares for her: "He gave me something of himself and it's still in me. I know all his bones. I know his eyes and the way they look out at me. I can hear him breathing in the night. What do I do with all that? Where can I put it?" (20-21). In a culture which sanctions female sexual appetite only within marriage, there is nowhere to put Nellie's desire—or her anger. She is beyond the pale of social convention; like Dora Weck, there is "no place in the world" for her.

Nellie's unrequited desires apparently have as much to do with her longing for a child as with her longing for Dorr himself. Regarding this, the narrator distances herself from Nellie, claiming not to share this particular desire; Latimer here locates the urge for "the vast power for happiness in the body, in the womb" with Nellie Bloom, and ambitious "head-fancies" with the woman of a later generation (21). Although Nellie manages to continue her strained relationship with the childless couple, it is Bird's eventual pregnancy that finally devastates her. Expected to pay a social call after the birth, Nellie musters her self-control and visits. When Bird lays the child in her lap, Nellie is unable to process what is happening: "She heard Bird come into the room and she was conscious that something lay soft and heavy in her lap, but she was also aware of not noting these things or commenting on them. She told Bird it would be a good thing if they would put in cement walks all over town" (25). Unheeding of the bundle in her lap, Nellie converses for a while about civic developments, but her acknowledgment of the child precipitates a crisis: "Nellie looked around the room strangely and then down at the child in her lap. 'Oh, God,' she said faintly and stood up, but Bird had her baby in her arms before it fell" (26). That night, Nellie dies a mysterious death, a death by sheer anguish, as it were. Latimer describes the death as a stiffening, a freezing; Nellie keeps "clearing her throat as if she were trying for the last time to force herself to say that she loved them, but her throat must have been frozen" (27). Nellie's agony is limned a constriction of the throat; she dies, the narrative suggests, because she cannot speak.

"Mr. and Mrs. Arnold," originally published in the *Reviewer* in 1924, is Latimer's earliest fiction to deal explicitly with marital relationships and reveals much about her stance toward traditional gender relations. In the story, which transpires within a single day, a long-married husband and wife have a chance to rejuvenate their relationship—to "only connect," in E. M. Forster's famous phrase. The characters, however, fall back into their traditional roles and fail to renew their intimacy. The chance for epiphany is missed.

Curiously, Latimer diffuses the impact of her simple plot with the characters' confusing speech patterns. Their dialogue, marked by abrupt switches in meaning, almost obscures the larger action of the story. Performing roles rather than communicating, Mr. and Mrs. Arnold are reduced to self-contradictory, nonsensical babble, oscillating between poles of signification. The reader, startled into amusement by the contradictions, tenuously constructs meaning as the dialogue lurches from assertion to counterassertion. Oddly comic, the story has a grim absurdity that anticipates Beckett's work: words have come slightly unhinged from their meanings, and everything is askew just enough not to work, yet still familiar enough that the characters keep trying. This lack of communication and its attendant despair emphasize Latimer's views of traditional marriage.

Fittingly, the text opens by acknowledging the couple's lack of forthrightness: "No one knew what Mrs. Arnold believed; she never said much. Mr. Arnold played extravagantly with words but no one knew what he believed. They thought they loved and hated one another but they could never be sure" (51). Both characters conceal themselves in a stereotypically gendered manner. Mrs. Arnold masks her true feelings by acting as the silent nurturer, gentle and serene, a veritable angel in the house. Although her husband harshly criticizes her appearance, behavior, and speech, she does not retaliate but rather moves to help and support him in quiet humility. Withdrawing into an acceptably feminine silence, she does not have to risk a confrontation.

While Mrs. Arnold disguises her true emotions with the absence of language, Mr. Arnold masks his with a surfeit. Although the narrator charitably describes his verbal vacillation as "play[ing] extravagantly with words," the story presents his contradictions as irritating, even maddening. A self-made authority on every topic he encounters, Mr. Arnold opines, critiques, passes judgment, and gives advice—no matter that his opinions conflict, his judgment about the weather turns out to be wrong, and his advice to his wife (about crossing streets carefully) would be best heeded by himself. He blusters on, convinced of his mental prowess: "If I'd known thirty years ago what I know now, I'd have set the world on fire" (55). He feels confident enough in his role as household authority to lay down contradictory edicts: " 'Darling,' said Mr. Arnold. 'Oh, nothing, nothing at all,' he shouted suddenly at her mild face. 'I wish you wouldn't wear that confounded cap, please. Oh, wear it if you want to. . . . What do I care! If women want to wear caps let them.' " His wife, silently obliging, "removed her cap, smiled up at him, and suddenly replaced it" (51). But though she tries throughout the narrative, she cannot accommodate his shifting demands. His remarks switch back and forth, a dialectic of disagreement he never resolves.

While both characters hide their true feelings, Mr. Arnold's mastery of language gives him the power to pronounce and define. Amid the banter about caps and apple cider, there is also a more serious debate occurring. While Mrs. Arnold deflects his derogatory comments, remaining apparently serene, her husband is defining her very sanity. For instance, when Mrs. Arnold, foreseeing rain, suggests that he take an umbrella,

His mouth fell open and he stared out at the bright maple leaves on the lawn. "Are you crazy?"

"I am always sane," she said and added in the same voice, "never sane." (52)

Crazy? Sane? She accepts and repeats her husband's fluctuating assessments of her, just as she removes and replaces her cap at his whim. (It later does, in fact, rain.) Because her tone is flat, we wonder how engaged or invested she is in the whole debate—if she has not rather withdrawn altogether into a private world of tatting and housework. She has tuned out emotionally: "Her laughter was neither bitter nor amused. It was a plain flat sound" (54). An air of detachment pervades her every move: "Mrs. Arnold took the breakfast dishes into the kitchen and filled the dishpan. She made suds with flakes of soap and watched the water make the glasses clean. Then she wiped the dishes and noted reflections on their surfaces; she wiped the dishpan and hung it up" (53). Here, Mrs. Arnold is merely a passive observer: she "watche[s] the water make the glasses clean." The water, rather than the character, is given agency, as if she herself has no impact upon her environment. Although she "note[s] reflections," we are not told if those reflections are of her own face or of other objects. To Mrs. Arnold, it does not seem to matter. Overwhelmed by her husband's definitions of her, she has disengaged from the discussion and become a neutral observer of her own life.

Latimer's depiction of Mrs. Arnold anticipates the compliant facade of Mrs. Ramsay in Woolf's *To the Lighthouse,* published three years later. Mr. Ramsay, upset that his wife has disagreed with his impromptu weather forecast, curses her in an angry outburst. She restores his good humor by silent submission:

. . . without replying, dazed and blinded, she bent her head as if to let the pelt of jagged hail, the drench of dirty water, bespatter her unrebuked. There was nothing to be said. . . .

Very humbly, at length, he said that he would step over and ask the Coastguards if she liked. (51)

Mrs. Ramsay uses silence as a strategy to restore order and peace, rather than risk provoking a direct confrontation. Similarly, when Latimer's patriarch has a self-contradictory outburst, his wife responds submissively: "From Mrs. Arnold radiated silence" (51). Mrs. Arnold's withdrawal, like Mrs. Ramsay's, functions as a survival strategy, a method of gaining freedom and transcendence while remaining in a hostile environment she cannot escape. Faced with a controlling, critical husband who constantly seeks to define her, Mrs. Arnold emotionally excuses herself, like the wife in Doris Lessing's *The Summer before the Dark,* who pours coffee for her husband and his colleague and then "set[s] an attentive smile on her face, like a sentinel, behind which she could cultivate her own thoughts" (14). With the character of Mrs. Arnold, Latimer exposes the speechless angel-in-the-house role as a facade, a cover for the private selves of women who find themselves powerless in the traditional family structure.

Latimer also demonstrates the vulnerability, fallibility, and mortality that Mr. Arnold's masculine role conceals. In describing his physical appearance, she also reveals his character: "His skin was sulphur-colored, his face solid, his body big and broad, but his eyes proved him perishable" (54). Here Mr. Arnold is described as massive, a statue; his sheer bulk, his dominant physical mass, obscures recognition of his human frailty. Yet his eyes, with the capacity both to see others and to express emotion, render him vulnerable. His physique echoes the way he positions himself as an authority—on topics from politics to the weather to his wife's foibles—but is proven fallible by the events of the story. Mr. Arnold, contrary to his own high opinion of himself, is neither impervious nor unerring: he is knocked down by an automobile, the very thing about which he has warned his wife. He is not seriously injured; two men bring him home, and Mrs. Arnold attends to his comfort.

When the men leave, the plot opens as if for some sort of mutual epiphany, some chance for renewed intimacy between husband and wife. Spurred by the memento mori of the accident, Mrs. Arnold makes her first impulsive, spontaneous gesture of the story: "She came back to her husband and suddenly kissed him. She took his hands and they looked at each other" (56). For the first time, she acts "suddenly," as if moved by strong emotion, rather than with her usual expressionless serenity. This is also the first moment in the story when the husband and wife make eye contact. The moment seems ripe, almost begging for an emotional breakthrough to function as the climax of the narrative.

The opportunity, however, is lost. Terrified, Mr. Arnold falls back on a self-aggrandizing cliché: "I tell you I could set the whole world right if they'd only listen." Mrs. Arnold withdraws again, and the final lines of the story stamp on the reader's mind the couple's return to their usual mode: "His wife moved softly and slowly away. 'There's something quite good for supper,' she said without intonation" (56). He is again blustering, opinionated, and ultimately frustrated; she again moves "softly and slowly" rather than "suddenly," and her voice reveals no emotion. They have reinhabited their roles, refusing the chance for reconnection and rapport.

The story deconstructs assumptions about the primacy of the public sphere, shifting the reader's perspective away from the privileged world of politics and economics and into the domestic arena. Describing only those actions that occur inside the home, the narrative places the reader in the same subject position as the housebound Mrs. Arnold. The reader, like Mrs. Arnold, sees Mr. Arnold only in the morning, then during his lunch break, and finally in the evening when the two men bring him home. While he is absent from the house, the reader knows nothing of his whereabouts and activities. His work life—and even the pivotal event of his accident—occur offstage, outside the scope of the narrative view.

While the focus remains with Mrs. Arnold in the confines of her house, the dishpan details of her day are richly imagined. Latimer imbues Mrs. Arnold's relation to ordinary household objects with telling detail: "She lingered at the table and watched the suppressed look of the heavy silver imprisoned there on the white cloth. She moved a spoon close to the sugar bowl and fenced a delicate cup with forks" (55). Latimer invests Mrs. Arnold's smallest domestic actions with emotional weight, implying that the character perceives herself, at some unarticulated level, as "suppressed," "imprisoned," and "fenced."

But the narrative, while foregrounding the vantage point of the feminine social role, does not side simplistically with Mrs. Arnold. Although her plight in the marital situation is depicted with authorial sympathy, we also hear that "Her smile pricked the stiffness of her face," suggesting the strain of the angel-in-the-house charade (53). Mrs. Arnold's lack of spontaneity, of impulsiveness, has resulted in an emotional life as frozen as her countenance. In addition, Mrs. Arnold's strategy of emotional withdrawal, while perhaps a survival strategy, is also portrayed as potentially damaging. After another of Mr. Arnold's diatribes, she retreats inward: "Again she withdrew, into unlimited space, he judged, from her look" (55). Though this emotional evasion functions as a mode of transcendence for Mrs. Arnold ("unlimited space"), it also damages the couple's ability to communicate. This is the sole instance in the story when the third-person narrator focuses on Mr. Arnold's perceptions ("he judged"); elsewhere, the narrative sticks fairly closely to Mrs. Arnold's experiences. This apparent slippage in narrative control can be read as a telling signal of authorial sympathy for Mr. Arnold's plight: Mrs. Arnold's smooth surface, Latimer suggests, can frustrate attempts at genuine interaction as surely as can her husband's repeated clichés. The failure to "only connect" is mutual.

Given its pessimistic content, "Mr. and Mrs. Arnold" is surprisingly amusing. But Latimer's is an edgy kind of comedy, a humor of the absurd, a laughter on the edge of madness. Yet this brief narrative, immersing readers in the private experience of the couple as if the reader were a quiet, observant child witnessing parental interactions, reveals much about Latimer's stance toward traditional marriage and the traditional family. The reader, forced to piece together meaning from contradictory statements, wavers among hilarity, confusion, and despair.

"The Family," by far the longest story in *Nellie Bloom,* traces the progress of an artist from childhood to adulthood in a conventional household, chronicling the maturation of a sensitive young woman whose parents are much like Mr. and Mrs. Arnold. Though the protagonist, Dorrit Beale, depicts in paintings her vision of the ideal family, bathed in mutual affection, respect, and delight, her attempts to communicate that vision to the members of her own family meet with only embarrassment and dismay.

On a visit home from college, she arranges her paintings on the walls of her room and brings her parents to see them. The vision she has labored to portray is not a detached, neutral one, but has immediate personal relevance. Her paintings are not only aesthetic objects but also a direct emotional appeal to her parents:

The walls were covered with pictures of happy families, the father, the mother, and the child, painted in bright sun among flowers and birds, painted with love in their faces and hands, love in their hands and arms that touched each other, and all three in some strange way were entirely separate and yet interchangeable, as if they understand each other's parts, as if they understood so well that they need not speak. And here there was no love withheld, it was all over them, it was part of the bright light that came from their flesh and their deep happy eyes. Each was a picture of a family, but a family that had never appeared upon the earth. (155)

Keeping such a vision at bay, however, her father responds with a lecture about realism and the laws of anatomy, overwhelming her mother's murmured vague support.

Yet Latimer, sensitive to the contours of American history, attributes the oppressive frustration of her WASP patriarchs to their unmet, unacknowledged yearning for the frontier past of their childhoods. After bellowing at his wife and daughter so that both flee the dinner table, Mr. Beale exclaims with an outraged sense of entitlement,

"When I take a day off from the store I expect to be entertained, I expect to have a little consideration shown me and look at this!" He waved his hands over the loaded table and the empty chairs. His heart felt so sore and open that he could not speak. . . . He remembered the day his father took him to see Dick Bacon's sick bull. He could see the mud, the flies stuck in it and circling above, singing like hornets. Home in the wagon, buckwheat cakes for supper, a lamp in the center of the table. He bent his head lower. "Pass the bread, if you please." Plates piled with bread white as snow, platter heaped with hot sausages, his father saying the blessing, freckles on his mother's hand seen through eyelashes in the lamplight, in the peace, amen. (137)

His rural background rendered irrelevant, Mr. Beale has become one of a nation of shopkeepers. Though he longs for the closeness of his family, all he can muster are diatribes about woman's place, dirty foreigners, and the glorious superiority of the United States, like the father in "Marriage Eve" who, "standing fixed in a strange rock-like position, his head thrust forward like a bull's," can only offer his grown daughter a book of Woodrow Wilson's collected speeches—"Real American stuff. A-number one"—when she comes home seeking rapprochement (*Guardian Angel* 277, 282). Bull-like in their stubborn strength, "their broad tough shoulders spread solid and dark and impregnable," Latimer's patriarchs reach for communion yet alienate the women around them (277).

Dorrit eventually leaves her home and the provincialism of the small-town Midwest to become a successful and well-known artist, yet her father is never able to accept her work, and her mother, initially supportive, becomes increasingly frightened by it. When Dorrit's paintings are exhibited at the Art Institute of Chicago, "The one reproduction Mrs. Beale saw in a city paper made her shake with grief and fright. It made her think of their position in town, of the butcher and the postman and the clerks everywhere" (187). Mr. Beale, outraged, takes the train for Chicago in an attempt to have Dorrit's paintings taken down. When he sees them, the "sweat came out on him" and he imagines himself telling someone, "My daughter painted these freaks that have never been seen on earth. I brought her up right but my wife spoiled her" (191).

Dorrit's vision is indeed disruptive. The first painting Mr. Beale views foregrounds

> a naked woman in sand. Bright sky and water. Two enormous gulls with opened wings. A huge happy baby seated squarely on the woman's stomach and the woman's head pushed deep in the sand, chin up, a look of such definite animal delight in her face that Mr. Beale shivered. He went on until the room seemed to fill up with the happy naked figures of men and women and children, until the sun was there behind him and his shoulders were hot with intense gold light. Sea gulls were in the room, you heard their enormous wings, the ocean was there, and everywhere he looked he met one of the supreme bright looks of radiant bliss. (190)

Like her earlier work, Dorrit's show in Chicago depicts humans in ecstatic connection with each other and the natural world. Rather than keeping their aesthetic distance, Dorrit's paintings cause feelings and sensations: Mr. Beale is "hot with intense gold light," and Latimer, breaking with narrative convention, employs the second person to involve the reader as well: "you heard their enormous wings." Dorrit's artistic vision is one of engagement, participation, emotion, and freedom. It is a vision of an ideal world.

Perhaps conscious of the futility of trying to have the loving family she envisions so clearly, Dorrit never does go home again, substituting the increasing approbation of the larger world for the understanding of her parents. This wider acclaim, though, does not entirely suffice: the narrative closes in Paris, where a drunken young Dorrit caricatures her father's speeches for a table of laughing men. Though she can envision and portray the happy, egalitarian family she desires, Latimer's artist figure is unable to construct such a family in her life, either with her parents or with a partner. A neighbor of the family, vacationing in Paris, witnesses the café episode and wonders if the young woman can possibly be happy. Latimer leaves the question unresolved.

This Is My Body

In the 1930 novel *This Is My Body,* her most explicitly leftist work, Latimer weaves autobiographical elements into a *Künstlerroman* to present the difficult truth about her life in the medium of fiction. Challenging genre boundaries between fiction and memoir, she ties the protagonist repeatedly to public images of her own body to tell the story of a young woman who, like herself, wrenches away from the small town of her upbringing, attends college, and finally settles in New York, where she faces poverty and sexism while struggling to become a writer and form an egalitarian heterosexual relationship. At once liberating and apocalyptic in its revelation of female experience, *This Is My Body* stands as one of the few portraits of the artist as a young woman in early twentieth-century literature. It refutes, moreover, masculinist assumptions within leftist, high modernist, and futurist circles about reproductive choice and women's creativity, thus participating in culture-wide conversations among multiple movements of the period.

The novel opens with a physical description of Megan, who is "rather large with a full sweet body" and red-gold hair (3). Focusing immediately on her body and her hair, this description of Megan is not incidental, for it overtly links her to Latimer, who herself was tall for a woman of the period—about 5'8"—and whose hair formed a focal point for contemporaries' physical descriptions. Given the risks *This Is My Body* takes in telling the coming-of-age story of a woman artist, this linkage is a daring one. As Virginia Woolf pointed out one year prior to the novel's publication in *A Room of One's Own* (1929), issues of sexuality and the body remained, for women, extremely difficult to address: "Chastity . . . has even now, a religious importance in a woman's life, and has so wrapped itself round with nerves and instincts that to cut it free and bring it to the light of day demands courage of the rarest" (51). In *This Is My Body,* Latimer brings both female sexuality and its frequent result, unplanned pregnancy, "to the light of day," for the portrait of the artist as a young woman is here climactically punctuated by abortion.

The issue of pregnancy was particularly vexed within socialist circles. It may seem counterintuitive that women would be viewed as second-class citizens within a political movement predicated precisely upon the struggle for human equality, yet recent scholarship by Laura Hapke, Constance Coiner, and others has illuminated the many obstacles facing leftist women of the twenties and thirties: the refusal of leftist party politics to address women's issues, the resistance to women in positions of leadership, and the ideology that discouraged women's literary production. Mike Gold's famous description of the ideal proletarian writer—"a wild youth of about twenty-two, the son of working-class parents, who himself works in the lumber camps, coal mines, and steel mills"—excludes women by definition (qtd. in Nekola and Rabinowitz 3).

While the increased availability of contraception and abortion during the period may appear—from our post-*Roe-v.-Wade* perspective—to have been a guarantor of female freedom, the ramifications of such technologies must be understood differently within the context of American socialism, a movement whose dominant voices saw children largely as either impediments to class struggle or fodder for the factory and battlefield. Women who found themselves pregnant could be compelled, in the interests of leftist political ideology, to reject childbirth regardless of their own desires.

Pregnancy was also a contested issue within high modernism. When influential modernist critic Cyril Connolly pronounces in *Enemies of Promise,* for instance, that "there is no more sombre enemy of good art than the pram in the hall," he speaks for a significant strain of high modernism that would reject women, children, and the whole of family life as antithetical to literary production, a rejection that male writers on the left largely echoed (116). The opening phase of Anglo-American modernism, propagated by Pound, Eliot, Wyndham Lewis, T. E. Hulme, and others relied, as Peter Nicholls has argued, on a kind of "technical and ethical self-discipline, on an *ascetic* refusal to collapse art into life . . . [which] den[ies] itself the immediate pleasures of the 'caressable' and the mimetic. . . . The literary values of this type of modernism are founded, then, . . . on the appeal to the visual and objective which affirms distance and difference" (197). Pregnancy and childbirth, with all their attendant intimacy and messiness, fly in the face of such an aesthetic.

Futurism, "The Other Modernism," as Cinzia Sartini Blum has termed it, also problematized the issue of female reproductivity. The basic insight of F. T. Marinetti, the founder of Italian futurism, was that the struggle between cultural tradition and the forces of industrial innovation was "relentless, unpitying, and weighted in favour of the modern." His first manifesto, published in 1909 in the Parisian paper *Le Figaro,* argued in favor of expunging from art and literature all human sentiment in order to valorize the inhuman speed and technology of the machine age (Nicholls 85). The fundamental misogyny of futurism has long been accepted; Marinetti's own creative vision produced the novel *Mafarka le Futuriste* (1909), which finally dispenses with women's bodies altogether: in *Mafarka* reproduction is performed solo by a male.

Because of this gender tension within the leftist, high modernist, and futurist movements, the issue of reproductive choice becomes particularly fraught in women's writing of the period. In *This Is My Body* Latimer uses the issue of abortion to vet the inconsistencies of leftist politics and to reveal the contradictions of the left's promise of freedom for women. Exploring the ways in which women's bodies and desires are controlled and women *as a class* are exploited, she contributes a pointed feminist critique to leftist writing of the period. Moreover, by linking the negative aspects of abortion to images of technology, the novel critiques the futurists' enthusiastic denial of the human in favor of the machine. Rejecting a vision of the future that edits out connection, relationship, and the female sex itself in its rush to embrace efficiency, *This Is My Body* negates such an unquestioning celebration of technology. Finally, it functions as a profound interrogation of that strain of modernism that would turn away from the caressable pleasures of the natural world.

The abortion story can serve, as Judith Wilt has argued, as a rich and productive narrative moment, since it is always a site of profound anxiety, both for the storyteller, who stands revealed as a potential locus of moral culpability, and for the reader, who must contend with a morally contested, emotionally explosive issue. Significantly, the structure of Latimer's novel does *not* conform to Wilt's analyses of abortion plots. Interpreting the work of more recent authors (Didion, Barth, and others), she argues that abortion functions to resist control. Thus if a man tries to control a woman with pregnancy, the plot resists with abortion. Conversely, if a man tries to control a woman by coercing or forcing her to have an abortion or if a woman tries to control "nature" by having an abortion, then the plot resists with continued pregnancy. Such resistance, however, is not operative in this novel from the Depression era. Instead, the female protagonist is pressured by her male partner to terminate a pregnancy she clearly wants. Backed by leftist rhetoric, the male character attempts to control her, and she submits. Later, she suffers from not only physical and emotional pain but also the sense that she has betrayed her values. Given the overt commitment of the left to struggle and resistance, this *lack* of resistance required of its women works as a telling indictment from within.

The abortion in Latimer's text functions structurally as the climax of the plot, an ironic and bitter dashing of the protagonist's hopes; the denouement records the emotional aftermath of the experience. Since the abortion itself is never described—only the events immediately before and after it—the climax itself is a silence, an emptiness, a hollow center. Abortion, moreover, functions in this text as a trope for more general kinds of loss or failed potential: the failure of the bourgeois ideal of maternity to translate to lives of political commitment and financial instability, the failure of leftist party politics to comprehend important aspects of women's experience and women's desire. Latimer plays on abortion's metaphoric possibilities and multiple meanings, then, in order both to critique capitalist culture and to interrogate masculinist assumptions of the left.

Latimer offers an incisive critique of the intersections of class difference and sexual politics at the locus of pregnancy. The narrative hinges upon the heroine Megan Foster's reluctant agreement to abort the pregnancy her lover does not want. A subplot focuses on

Megan's friend, a fellow university student who, impregnated by
the married dean of her college—a representative of bourgeois re-
spectability—is tricked by him into visiting a doctor, who performs
a forced abortion while she struggles and screams.

In each narrative thread the young woman wishes to keep her
pregnancy, both presenting verbal arguments in favor of continued
pregnancy and exhibiting emotional distress at the prospect of ter-
mination; in each, her male partner pushes her to abort for a complex of social, political, and economic reasons, which—the narratives make clear—function to conceal personal reluctance to make
public an illicit relationship, to reconceive the relationship as other
than a sexual playground, or to cede primary importance in the
eyes of the female. The Kenneth Fearing figure, Ronald Chadron, is
a bohemian poet who derides bourgeois morality and espouses socialist ideals, yet he listens to his partner no more than does the
dean to his. Although he does not, like the dean, employ physical
restraint, the narrative carefully delineates his emotional violence:
after using economic and political arguments to convince Megan to
terminate her wanted pregnancy, he makes her go for the abortion
alone and pay for the procedure herself. It is only after Megan ac-
quiesces, moreover, that Ronald at last consents to touch her again,
"press[ing] her arm warmly like a comrade or a husband," suggesting Latimer's equation of party power structures and the male-
dominant structure of the bourgeois household (325).

The narrative is beautifully attentive to material detail, yet
Latimer blends a leftist focus on material conditions with a high
modernist use of archetypal symbolism. The abortion itself, when
described by Miss Bradley, a Greenwich Village waitress and fellow
aspiring writer, is figured as an everyday economic transaction, re-
quiring the performance of class position: "He'll do it for thirty dollars," she tells Megan, "wear old clothes or he'll charge a hundred"
(326). Later we learn that Megan has in fact dressed the part, performed her class position, for when Ronald asks the cost, she replies, "Thirty." Latimer twice notes the price; its resonance with the
thirty pieces of silver for which Judas betrays Christ is not coinci-
dental, for the passage is infused with the language of betrayal:
"Oh, you've let me betray myself," she tells Ronald. "I've betrayed
myself. I've punished and violated and betrayed my own self" (329-
30). We remember the novel's title, *This Is My Body,* and realize that
Latimer has audaciously couched the abortion narrative in Christ
imagery; the epigraph reads: "'I'll give them my body—I will say—
'This is my body, friends, world—Oh, take my body and eat—Oh,
take my soul and do not be afraid—.'" Latimer details her intention
to employ Christian symbolism—and her resultant anxiety over

such a move—in letters to friends, writing to Matthias in the winter of 1929: "Your Christmas present is going to be a copy of my new book which will be out the twentieth of January, published by Jonathan Cape and Harrison Smith. Did I tell you the title? It is called "This Is My Body" and I mean in the same way Christ meant when he said—'This is my body; take, eat.' I felt so fulfilled giving myself that way, my blood, my illusions, my life, the last atom of my self to all. . . . O I hope they don't laugh." Latimer's biblical allusions, however, go unremarked in reviews of the novel, suggesting the lack of understanding with which most women's explorations of such structures met during the period. As Elaine Showalter explains, "Even when women produced feminine versions of modernism, reimagining myths, for example, from female perspectives (such as Bogan's 'Cassandra' and 'Medusa,' Millay's 'An Ancient Gesture,' describing Penelope, and H. D.'s 'Eurydice'), as James Joyce and T. S. Eliot had modernized the myths of Ulysses and the Grail, [their] experiments were ignored and misunderstood" (109). Reviewers of *This Is My Body* fell so wide of the mark in interpreting Latimer's allusions, in fact, that the *New York Times Book Review* attributes the title and epigraph ("This is my body, friends, world—Oh, take my body and eat—") to Walt Whitman: "Miss Latimer has taken for her text a paraphrase of Whitman's introduction to 'Leaves of Grass'—'who touches this book touches a man.' Only her version of it is somewhat more diffuse" ("Hungry" 9). Latimer's deliberate linkage of Megan's story to the primary Western narrative of self-sacrifice went unnoticed by critics, who failed to suppose that a young woman's story could be meaningfully related to Christ's.

Latimer also recasts elements from traditional fairy tales to underscore the narrative's *Künstlerroman* plot and suggest that the roles women have inherited are inadequate and destructive, anticipating the work of feminist writers like Anne Sexton and Angela Carter. In the apartment Megan shares with Ronald, for example, hang prints depicting scenes from childhood tales such as "Little Red Riding Hood." Initially, the prints are described in neutral ways, but as she faces the more sordid aspects of men's sexual exploitation of women, Megan's perceptions of the pictures become progressively more sinister: the wolf begins to leer at Red Riding Hood, at the "good things under her round red cape" (317). After acquiescing to her lover's demands by terminating the pregnancy she wants to keep, Megan stumbles through the city, seeing the men around her as vicious predators: " 'Oh, save me from the hungry wolves,' she cried as sun gleamed on those twitching canes, those dark sleek faces under stiff formal hats, those bunched grey gloves" (350).

The novel ends ambiguously. While the narrative thrust of the *Künstlerroman* is fulfilled—Megan's book is finally accepted by a publisher—she suffers such severe physical and emotional pain that it is unclear whether her sexual and social coming-of-age has succeeded or failed. In a 1930 letter to Matthias, Latimer explains her intentions for the novel in fairy tale terms as well:

I meant it to be like a fairy tale in substance. You know the prince who is sunk in a snake skin and looks horrible from the outside? The princess faces his horror and he emerges beautiful? I thought of this girl as being wrapped in all the horror of fear, the darkness of inexperience, the death of hatreds, indifference, egoism. I meant her to slowly have her wrappings withdrawn and with each loss, a gain in understanding, so that at the end, completely revealed through love and defilement she faced a new world and faced the possibility of living a new life through effort.

But in Latimer's gender reversal of the traditional plot, the catalyst for transformation—the prince who would fulfill for Megan the function of the all-accepting princess in various tales of male beast-liness—is nonexistent.

Latimer's focus on the experience of the female body as a locus for cultural critique is highly self-aware. Early in the novel, Megan goes to the dean of the college—the same dean who later tricks his young lover into a forced abortion—and, claiming that her pre-scribed courses do not interest her, requests a special seminar on Descartes and Spinoza (35). Latimer thus anticipates the work of contemporary feminist theorists such as Elizabeth Grosz, who sees the philosophical differences between Descartes and Spinoza as so fundamental to our contemporary understanding of the body that she opens her 1994 *Volatile Bodies: Toward a Corporeal Feminism* with a discussion of their work (6). While the Cartesian attitude to-ward the body—that it is "a self-moving machine, a mechanical de-vice"—lends support to the arguments of characters like Ronald—or like Hemingway's famously oblique male character in "Hills Like White Elephants," who insists to his girlfriend that the operation will have no significant consequences—Latimer's work functions to resist this "exclusion of the soul from nature, this evacuation of con-sciousness from the world" (Grosz 6, 10). In rejecting definitions of body-as-machine, Latimer traces the sexual politics of her time to their root in Enlightenment philosophy and decries the mechanistic philosophy of the futurist argument.

Technology and machines are allied in the text with the degrada-tion of female subjectivity. After hearing her friend Arvia's experi-ence of being strapped down for an abortion, Megan is deeply shaken. In contrast to the high modernism that would repudiate the "immediate world" "of nature and natural things," Megan responds by craving vegetation, water, and soil as sources of comfort, rereading the "messiness and confusion" of nature as something stable and reassuring:

> She could feel nothing but fear and nausea, a great panic as if she must catch hold of wood, earth, anything solid and clean. . . . She thought in a flash of a tree that she could bind her arms around and clench herself close to so that when lightning came she would be holding a part of the tree even if it split apart and went rolling down the cliff. Then when the great tremendous floods of water came she would be holding part of the sweet firm wood. She would be borne out into the dark sea clinging to part of it, her arms wrapped around it. (310-11)

The passage combines both the imagery of a fundamental split and flood imagery of retribution for sexual transgression. As long as she can hold on to part of nature before it is bifurcated, Megan believes, she will be saved. But the modern world offers no such refuge. When the two women leave the restaurant in a taxi, "Megan pressed against the glass. She tried to find something hard to grip hold of but there was nothing but the steel bar on the driver's seat. She crouched closer and smaller, one shoulder drawn up as if she thought someone was going to strike her, the other down against the glass" (311-12). Technology, machinery, offers no comfort; Latimer repeatedly uses the word *against* to describe its relationship to Megan's body.

The abortion scene itself is pervaded by an emphasis on technology, since the literal tools of the procedure command center stage. In Latimer's text the abortion occurs entirely offstage. The doctor announces, "It will take one hour to sterilize the instruments. You can wait in there" (327), and a section break abruptly follows. The opening line of the next section finds Megan entering her apartment: "It's over," she tells Ronald (328). Readers must infer the entire procedure. The focus thus falls on the technology, the instruments, and upon Megan's own lack of agency in the face of technology's power.

Afterward, she expresses her grief in terms of the material detail of abortion: "I ache. That iron scrapes all the time in my head" (330). Associating the technology of abortion with the changes of modernity and urbanization, the novel's final line returns us to the image of flesh being scraped from flesh in its depiction of Megan's acceptance of a bifurcated self: "And now it seemed as if she walked on her knees behind herself, pushing her body forward through the waves of mindless faces, her stockings, her skin scraped off her moving knees, the raw flesh at last on the dull cement" (351).

Melding high modernist structure and symbolism with socialist attention to material contingency, *This Is My Body* thus complicates traditional boundaries between leftist and modernist canons while offering a feminist critique of high modernism, leftist sexual politics, and futurism's dehumanizing ideology, indicting the mind-body bifurcation that underpinned all three.

Guardian Angel and Other Stories

The title novella and eight stories of the 1932 *Guardian Angel and Other Stories,* Latimer's final book, offer finely detailed, unsentimental portraits of the impact on girls' friendships of class difference, family dysfunction, and awakening sexuality (in "Gisela" and "The Little Girls") and examine the lingering psychological impact of old love affairs (in "Married," "Monday Morning," and "Daisy Turlock," in which the protagonist rushes to her room after her parents "had bent over a big map, trying to locate the places where Christianity hadn't penetrated" (217)). The stories explore a young woman's struggle to escape from her overbearing father ("Marriage Eve"), campus literary politics ("O Clouds, Roll Back"), the last-minute epiphany of an elderly woman ("Death of Mrs. Vanderwood") and, again, in "Guardian Angel," the Latimer-Gale relationship.

In "Guardian Angel," Latimer's final depiction of her relationship with Gale, the young woman Vanessa successfully breaks away from the sexual and emotional restraints of her mentor Fleta Bain. She leaves for the city to pursue her artistic goals, and the narrative implies that she will enjoy an active and satisfying personal life. "Guardian Angel" employs a first-person narrator, but the voice speaks not from the position of the immature Latimer figure, who is viewed with ironic detachment, but from that of Vanessa's Aunt Grace, who (married with children) serves to represent the traditional mother figure. That Aunt Grace narrates the novella indicates a significant development from *We Are Incredible,* in which Myrtle Fry is the only major character who does not have a section of her own: although readers hear plenty of Myrtle's words, they are always filtered through the perspectives of Stephen, Dora, or Hester; we never hear the voice of Myrtle's interior life. In "Guardian Angel," however, the entire narrative is told from the first-person point of view of Aunt Grace, who occupies the same position as Myrtle does in *We Are Incredible*—the wife and mother, the older woman relative who functions as a potential role model for the Latimer figure (though here an aunt rather than an older sister). It is Aunt Grace's family that functions as a backdrop for the main action, as do the Frys in *We Are Incredible*. Yet while Latimer's earlier work provides a bitter, disturbing portrait of marital turmoil and destructive parenting, "Guardian Angel" is narrated by a mature, intelligent, creative woman who deeply loves her husband and children yet retains an undimmed critical sensibility, a wry sense of humor, and narrative authority.

The bifurcation between traditional mother and countermother roles in "Guardian Angel" is not as strict as that presented in *We Are Incredible,* suggesting an ideological movement toward rapprochement. Grace achieves a satisfying sexual life and raises affectionate, psychologically healthy children in a situation that affirms both self and others. However, she is still faced with an either/or situation; her successful home life has come at the cost of her singing career. Yet although she has relinquished artistic and professional goals in favor of family life, Grace is depicted by Latimer as thoughtful and mature. She chooses and supports her children and is nurtured by her husband in a mutually satisfying relationship. Although she has not struck an ideal balance, as Vanessa (the text promises) will, she has certainly come closer than Myrtle Fry.

Likewise, just as Grace functions as a traditional mother yet remains intellectually alive and independent, the countermother figure Fleta Bain incorporates elements of the opposing paradigm. Fleta possesses many of Hester Linden's characteristics: though lovely and charming, she suppresses the spontaneity and warmth of everyone around her, constantly denying and denigrating embodied experience. Yet during the course of the novella, she chooses to marry, and—significantly, given Latimer's emphasis on vegetal imagery as representative of female sexuality and spirituality—she begins to garden in an effort to connect with nature. Though she does so imperfectly—the flowers stand "in straight rows, in full bloom, newly transplanted from a greenhouse"—effort is nonetheless being made (105). With "Guardian Angel," Latimer moves closer to a synthesis of women's two divergent social roles.

In "Guardian Angel" Latimer seems to explore several of the elements in Woolf's *The Voyage Out* (1915). Both Woolf's Aunt Helen and Latimer's Aunt Grace are mature women who are artistic and intellectual yet devoted to their children and happily married. Both have immature, vague, beautiful nieces with an artistic bent: Rachel Vinrace plays piano, and Vanessa draws. Both nieces admire older women who represent glamour, society, and art: Rachel idealizes Clarissa Dalloway, and Vanessa idealizes Fleta Bain. However, Fleta Bain discourages heterosexual romance, while Mrs. Dalloway encourages marriage, arguing for its efficacy as a sexualized emotional balm for the wound of Rachel's lost mother:

Mrs. Dalloway went on:

"Are you like your mother?"

"No; she was different," said Rachel.

She was overcome by an intense desire to tell Mrs. Dalloway things she had never told any one—things she had not realised herself until this moment.

"I am lonely," she began. "I want—" She did not know what she wanted, so that she could not finish the sentence; but her lip quivered.

But it seemed that Mrs. Dalloway was able to understand without words.

"I know," she said, actually putting one arm round Rachel's shoulder. "When I was your age I wanted too. No one understood until I met Richard. He gave me all I wanted. He's man and woman as well." Her eyes rested upon Mr. Dalloway, leaning upon the rail, still talking. (59-60)

Here, Rachel apparently wants her mother, who is dead, yet she cannot speak that desire for the feminine, reduced to the wordlessness of compulsory heterosexuality. Mrs. Dalloway urges the transmutation of that longing into a heterosexual love which will satisfy all desires, in which a husband will be "man and woman as well." Yet this solution unravels as the plot does, for Richard Dalloway betrays his wife's trust; when she is seasick, he turns to Rachel for erotic gratification, revealing an underworld of untrustworthy male desire similar to that in *We Are Incredible* or *This Is My Body*.

In "Guardian Angel," on the other hand, Latimer presents a more optimistic vision of the potential of heterosexual love. It is noteworthy that not Vanessa's but Grace's mother has died; Grace's maturity seems to be predicated upon her acknowledgment of that loss. Her husband Wendall, unlike Richard Dalloway, makes no corresponding overtures to other women. He and Grace remain loyal to one another, and he in fact functions as a catalyst for Grace's mourning of her mother. Rather than the death of a child (like Deva in *We Are Incredible*), Grace's mutually enriching relationship with her husband, which acknowledges and grieves the loss of her mother, produces new life; she confides happily to the reader that she has become pregnant. Similarly, rather than dying—as do Rachel Vinrace and Dora Weck—Vanessa (a generation removed from Grace's grief) succeeds in leaving old roles behind for a life which combines both work and love. With the character of Wendall, Latimer reimagines the male role as one that encompasses nurturing and loyalty in addition to traditional gender expectations, leaving ideological room for egalitarian heterosexual romance. Latimer's narrative, like Woolf's, seems to situate women's health and happiness as dependent upon both their acknowledgment of their lost mothers and the trustworthiness of male desire. Yet, unlike *The Voyage Out*, Latimer's "Guardian Angel" provides a successful resolution.

This preoccupation with the death of the mother represents a departure from Latimer's autobiographical representations, for while Latimer litters her literary landscape with maternal remains, her own mother outlived her by several years. The textual death of the mother instead serves to symbolize the powerlessness, the social silencing of the traditional mother figure in nineteenth- and early twentieth-century American culture. The ambivalence of the daughter figures stems from the fact that to join the mother, to become like her, is to die in terms of autonomy and public achievement. Conversely, to live—to participate in the sort of active political and social engagement typified by such figures as Gale, Addams, and Gilman—is to reject the mother, to betray and lose her in one motion. By acknowledging and grieving what has been silenced, Latimer argues via Aunt Grace, women could begin to make the transition toward integrating and enlarging their options.

Latimer's various fictional interrogations of the mutually exclusive life-choices available to women function, in Carolyn Heilbrun's words, as an effort to "write her own life in advance of living it," as a way to write her way through to a new reality for women (11). In "Guardian Angel" Latimer seems to resolve those aspects of her relationship with Gale which she found so problematic: Gale's magnetic appeal, her vague metaphysics, and particularly her repudiation of physicality and sexuality. The novella holds the opposing terms of the available paradigms of womanhood in tension, yet in Latimer's creation of Vanessa, "Guardian Angel" holds a clear promise of future synthesis.

The results of the feminist project of recovering lost or historically undervalued women writers are now so successful as to have become commonplace: "When I grow up," a little girl tells her companion in a recent New Yorker cartoon, "I want to be rediscovered." As a theoretical exercise, scholar Mary Poovey recently recovered the work of nineteenth-century British novelist Ellen Pickering— not for its own sake, but in order to test the contemporary critical practices and assumptions that inform such projects. Citing the arbitrarily selected novelist's conventionality, Poovey concluded in the Yale Journal of Criticism, "Do I think that Pickering's works should be canonized? No, frankly, I don't" (448).

In contrast, Latimer's work urges our serious examination on its own merit. Critics encountering her fiction in recent years have called repeatedly for recuperation. Former MLA president Louis Kampf closes his 1984 essay on Latimer with the assertion that she "richly deserves a place of honor in the history of American modernism" (246), and Daniel McCarthy argues that "a closer look at her is overdue" (475). Toomer's biographers Kerman and Eldridge assert that her "phenomenal career" deserves critical consideration (192), and a recent study of Fearing calls Latimer "immaculate, luminous, mystical, otherworldly," an "exceptionally gifted young writer" (Ryley xii). At the college level, her work teaches well in conjunction with that of her American contemporaries Faulkner, Fitzgerald, and Hemingway; students find Latimer equally challenging, stimulating, and revealing. Erudite and experimental, her work participates equally in the modernist project yet offers a feminist perspective on issues of sexuality, social structure, urbanization, and technology.

Do I think that Latimer's works should be canonized? Yes, frankly, I do. Appreciating Latimer's groundbreaking contributions to literature complicates and enhances our understanding of both modernist and American literary canons, and recognizing her reinterpretations of material by her female predecessors unearths intertextual links within women's literary traditions. Like the important female modernists whose work has been excavated in recent decades and like the rediscovered American women writers Kate Chopin, Charlotte Perkins Gilman, and Zora Neale Hurston, Margery Latimer was lost for too long. It is time to find her.

WORKS CITED

Ammons, Elizabeth. *Conflicting Stories: American Women Writers at the Turn into the Twentieth Century.* New York: Oxford UP, 1995.

Blum, Cinzia Sartini. *The Other Modernism: F. T. Marinetti's Futurist Fiction of Power.* Berkeley: U of California P, 1996.

Buss, Carl Alfred. "Margery Latimer—Wisconsin's Newest Writer." *Wisconsin Magazine* February 1929: 14-15.

Chopin, Kate. *The Awakening and Selected Stories.* New York: Random House, 1981.

Cixous, Hélène, and Catherine Clement. *The Newly Born Woman.* Trans. Betsy Wing. 1975. Minneapolis: U of Minnesota P, 1993.

Coiner, Constance. *Better Red: The Writing and Resistance of Tillie Olsen and Meridel Le Sueur.* Champaign: U of Illinois P, 1995.

Connolly, Cyril. *Enemies of Promise.* New York: Macmillan, 1938.

Dane, Gabrielle. "Hysteria as Feminist Protest: Dora, Cixous, Acker." *Women's Studies* 23 (1994): 231-55.

Dawson, M. C. Rev. of *This Is My Body,* by Margery Latimer. *Nation* 7 May 1930: 552.

Derleth, August. *Still Small Voice: The Biography of Zona Gale.* New York: Appleton, 1940.

Diamant, Gertrude. Rev. of *Nellie Bloom and Other Stories,* by

Margery Latimer. *New York World* 16 June 1929: 7.

Eisler, Benita. *O'Keeffe & Stieglitz: An American Romance*. New York: Penguin, 1991.

Friedman, Susan Stanford. Personal E-mail to author. 23 August 2000.

Gregory, Horace. Rev. of *Guardian Angel,* by Margery Latimer. *New York Herald Tribune Books* 6 November 1932: 2.

Grosz, Elizabeth. *Volatile Bodies: Toward a Corporeal Feminism*. Bloomington: Indiana UP, 1984.

Rev. of *Guardian Angel and Other Stories,* by Margery Latimer. *Saturday Review of Literature* 15 October 1932: 179.

Rev. of *Guardian Angel and Other Stories,* by Margery Latimer. *New York Times Book Review* 16 October 1932: 6.

Hapke, Laura. *Daughters of the Great Depression: Women, Work, and Fiction in the American 1930s*. Athens: U of Georgia P, 1995.

Haxton, Florence. "Irradiations in Prose." Rev. of *Nellie Bloom and Other Stories,* by Margery Latimer. *New York Herald Tribune Books* 12 May 1929: 3-4.

Heilbrun, Carolyn. *Writing a Woman's Life*. New York: Ballantine, 1988.

Hite, Molly. *The Other Side of the Story: Structures and Strategies of Contemporary Feminist Narrative*. Ithaca: Cornell UP, 1989.

Huf, Linda. *A Portrait of the Artist as a Young Woman: The Writer as Heroine in American Literature*. New York: Frederick Ungar, 1983.

"Hungry for Life." Rev. of *This Is My Body,* by Margery Latimer. *New York Times Book Review* 2 March 1930: 9.

Jewett, Sarah Orne. *The Country of the Pointed Firs and Other Stories*. 1925. New York: Doubleday, 1989.

"Just Americans." *Time* 28 March 1932: 19.

Kampf, Louis. "Afterword: The Work." *Guardian Angel and Other Stories*. By Margery Latimer. Old Westbury, NY: Feminist Press, 1984. 236-46.

Kerman, Cynthia Earl, and Richard Eldridge. *The Lives of Jean Toomer: A Hunger for Wholeness*. Baton Rouge: Louisiana State UP, 1987.

Latimer, Margery. *Guardian Angel and Other Stories*. New York: Smith & Haas, 1932; Freeport, NY: Books for Libraries Press, 1971.

——. Letter to Blanche Matthias. 1929. Margery Latimer Collection. Department of Special Collections. University of Wisconsin Memorial Library, Madison.

——. Letter to Blanche Matthias. September 1930. Margery Latimer Collection. Department of Special Collections. University of Wisconsin Memorial Library, Madison.

------. *Nellie Bloom and Other Stories*. New York: Sears, 1929.

------. *This Is My Body*. New York: Cape and Smith, 1930.

------. *We Are Incredible*. New York: Sears, 1928.

Lessing, Doris. *The Summer before the Dark*. New York: Knopf, 1973.

Le Sueur, Meridel. "Afterword: A Memoir." *Guardian Angel and Other Stories*. By Margery Latimer. Old Westbury, NY: Feminist Press, 1984. 230-35.

Loughridge, Nancy. "Afterword: The Life." *Guardian Angel and Other Stories*. By Margery Latimer. Old Westbury, NY: Feminist Press, 1984. 215-29.

Matthias, Blanche. "My Friendship with Margery Bodine Latimer." Unpublished essay, 1977, ts. Margery Latimer Collection. U of Wisconsin, Madison.

McCarthy, Daniel. " 'Just Americans': A Note on Jean Toomer's Marriage to Margery Latimer." *CLA Journal* 17 (1974): 474-79.

Nekola, Charlotte, and Paula Rabinowitz, eds. *Writing Red: An Anthology of Women Writers, 1930-1940*. New York: Feminist Press, 1987.

Rev. of *Nellie Bloom and Other Stories,* by Margery Latimer. *Saturday Review of Literature* 10 August 1929: 42.

Nicholls, Peter. *Modernisms: A Literary Guide*. Berkeley: U of California P, 1995.

Poovey, Mary. "Recovering Ellen Pickering." *Yale Journal of Criticism* 13.2 (2000): 437-52.

Rakosi, Carl. *The Collected Prose of Carl Rakosi*. Orono: National Poetry Foundation, 1983.

Rich, Adrienne. *Of Woman Born: Motherhood as Experience and Institution*. 1976. New York: Norton, 1986.

Robbins, F. L. Rev. of *This Is My Body,* by Margery Latimer. *Outlook and Independent* 154 (1930): 148.

Ryley, Robert M. *Kenneth Fearing: Complete Poems*. Orono: National Poetry Foundation, 1994.

Scott, Bonnie Kime, ed. *The Gender of Modernism: A Critical Anthology*. Bloomington: Indiana UP, 1990.

Seaver, Edwin. Rev. of *This Is My Body,* by Margery Latimer. *New York Evening Post* 12 April 1930: 10.

Showalter, Elaine. *Sister's Choice: Tradition and Change in American Women's Writing*. Oxford: Clarendon, 1991.

Smith, Patricia Juliana. *Lesbian Panic: Homoeroticism in Modern British Women's Fiction*. New York: Columbia UP, 1997.

Spacks, Patricia Meyer. *The Female Imagination*. New York: Knopf, 1975.

Rev. of *This Is My Body,* by Margery Latimer. *Bookman* 71 (1930): 216.

Rev. of *This Is My Body,* by Margery Latimer. *New Republic* 62 (1930): 227.

Rev. of *This Is My Body,* by Margery Latimer. *Saturday Review of Literature* 24 May 1930: 1073.

Wakefield, Eleanor. Rev. of *This Is My Body,* by Margery Latimer. *New York World* 23 February 1930: 10.

Rev. of *We Are Incredible,* by Margery Latimer. *Milwaukee Journal* 26 May 1928: 17.

Rev. of *We Are Incredible,* by Margery Latimer. *New York Evening Post* 26 May 1928: 8.

Wilt, Judith. *Abortion, Choice, and Contemporary Fiction: The Armageddon of the Maternal Instinct.* Chicago: U of Chicago P, 1990.

Woolf, Virginia. *A Room of One's Own.* 1929. New York: Harcourt Brace Jovanovich, 1957.

———. *To the Lighthouse.* 1927. New York: Harcourt Brace Jovanovich, 1955.

———. *The Voyage Out.* 1915. New York: Signet, 1991.

A Margery Latimer Checklist

"The New Freedom." *Reviewer* 4 (1924): 139-40.

We Are Incredible. New York: Sears, 1928.

Nellie Bloom and Other Stories. New York: Sears, 1929.

This Is My Body. New York: Cape and Smith, 1930.

Guardian Angel and Other Stories. New York: Smith & Haas, 1932;
Freeport, NY: Books for Libraries Press, 1971.

"Letters to Georgia O'Keeffe." *The New Caravan*. Ed. Alfred
Kreymborg, Lewis Mumford, and Paul Rosenfeld. New York:
Norton, 1936. 488-93.

Guardian Angel and Other Stories [collected from *Nellie Bloom* and
Guardian Angel]. Old Westbury, NY: Feminist Press, 1984.

Book Reviews

W. G. Sebald. *Austerlitz*. Trans. Anthea Bell. Random House, 2001. 300 pp. $24.95.

The fourth novel by the German expatriate author W. G. Sebald records the life story of Jacques Austerlitz, an eccentric architectural historian born in Prague and raised by foster parents in Wales. Battling the alienation that has wrecked his life, Austerlitz eventually reclaims his origins from the darkness of the Holocaust, aspiring to "a kind of historical metaphysic, bringing remembered events back to life." Sebald's narrator, driven by a similar impulse, shudders to think "how everything is constantly lapsing into oblivion with every extinguished life, how the world is, as it were, draining itself, in that the history of countless places and objects which themselves have no power of memory is never heard, never described or passed on." Sebald employs an old-fashioned, scholarly manner to entirely fresh ends, fusing learning and sensitivity into a kind of neurotic sublime. He stares into the abyss, yet engages in an act of affirmation: of the individual against the mass, of the detail against our habitual inattention, of recollection against oblivion. The repressed memories of Jacques Austerlitz serve to indict the entire postwar age of denial through forgetting. Identity is fragile, we are reminded, and the individual is forever at the mercy of fanatical ideologies, whether religious, capitalist, or totalitarian. Sebald's new translator, Anthea Bell, proves a worthy successor to Michael Hulse: the language is exquisite. But how to evoke the reach and the immense appeal of Sebald's vision, with its uncanny anecdotes, its quirkiness, and its compassion? His humanist stance is qualified by an annihilating sense of historical contingency, yet he never succumbs to cynicism. The sheer quality of the writing seems a statement of value. *Austerlitz* shines like a light. [Philip Landon]

Mary Caponegro. *The Complexities of Intimacy*. Coffee House, 2001. 220 pp. Paper: $14.95.

The Complexities of Intimacy, which includes four darkly humorous, richly imagined stories and a novella, examines the nuclear family in all its crippling yet structurally crucial intimacies and disjunctions. Due to the nature of this subject, as well as Caponegro's use of images with strong psychoanalytic and feminist currency (such as the father's house, the daughter's phallic tail, and the mother's milk which "transubstantiates" into ink), the stories lend themselves to readings à la Jacques Lacan and Luce Irigaray. However, while the stories invite such readings, they also wriggle out of them via the polyvalent capacity of Caponegro's prose. Language in this collection is a wondrous beast, both precise and mutable. This paradoxical quality perhaps figures most prominently in the opening story, "The Daughter's Lamentation," where the journey from the beginning of a paragraph to the end, or the transition from one sentence to the next, often seems to be as much effected by a felicitous turn of word or phrase as it is by the reins of thought. The author gracefully guides language in the direction of the fictions she is exploring—both the stories themselves and the family under patriarchy—and at the same time seems to follow its lead, pursuing its possibilities for play and ambiguity. Caponegro's ability to exploit so deftly the resources of language is what makes the moments when the stories take a decidedly surrealistic turn (when, for instance, the mother and daughter in "A Father's Blessing" crawl together inside the daughter's womb for a little respite from motherhood) work so well: it seems perfectly natural, given the supple and miraculous nature of her prose, that the world it originates should be equally so. [Elisabeth Sheffield]

Juan Goytisolo. *The Garden of Secrets.* Trans. Peter Bush. Serpent's Tail, 2000. 147 pp. $24.00; *Landscapes of War: From Sarajevo to Chechnya.* Trans. Peter Bush. City Lights, 2000. 225 pp. Paper: $16.95.

Following up his translations of *Quarantine* and *The Marx Family Saga,* Peter Bush has rendered into English two more works by the cosmopolitan Spanish writer Juan Goytisolo. *The Garden of Secrets* is a brief novel that continues the formal experimentation Goytisolo initiated in *Marks of Identity.* Like most of his fiction, it meditates on the Spanish Civil War and its repressive aftermath. It also explores the Christian-Jewish-Arab encounters his writings have focused on for decades, beginning with his most celebrated novel *Count Julian.* Emulating the creators of *The Arabian Nights, The Decameron, Don Quixote, Tristram Shandy,* and *Absalom, Absalom!,* Goytisolo constantly calls attention to his fiction's means of invention. Rather than presuming to represent reality, his experiments in narrative perspective reflect his distrust of realist pretensions. Accordingly, this novel consists of a collective story concocted by twenty-eight members of a professionally and culturally diverse reading group. In reconstructing the life of a poet named Eusebio who fled Franco's Spain, their collaborative aim is to demolish "that disposable entity, the novelist" and "realise a creative mix of perspectives and possibilities." Eusebio bears biographical resemblance to Goytisolo himself, and his story develops the author's frequent Joycean theme of exile as both liberation and alienation. In typical postmodern fashion, the facts of Eusebio's life remain a mystery, and his poetic reputation may have been a complete sham. But the patchwork, eclectic fiction about him stands as another important addition to Goytisolo's attempt to reinvigorate Spanish fiction by "poisoning" it with a transhistorical and international range of subject matter and with formal innovations that aim to open up new channels for thought.

While *The Garden of Secrets* will probably be of interest to those already familiar with Spanish and Arab literature and culture, *Landscapes of War* has a more direct appeal because of the depressingly persistent urgency of its subject matter. Written for Madrid's *El País* from 1993 to 1996, Goytisolo's journalism confidently covers a wide variety of topics: the psychological effects of warfare; the urban geography of bombed-out, sniper-riddled Sarajevo; the reassuring aims and unfortunate excesses of collective Islamic consciousness; the semiology of everyday life in occupied Palestinian territories; and the history of Russia's occupation of Chechnya. The collection is nicely rounded off with a long informative essay that offers a recent history of Islamic relations with the West and calls for a more respectful inclusion of Muslim countries in global society. Goytisolo's fiction parodies traditions, dwells on solipsistic estrangement, and with coy postmodern irony questions the attempt to represent reality. But his journalism bleeds sincerity, and it uncompromisingly insists that ideals like toleration, respect, and magnanimity be put into political practice. Take, for example, his thoughts on leaving war-torn Sarajevo: "One's sense of morality is refined and improved. . . . Things that previously seemed important wane and lose substances; others slight in appearance suddenly acquire greatness and stand out as self-evident truths. Direct contact with the brutality and cowardice of the paladins of ethnic cleansing and the courage of the women and men who, defying sniper bullets and Serbian nationalist shelling, go out in search of water armed only with their faith and attachment to life, creates experiences and images that don't fade from the mind." By so movingly expressing "the need for commitment, the urgency of solidarity," Goytisolo invests his outrage at overdue political solutions with a power that one hopes would become infectious. [Thomas Hove]

Sheila Kohler. *Children of Pithiviers*. Zoland, 2001. 204 pp. $21.00.

This novel is an astonishing, seductive, sinister nocturne. The narrator returns in her memory to a small town in France she knew when she was turning eighteen. She describes a decaying castle in which she resided after being exiled from Paris because of an abortion that shocked her family. Her descriptions are disturbing: "The elegance of that room always made me uneasy. Did I notice it at first? Or was it only later that I became aware of the dark marks of the paintings no longer hanging on the walls, of the faint stains around the edges of the silk curtains, a dimness that suggested something slightly soiled?" And when she meets the occupants of the castle—Madame and Monsieur, Luis and Dubres, the servants—she is unsure about them, their subtly orchestrated remarks and movements. She remarks: "Madame sighed again and said youth lasted too short a time, and one should enjoy every moment of it. Somehow it sounded almost a threat, and I felt the same sense of unease I had earlier. An expectant silence hung in the big half-empty room. All we could hear was the sob of water beneath the house." The omens she senses will bear fruit later when she finds out the significance of the water and the obscure alliance of unspoken words and polite conversation. Clearly, we are caught in some elaborate, perverse ritual. The young woman slowly understands that she is a victim, a sacrificial lamb who will be exploited by all the occupants of the castle. And she will also grasp the fact that she wants to be violated, and at the same time to violate the others. These perverse pleasures echo events that occurred in 1942 when children hid in the castle to escape Nazi occupation. Exile, betrayal, the loss of innocence—these elements become more pronounced as the novel plays with revelation and concealment. *Children of Pithiviers* is an unforgettable performance of dread and pleasure—a stunning experience. [Irving Malin]

Dimitri Anastasopoulos. *A Larger Sense of Harvey*. Mammoth, 2001. 413 pp. Paper: $18.00.

A Larger Sense of Harvey is a challenging, multilayered—structurally and thematically—first novel. The work is a book of parts: selections from journals and documents amassed from a lifetime's work by Harvey Rocketsch, a seemingly insignificant journalist from Russia who suddenly finds himself in a research project of international intrigue. From his earliest days, Harvey has lived most fully in his imagination and in the language he manipulates to express it. His connection with the empirical is tenuous, though he lives by an aesthetic of inclusiveness—whatever is felt, seen, experienced (down to the most minute ticks or bodily functions), or thought— that defines his identity and his prose. He is commissioned to work on *langoo-adj*, a new age Esperanto, designed to cut the imprecision, overabstraction, and profligacy of words that engender unclean reasoning. During this work he falls into a love triangle with Bete, coordinator of the project, and Ambrose, his translator, mentor, and alter ego. The densely coiled relationship between the two men forms the center of the novel and its narrative concerns with identity and language as a medium of expression. À la Kinbote in Nabokov's *Pale Fire,* Ambrose has so thoroughly interposed himself between Harvey and the reader that one is never sure of the authorship of any passage, and the novel even begins with a preface acknowledging the indecipherability of authorial identity. The novel is as postmodern as it sounds, a deconstructive delight (or nightmare), with each incident undone by its parallel or opposite. For this reason the novel is a bit too clever. Its very aesthetic of inclusiveness leads to sections that are simply diffuse and poorly focused. There is no question that Anastasopoulos is a talented writer who has read widely and possesses a fertile imagination; it will be interesting to see where his career takes him. [David Madden]

Josef Škvorecký. *Two Murders in My Double Life*. Farrar, Straus & Giroux, 2001. 175 pp. $22.00.

Josef Škvorecký's new novel is playful in form, pitting two story lines against each other to create effects at once tragic and comic, disturbing and absurd. As the novel opens the reader is introduced to the first story line: a murder mystery set against the backdrop of academic politics and pettiness at the fictional Evandale College, where the narrator, a Czech exile, teaches classes in detective-fiction writing. Dorothy Sayers, a student in the narrator's class and a member of the campus police force, leads an investigation into the death of Raymond Hammett, a handsome womanizer whose wife teaches mathematics at Evandale. During tutorial sessions with Sayers, the narrator pumps her for information about the murder and offers his advice (using the tenets of good detective writing as a guide) for how to proceed with the investigation. Gradually he pieces together a theory of Hammett's unfortunate demise, involving campus sweetheart Candace Quentin, a groundbreaking mathematical theory, and a colleague's quest for academic fame and fortune. But the foundation of this novel is the second and more sober story line: a murder in the form of a character assassination that transforms this detective story into a work of serious literary fiction. The story here revolves around the narrator's wife Sidonia and "the List" published by the Czech magazine *Kill Kommunism!,* which accuses her of providing information to the communist secret police. Sidonia is devastated by the accusation, and she enters a downward spiral of alcoholism and depression as she fights to clear her name. By juxtaposing the events at Evandale with the more serious consequences of Sidonia's plight, Škvorecký emphasizes the difference between the death of a body and the more serious consequences of the murder of a soul. *Two Murders in My Double Life* is witty and compelling to the end, a very smart, funny, and utterly engrossing book. [Christy Post]

Javier Marías. *Dark Back of Time*. New Directions, 2001. 336 pp. $26.95.

When explaining "dark back" near the end of the novel, the narrator—a character named Javier Marías—explains that it is "the kind of time that has not existed, the time that awaits us and also the time that does not await us and therefore does not happen, or happens only in a sphere that isn't precisely temporal, a sphere in which writing, or perhaps only fiction, may—who knows—be found." While this exposition informs the strategy of Javier Marías's superb novel, its success stems from the effective interweaving of compelling narrative threads. The novel begins with the circumstances surrounding the reception of Marías's earlier novel, *All Souls*. The narrator finds it impossible to convince former colleagues, acquaintances, and students that the novel is fictional; they believe the work to be a roman à clef. In order to establish control, the narrator proceeds by digression, first exploring the death of Wilfred Ewart, an English novelist who was shot through the eye by an errant New Year's Eve celebratory bullet in Mexico City. The seed for the Ewart digression comes from another Marías novel, *Tomorrow in the Battle Think on Me*, where he examines the circumstances surrounding a peculiar death. The final substantive digression deals with the small Caribbean island nation Redodna, where the minor poet John Gawsworth is the island's second leader. Javier Marías, it turns out, is the island's fourth and current leader, as the regime is passed by way of appointment rather than heredity. Within this digression, there is also an inquiry after Oloff de Wet. Oloff is not only the man who made Gawsworth's death mask; he is also an intriguing figure in Spanish folklore, as he made an appeal to Franco on behalf of a rogue group hoping to gain support for a guerrilla campaign against the Russians in the Carpathians. The strength of *Dark Back of Time* rests with the successful integration of the digressions. Javier Marías, a prolific writer whose works have been widely translated, rightly deserves the acclaim he is receiving. [Alan Tinkler]

José Manuel Prieto. *Nocturnal Butterflies of the Russian Empire*. Trans. Thomas and Carol Christensen. Grove, 2000. 322 pp. $24.00.

Prieto tells the hidden story of the cold war's frantic swan song. Like Nabokov in *Sebastian Knight*, he gives us a V. and a quest; like Pynchon, he searches amid literary burrowings and apocalyptic agitation. Going from Cuba to Novosibirsk in 1986, the author can report on what, for American readers, is the other side of history. Prieto renders the incongruous into the irresistible. The narrator wanders through ruins, looking for his lost love and the shards of his own consciousness. The woman is no longer there, and when she was there she was clouded by Leilah, a third term, a specter of the night. The narrator scans people who have spent whole lives under tyranny, searching for signs of hope. His sole activity is "crossing the membranes of states (borders), taking advantage of the different values between one cell (nation) and another." Anchored in the mournful Crimean seaside palace of Livadia, the narrator traverses a de Chirico dreamscape. And whence the butterflies? They are rarities made commodities, objects of mass desire for their obscure aura. The narrator, a foundling of the new world, scavenges among the detritus of the old. Competently translated by Thomas and Carol Christensen, Prieto's prose keeps us interested even as it keeps us wondering. Quests take place across landscapes, but what happens when the political contours of the landscape shift so drastically? And how does the receding object of the quest, in her alluring elusiveness, affect the perceiver's "lines of transmission"? Post-Soviet, yet more than omni-American, Prieto's butterflies bypass usually traveled cultural itineraries and flutter their way toward a new route for globalization. [Nicholas Birns]

Harry Mulisch. *The Procedure*. Trans. Paul Vincent. Viking, 2001. $24.95.

Harry Mulisch, a Dutch writer of considerable international stature, perennially shortlisted for the Nobel, writes old-fashioned novels of ideas or, more specifically, novels about characters unafraid to tangle with ideas. Although that genre may suggest plotless contrivances where characters-qua-philosophical positions engage in artificial debates, Mulisch—like Mann and Bellow and, more recently, DeLillo and Richard Powers—deploys articulate characters who engage in the exhilarating endeavor to think through Big Questions within a mystifying universe. In *The Procedure* Mulisch interrogates the act of creation, braiding theology, biology, and literature. He focuses on the Jewish tradition of the golem, vividly recounting the disastrous consequences of such an artifact conjured by a sixteenth-century Czech rabbi; explores the (extra)ordinary intricacy of biological conception itself; and throughout considers the literary process, an author engendering characters out of letters. *The Procedure* largely centers on Victor Werker, a chemist who has created from inorganic stuff a crystal that reproduces, in essence, life itself. Mulisch downplays the science to dramatize the human implications of such a discovery. Victor is a character, not a philosophical position. He is haunted by his past. We share heartrending letters he posts to his estranged wife, letters addressed to a stillborn daughter whose death testifies to the intrusion of accident into the imperfect process of creation. *The Procedure* is a powerful inquiry into the implications of conception, an intricately constructed speculation that audaciously links Adam and Eve, Pygmalion and Frankenstein, and Crick and Watson. But as with the finest novels of ideas, what lingers here are not the Big Questions posed about life but rather the characters, proud and passionate, who here pose them. [Joseph Dewey]

Assia Djebar. *So Vast the Prison*. Trans. Betsy Wing. Seven Stories, 2001. 363 pp. Paper: $16.95.

The fragmented narrative of *So Vast the Prison* offers spaces of light—views between the bars, the breaks between segments. Ostensibly, Isma, called "the name," narrates the novel, which relates her autobiography, her family history—especially the women's side—and Algerian/Islamic history. The narration begins with the platonic love Isma has for a young journalist, "the Beloved." This story serves as the seed for the first narrative—Isma's repudiation by/of her husband, who attempts to blind her by beating her badly with a broken whiskey bottle, and her life to follow—and also as the seed for the imagery, repetitive occurrences, parallels in character and action in the rest of the novel. The magic of the book presents itself first in the recollection of "the Beloved," who is raised from the ruins of the past ten years after the brief summer of acquaintance. Then family history, moments of autobiography, and stages of the historical past rise into sharp focus in passages that detail the most minute factual matter yet fix nothing fast. The importance of movement, especially for the women of the family but also out of the Berber tradition, reflects the desire for and movement toward "freedom," though, as the deaths of Isma's friends at home while she lives in France suggest, the prison—of consciousness, of memory—*is* vast. Ms. Djebar has a formidable intellect, a sure aesthetic sense, and a complex emotional involvement with the present life and history of Algeria. Reverberations of Baudelaire, references to *Don Quixote,* Alain-Fournier, Rivière, Camus, only hint at the fertile depths beneath this work. I would recommend it to anyone with an interest in experimental, cinematic fiction. [Richard Murphy]

Ariel Dorfman. *Blake's Therapy*. Seven Stories, 2001. 175 pp. $21.95.

Most of Ariel Dorfman's work to date has addressed the detrimental effects of dictatorships upon the body and mind (*Hard Rain, Konfidenz, Death and the Maiden*), but in his newest novel, he leaves Latin American politics behind to explore the corruptive power of corporate culture. The premise of *Blake's Therapy* is simple enough: Graham Blake, the marketing mastermind behind Clean Earth Inc., is suffering from chronic insomnia, forcing him to check into a radical psychological institute designed to treat wealthy businessmen. Blake's therapy resembles an insane "reality TV" show—he is assigned a family that he can monitor twenty-four hours a day. Beyond that, he is given a godlike opportunity to change their lives forever, because the true "therapy" occurs when all of his whims (both good and bad) are enacted on the family. Blake immediately becomes obsessed with one member of the family, Roxanna, a young Latino girl, and orchestrates a string of misfortunes with the hope of winning her love after the treatment is completed. Then Blake finds out that the family is actually a set of actors and actresses, and the metaphorical rug is yanked out from under both him and the reader, transforming the very structure of the book into a playful (and deceptive) exploration of truth and falsity. The post-therapeutic Graham Blake is no saner than the man who entered therapy; he becomes more and more obsessed with retaining control of his life, friends, and business, primarily by videotaping all of his acquaintances and spending sleepless nights pouring over their interactions. After discovering that Roxanna was modeled after a real worker at one of his factories, Blake grows increasingly paranoid that someone may be behind the scenes, controlling his life. Both Blake and the reader are drawn into a complex quest to uncover what is real, what is a simulacrum, and who's truly calling the shots. Although the plot of this novel is not as compelling as some of Dorfman's earlier works, the mastery with which he manages to dupe the reader time and again gives rise to his main concern—the nature of narrative and its manifold possibilities. The games that he plays with both the style and framing of his story line recall the writings of Borges and Cortázar, solidifying Dorfman's place within the grand tradition of experimental Latin American novelists. [Chad W. Post]

Orhan Pamuk. *My Name Is Red*. Trans. Erdağ Göknar. Knopf, 2001. 413 pp. $25.95.

Colors figure prominently in this historical mystery, set in sixteenth-century Istanbul, which takes us into the lives of a handful of miniaturist painters, one of whom is murdered by a fellow artist in the first chapter, narrated by the corpse itself. "Try to discover who I am from my choice of words and colors," we are told toward the opening of the novel in a chapter entitled "I Will Be Called a Murderer." The ensuing narrative, in a manner similar to Umberto Eco's *The Name of the Rose,* gradually pushes toward a resolution of the mystery while at the same time giving us a flavor of life in the days of Sultan Murat III and introducing us to the rich traditions of miniaturist painting. At stake is that very way of life. The murders (yes, there is more than one) seem to be motivated by wishes to adhere strictly to Muslim prohibitions on representational art and stave off the corrupting Western influences of Venetian portrait painting that elevate the individual at the expense of more selfless, collective endeavors. The themes of Pamuk's novel are highly relevant for a Turkey that even today is caught in the crosswinds of the competing values of West and East. Near the end of the novel a mob enflamed by the words of Preacher Nusret Hoja of Erzurum attacks a coffeehouse, killing a storyteller who they have determined is corrupting morals and overstepping the bounds of religion. Pamuk, however, is not at all didactic; rather, he simply displays the cultural dynamics at work. As in Faulkner's *As I Lay Dying,* the story's baton is handed from one character to another and moves through time, producing a clever narrative scheme we only wholly grasp on the last page. [Allen Hibbard]

Han Ong. *Fixer Chao.* Farrar, Straus & Giroux, 2001. 377 pp. $25.00.

Playwright Han Ong's first novel tells the story of two twenty-first-century confidence men: Shem C., a frustrated writer bent on scaling Manhattan society or, failing that, bringing the rarefied bunch, cocktail-party chatterers crashing down to his level, and William Narciso Paulinha, a Filipino street hustler who makes ends meet doing data entry and giving blow jobs in bathroom stalls. Shem devises a plan: Paulinha studies some Feng Shui books, assumes the name Master Chao, and pretends expertise in the ancient Chinese art of placing furniture in ways to guarantee a healthy life and obscene wealth. The two work the uptown crowd, taking full advantage of everyone's eagerness to be mystified by anything Asian. They charge a hefty sum for twenty-minute consultations, all the while exploiting their clients' anxieties over their spiritually bereft lives and the latest trend passing them by. Ong's novel is broadly satiric and filled with occasionally cutting observations on the upper class, high culture, and the hypocrisies of both. Sometimes the novel is too broad. At a bustling mixer, the characters are such standard types that it's hard to imagine even the most sensitive and easily bruised member of Manhattan society finding much difficulty laughing at their behavior. The novel becomes more complex when Master Chao decides that rather than take his clients' money and give them fake, casually invented advice on the placement of their beds, he'll take their money but endeavor to give them real advice. He'll try to help them; most of them anyway. Is he still a charlatan? When clients' lives improve, can he still be said to be cheating them? Ong's novel sufficiently muddies the distinctions between scammer and scammed, imposter and expert. His book becomes a brisk, glitter-studded catalog of the ways people deceive and are deceived, over and again. [Paul Maliszewski]

Sándor Márai. *Embers*. Trans. Carol Brown Janeway. Knopf, 2001. 224 pp. $21.00.

The General—scion of an old Hungarian family, the son of an Officer of the Guards who was the Emperor's friend—awaits his old friend Konrad, whom he has not seen for forty-one years, with profoundly mixed emotions. The first third of Sándor Márai's 1942 novel (the first of his fiction to be translated into English) recounts the General's anxious preparations for the arrival of his guest. Fortunately, his old nurse, Nini, will take care of all arrangements, as she so faithfully has attended the General since his birth. Yet even out on his estate in the Hungarian forest, at considerable remove from the world he assiduously has shunned since leaving the army, rumors of new carnage lately reach the General, as World War II begins to overwhelm Europe. When at length Konrad arrives, the General ushers him into the resplendently bedecked banquet room, unused since his wife Krisztina's death, then spends the rest of the book speaking to him across the table, re-creating the tragic theater of his waking dream of four decades—a series of events pivotal to their now being in this very room together. Gradually, in the General's urbane rendition of these painstakingly linked recollections, Márai, who died in San Diego at the age of eighty-nine, in exile from his native Hungary after having been driven out by the communists, fashions an acute edge to his perception of human nature and the modern world. In the General's elegantly precise, scrupulously detailed account of his own defining moments, the old man confronts with increasing tension the strong feelings that he has harbored for so long. Márai deftly fashions a parable of love, betrayal, and vengeance of great force and subtlety, compelling in its sheer, sustained narrative power. [Michael Pinker]

Oscar van den Boogaard. *Love's Death*. Trans. Ina Rilke. Farrar, Straus & Giroux, 2001. 152 pp. $20.00.

Boogaard's fifth novel (his first to be translated into English) is ultimately about loss: of life, family, love, and self. Spanning roughly fourteen years, *Love's Death* chronicles the story of Oda and Paul Klein, whose eight-year-old daughter, Vera, accidently drowns in the neighbors' pool. In the aftermath of the drowning, Paul leaves his wife to deal with her grief alone, as he takes a military post in Suriname. He returns seven years later to find a wife who has distanced herself from him and others. Soon after his return, the neighbors' house burns down, and a young girl—the same age as Vera would have been—emerges from the flames. Daisy, a fifteen-year-old from America who was staying with the neighbors, is taken in by Paul and Oda in a desperate attempt to re-create what they lost when Vera died. In the final section of the novel, Emil, a friend of Paul's and Oda's secret lover, speaks for the first time to reveal his involvement in both Paul and Oda's life and in the death of their daughter. Stylistically, *Love's Death* is astounding. Boogaard deftly stretches out time through acute attention to every detail, mirroring the attempts of the characters to keep ahold of something in the present. The narrative is told almost entirely in the present tense and at times with such sparseness, such directness, that the sense of loss permeating the text is truly experienced by the reader. In terms of plot, the majority of the book holds together well with a maintained sense of tension and grief. The final section, however, in which Emil speaks, feels almost too contrived (as if we couldn't guess from the previous sections what had happened) and moves us too far away from where our focus should be—on whether Paul and Oda will ever survive their multiple traumas. For its stylistic merits alone, though, more of Boogaard's work should find its way into English translation. [Jason D. Fichtel]

Yoel Hoffman. *The Heart Is Katmandu.* Trans. Peter Cole. New Directions, 2001. 144 pp. $22.95.

This is the fourth volume by Hoffman published in the last few years. It confirms that he is the most interesting and experimental novelist in Israel; and it also confirms that New Directions is still one of the most important, daring publishers in America. The plot is simple. Yehoahim, a thoughtful man separated from his first wife, falls in love with Batya, the mother of a mentally challenged infant. Both seem to have no need to converse; they are beyond words. However, the text assumes that even the most common relationships are more complex than we, or the characters, know. Thus the two characters think about their identities, their differences and similarities. Occasionally they speak to us or the author, and often the author speaks back. The distance between Batya and Yehoahim is symbolically patterned by spaces on the page itself. The text is divided into 237 frames and suggests that art cannot be linear. The imagery returns again and again to distances, connections, and attempts at connection. Language itself becomes problematic. For example, frame 140: "Take a word (Yehoahim says to himself). Take a word like son, thy son, thine only son, in that scene where Abraham drew the knife, like 'yes,' or like 'let there be,' or like 'Jehovah,' just so long as you don't make a mistake, for if you make a mistake creation will take everything back, as when one regrets a momentous act and reverts to no-thing. I can't afford to make a mistake, he thinks to himself, and, therefore, his lips mouth the only word that holds all of these worlds: Batya." Hoffman's wonderful book is both a love story and a meditation on the words *love* and *story*. It ends with this cryptic sentence: "Everything has its name, and the name has one as well." [Irving Malin]

Maureen Howard. *Big As Life: Three Tales of Spring*. Viking, 2001. 225 pp. $23.95.

Big As Life is the second book in Maureen Howard's projected tetralogy about the seasons, the first of which was 1998's *A Lover's Almanac*. *Big as Life* is composed of three novellas. Howard, like William Trevor, sometimes writes in a style that initially seems at the heart of convention. However, both she and Trevor possess a subtlety and a brilliance, an interest in the nature of narrative and narrative structure, which make their best work anything but traditional. In "Children with Matches" Howard begins with the meditations of an old man approaching death, then quickly moves to one of his descendants as she reflects in the old man's ruined house, hoping (and failing) to bring an element of fairy tale into her life. "The Magdalene" moves back and forth between two cousins—one cousin's narrative in first person, the other in third—covering the effect that their brief early relationship seems to have had on their lives as a whole. The final novella, "Big As Life" is divided into three largely unrelated parts that nonetheless inform one another and build to a larger whole. In the first, we see naturalist John James Audubon's wife Lucy abandoned while Audubon tries to forward his artistic concerns. The second depicts a mathematician's journeys back and forth between a harrowing summer workshop and his lover, a painter. The final short section presents an unnamed contemporary narrator's history of her relationship with the natural world. Combining elegant and cunning writing with a reconsideration of how stories can be pieced together, *Big As Life* is a strong text, with each novella having the impact of a larger novel. Howard is able to do three times in one book what it usually takes most writers an entire novel to accomplish not half so well. [Brian Evenson]

J. T. LeRoy. *The Heart Is Deceitful above All Things*. Bloomsbury, 2001. 247 pp. $23.95.

It's rare to be shocked, especially by a work of fiction, in an age of violent spectacle, when revolting images are as close as a few clicks of a remote or a mouse. J. T. LeRoy's collection of related stories is a tale of relentless torture from the point of view of an abused child who becomes a masochistic teenager. LeRoy writes with such honesty and authority about the subject that we have to believe him, even though these stories are so grotesque as to be unbelievable. They are desperate cries from darkest corners of the American landscape, painful howls from places that undoubtedly exist but seem the product of a madman's imagination. The two recurrent characters in this landscape are the narrator, Jeremiah, and his mother, Sarah, a shiftless, addicted prostitute whose maternal abuse is her only consistent quality. She torments her son to the point that he becomes completely passive. Even though Jeremiah is abused by almost everyone in the book, there is a sense of relief every time Sarah abandons him. What makes Jeremiah so unusual is that he genuinely loves his mother, though it is a desperate and irrational love, and this interplay of emotions adds considerable depth to the stories. With the shocking horror of Bret Easton Ellis and the penetrating gaze of Louise Erdrich, LeRoy succeeds in writing a book so gripping that it's difficult to put down, yet so disturbing that it is equally difficult to keep reading. The most successful stories deal with situations just outside of conventional experience—a mother forcefully reclaiming her child from his foster parents or the lives of truck-stop prostitutes. The less convincing stories are more sensational, such as Sarah's descent into the insane belief that coal is going to take over the world. The dominant note of systematic and relentless abuse of a child growing into a profoundly damaged adult is what will stay with the reader. This theme is rendered so accurately and so poignantly that it has the power to unsettle, if not destroy, complacency. [D. Quentin Miller]

Cristina Peri Rossi. *The Museum of Useless Efforts*. Univ. of Nebraska Press, 2001. 159 pp. Paper: $15.00.

The museum in Peri Rossi's title story is a library of thick, encyclopedic volumes cataloging by year thousands of "useless efforts." The efforts are movingly ordinary, not insane inventions undertaken by madmen, but a man pursuing an unrequited love for twenty years or children at the beach digging holes that are then washed away by the ocean. But whether the scopes of these useless efforts are large or small, it becomes clear that what is so powerful about them is that they are stories. In this way Peri Rossi aligns herself, and by extension the reader, alongside what the narrator of another story describes as those "melancholy activities certain to fail . . . which to me seemed like the only worthwhile ones." For Peri Rossi that worth is centered in language—in fact many of the stories take as their conceits language itself, usually figures of speech such as "Time Heals All Wounds," "Deaf as a Doorknob," or "Between a Rock and a Hard Place." Peri Rossi's technique is to literalize these clichés, revealing their metaphorical and lyrical potential as she pushes them to wonderful, dream-logical conclusions. If the mood of this book is one of Sisyphean futility, the stories themselves locate the beauty within that futile motion. [T. J. Gerlach]

Benjamin Anastas. *The Faithful Narrative of a Pastor's Disappearance*. Farrar, Straus & Giroux, 2001. 277 pp. $24.00.

Benjamin Anastas's first novel, *An Underachiever's Diary,* is a sweet, sad, hilarious, and perversely triumphant "memoir," written from the single point of view of its hapless narrator. *The Faithful Narrative of a Pastor's Disappearance,* Anastas's second novel, is more complex, as Anastas handles with consummate skill half-a-dozen points of view. The characters are a congregation of liberal, suburban New England parishioners—among them Margaret Howard, formidable realtor and mother of the local drug dealer, and Artemesia Angelis, an alarmingly pious housewife—and their spiritual leader, a young black pastor named Thomas Mosher. Also present are faithless souls tied to the congregants by kinship. When the pastor disappears without a trace, the never very orderly world of the parish is thrown into a crisis. Questions multiply. Did Bethany Caruso—unhappily married to a man who, although banished from her bed, loves her to distraction, mother of two small children, functioning depressive when on Zoloft— have an affair with the mysteriously absent pastor? Did Mosher's final sermon, "The Shapes of Love" (God is an infinite sphere whose center is everywhere and circumference nowhere), have something to do with his disappearance? Are the parishioners right in fearing that their inability to make their pastor feel welcome is partly responsible? Is the voracious hunger for someone to love and for an end to loneliness to blame? Only one thing is certain: God moves in mysterious ways. If he exists, that is. Anastas's novel is an unerring and very funny satire on life and mores in modern suburbia, a cautionary tale showing how unhappiness can seduce even the most upright heart, and an investigation of the blind search for a spirit that animates the universe. It is also a book of deep affection, affection for the good ship *Faith* and the good ship *World*—and for all who sail in them. [Evelin Sullivan]

Mohammed Dib. *The Savage Night.* Trans. C. Dickson. Univ. of Nebraska Press, 2001. 191 pp. Paper: $20.00.

Mohammed Dib's collection of thirteen stories vividly exemplifies the author's haunting narrative style. A prominent Algerian literary figure who has written for nearly fifty years from exile in France, Dib is one of the founding fathers of North African literature. He wields his pen to evoke memories of the Algerian war of liberation from France (1954-1962) as well as the aftermath of failed postcolonial, sociocultural, and political endeavors. The stories portrayed in *The Savage Night* take on global proportions, encompassing the austere life of war-torn Sarajevo as well as human suffering in Latin America. The universal message connecting these stories is that human brutality can reign where we least expect it. Dib does not cast stones, but sets his tales in front of his readers, forcing us to reflect on the tides of historical, cultural, and political events. From the bomb-planting Algerian brother and sister of the title story, who leave death and destruction in their wake, to the bullet that takes the life of a young burglar shot by a man defending his property in "A Game of Dice," Mohammed Dib coerces us to confront the persistence of senseless violence. His voice calls out to those caught up in the brutality of life—demonstrating that for millions of people from varying backgrounds, races, and nationalities, violence is a part of their daily routines. Dib pleads with us to turn our attention to the shameful indifference that often is the principal reason violence endures, generation after generation. [Valerie Orlando]

Zinovy Zinik. *Mind the Doors: Long Short Stories.* Trans. and adapted by Bernard Meares, Andrew Bromfield, and the author. Context, 2001. 192 pp. $21.95.

Zinovy Zinik's zanily comic portraits of Russian exiles who share a mordant sensitivity to cultural differences line this latest offering. The shock of displacement appears in strange guises, which the Russians may seldom overcome, for they cannot escape certain mocking reverberations of the Soviet past, echoes just beyond earshot, portending an ambiguous future. "A Pickled Nose" recounts the colorful tale of a louche artist's prize protuberant organ, which attains notoriety at tasks quite beyond the ken of your average hooter, according to the testimony of one London pub anecdotalist. In "No Cause for Alarm," a linguist plagued by unaccountable stomach rumbling repeatedly sets off London security alarms hither and yon, to his discomfort and frequent peril. "Double Act in Soho" transforms a sad, middle-aged Russian's desire for a beautiful young woman into a quest through Soho porn shops for an American video, only just avoiding falling victim to the shop-clerks' mysterious purpose. In "The Notification," a curiously destitute émigré provides a hallucinatory account of his seduction by a protean Jerusalem enchantress, for whom he writes letters to relatives of fellow exiles, keeping the fiction of their abiding concern alive. Finally, the title story depicts how a subway car becomes a trap for another émigré returning to Moscow post-*Glasnost,* who achieves minor celebrity trying to avoid embarrassment before an audience whose feeling for his plight cannot be predicted. Whether eluding a threatening gang of shop clerks or pinioned by a posh raincoat in a subway door, Zinik's hapless Pierrots misread the folly of their pursuits until they are involved past recovery. His fun at their expense is merciless. Unwitting marionettes in search of an evanescent liberty, always out of their depth, Zinik's doomed Russians present the comic potential of the artless émigré who never quite escapes his past. [Michael Pinker]

Tom Spanbauer. *In the City of Shy Hunters.* Grove, 2001. 504 pp. $26.00.

William Parker (aka William of Heaven) comes to New York (the Wolf Swamp) to find his lover/blood brother Charlie 2Moons (Fred) who has disappeared from the MFA program at Columbia University. Will appears in the Lower East Side in 1984 and immediately finds himself at the center of the performance art scene and in the darkest days of the AIDS epidemic. He is befriended by Rose (Argwings Khodek), a black drag actor of legendary fame in Alphabet City; by Fiona Yet (Muffy MacIlvain, Susan Strong), a child of an adoring, wealthy, liberal family; and by True Shot (Peter Morales), a handsome Latino who has started his own moving business, Spirit Schleppers, out of his Dodge van. By the time the novel ends, Will's closest friends are either dead, driven insane, or exiled from Wolf Swamp. Set during the Reagan years, this may be the first novel of the Bush II regime, for it blasts a compassionate conservativism that proved itself callous, mean-spirited, and smugly self-aggrandizing. It portrays a social hierarchy that is downright hostile to the dispossessed, the homeless, the different, the sick and the spiritually hungry—in short, all the "shy hunters" who are the true inhabitants of the city. As Ruby tells Will, the world is divided between Fools and Pharisees. If the politics are a bit simple, the lines between Them and Us a bit too easily drawn, *In the City of Shy Hunters* nevertheless speaks with a deep-throated passion for the downtrodden that is chilling, moving, and far too rare these days. [David Bergman]

Marie Bronsard. *The Hermitage*. Trans. Sonia Alland with the author. Northwestern Univ. Press, 2001. 69 pp. Paper: $14.95.

She writes this letter to him through the night. She has been writing to him ever since he left, ten years before. Those letters she has burned. This, she says, will be the final letter. They could have loved each other, but neither then had the capacity. Something came between them. Another man captured his attentions: "He had become necessary to you, like another self, spontaneous, immediate." She relives the memories of that experience through the night, memories of the other man's intensity, hostility, anger. Why did he leave? We wonder. Where is he now? Dead, we presume. He will always be with her. Dawn breaks, reminding her of the morning of his departure. Yet with the dawn also comes a calm, a possibility for regeneration. The form of the letter creates a hermetically sealed space determined by the intimacy between writer and addressee. Voyeurs, we read a letter addressed to someone else and peer into the innermost chambers of the relationship. Since so much is shared between the two, there is little need for specificity or elaboration. The narrative is elliptical. There are holes and gaps we, as readers, will never be able to fill in. Somewhat ironically, this most intimate means of expression opens up into a universal space. The prose is sparse and lyrical; the tone is that of mourning. The weight of the past, the profound sense of loss, is felt in the present, the time of writing: "Why write you this, you who cannot read what I write? Why do I still make use of you?" To get it all out. To give experience shape and meaning. To purge the pain. To break through. This letter is a scab created to cover the wound and allow it to heal. It is a crypt. It is also a beautiful gift. [Allen Hibbard]

Federigo Tozzi. *Love in Vain: Selected Stories*. Trans. and intro. Minna Proctor. New Directions, 2001. 164 pp. Paper: $14.95.

Tozzi's name won't be found heading many encyclopedia articles, but he was by all accounts a prolific and significant figure in premodern Italian literature. Although he didn't survive into his forties, his relatively few years of authorial productivity resulted in five novels and over one hundred short stories, among other works of poetry and drama. Of these considerable efforts, only the twenty tales in this volume are readily available in English. They range in date of composition from 1910 through 1919, and the highlight of the collection is the opportunity to trace Tozzi's growing facility with the story form. The early stories are barely more than vignettes, but the later ones show an increasing degree of sophistication, employing varying narrative techniques and more involved plots to explore a consistent thematic preoccupation: the confused psychology of semirural characters. In Tozzi's world, emotions swirl implacably, and motives are barely more intelligible to the reader than they are to the protagonists. Typically, in "First Love," Giacomo is "dizzy with youthful ecstasy" for Emilia but can't find words or even actions to express himself. Her kindly replies to his vague worries are met only with thoughts: "*You? I'm ashamed of you. I don't like you. I don't believe you.*" Here, as in every story, a character experiences conflicting impulses in a single moment. In this example, Tozzi yokes disparate emotions together with the abruptness of a clumsy lover, but with time, he learns to interlace them with an almost Chekhovian delicacy. [James Crossley]

Caren Gussoff. *Homecoming*. Serpent's Tail, 2000. 154 pp. Paper: $14.00.

At the thematic core of this complex, intriguing, multilayered work is the notion that observation is possession. What the first-person narrator, Katey, is looking for is an understanding of her murdered junkie sister Reese, a girl who "grew to hate touch, to be looked at at all, but always . . . watched." Clearly, the alignment here is of observation with power: the seer possesses the image. To underscore this, Gussoff pays repeated attention to photography, especially in descriptions of photographs of Reese and Katey (which Katey has stolen). Repetition itself becomes thematically important in the novel, as Katey repeats Reese's bad habits and overdoses on Valium while searching for her understanding of Reese. Katey loops through her mental tapes in order to get up the nerve to tell her family that Reese is dead. Curiously, saying the words is not what ultimately bothers Katey—it is how she'll *look* when she says them, whether she will be seen as sad enough. The sisters' preference for the visual is juxtaposed with the parental home, where no one really sees anyone clearly: the characters are blurry-eyed with drink or drugs and spend much of the time in separate rooms, yelling back and forth. The mother's philosophy, though, echoes Katey's: "If you cannot see, cannot hear, if it is not said, it doesn't exist." Katey is looking for Reese in order to possess her forever. However, even seeing and identifying Reese's body for the police cannot allow her this possession. Reese is gone and all Katey finds are shadows (another recurring motif), and "shadows can take on different shapes." This motif is reminiscent of Joyce's "The Dead," but in this psychologically complex debut novel, a novel more about impression than substance, shadows dwell in a darkened world where they are not so easily noticed. [Eckhard Gerdes]

Konstantin Vaginov. *The Works and Days of Svistonov*. Creative Arts, 2001. 161 pp. Paper: $14.95.

Originally written in 1929 and here translated into English for the first time, Vaginov's novel follows Andrey Svistonov, a fictional writer, as he mixes with Bolshevisk-era literary circles, attending the writers' union, parties, and readings. This mixing comprises Svistonov's research for a sprawling, many-charactered novel that encompasses all of life as it's experienced, or at least overheard. One moment Svistonov's wife is reading him newspaper clippings. The next moment, he's hastily transferring and lightly transforming the news into his novel. Did someone just quote Pushkin at that party? One of Svistonov's characters will surely repeat it moments later. In the manner of Pirandello, Svistonov's works and days could be summed up as one author in search of a novel. Like Nabokov, Vaginov was born in St. Petersburg in 1899. Unlike Nabokov, Vaginov remained in Russia, where he was conscripted into the Red Army, served at the Polish front, and returned to Petrograd, his renamed hometown. Where Nabokov is a stylist, complex and unabashedly lyrical, Vaginov, writing under considerable political pressure, conceals his complexity—his subtle parody and satire, his barbs and dismay for his present day—beneath an innocuous, almost unremarkable surface. What both these sons of St. Petersburg share is a lifelong, painful attachment to the past and its partial recovery through their imaginations. Vaginov never read Nabokov's suggestion that nostalgia is an insane companion, but he probably wouldn't have disagreed. His Svistonov is not merely desperate for characters, plot, and pages, he's racing to capture the people, places, and objects of a world disappearing around him. Svistonov doesn't enter a room without inspecting the books on the shelves, and like the conservator of a vanishing culture and heritage, he records their titles, details of their binding, and briefly appraises their content. Bakhtin was an admirer of Vaginov and his acts of literary preservation; now the publisher has preserved his work for us. [Paul Maliszewski]

Ludmila Ulitskaya. *The Funeral Party*. Trans. Cathy Porter. Schocken, 2001. 160 pp. $18.95.

In this novel, her first in English, Ulitskaya chronicles events surrounding the death of Alik, a Russian artist living in exile in New York, with exquisite irony and tenderness. His wives' and lovers' plaintive history of concern for him and themselves manifests the sensibility of a Russian genius whose mere presence is an occasion for happiness. The diverse yet congenial company of friends and neighbors crowding Alik's painting-strewn rooms during his last illness further suggest his variety and charm. And if dealers won't admit it while he's alive, Alik has created something indefinable, a perspective uniquely his own. Unaffectedly gifted and charismatic, Alik is also charmed: he brings laughter, sincerity, reconciliation. He cannot help himself; it is his nature. This clever, red-haired émigré is forgiven, doted-on, lovingly attended at his deathbed; none of the score of well-wishers arriving at his flat ever seems to leave. Then, as the shenanigans of Gorbachev and Yeltsin abruptly herald change for Russia, attention shifts to the television. Alik behaves better by fading faster. Cares and worries wash over him, who rests at peace in his dreams. As his world dims, Alik lives in memories, times past. When wife Nina wants to bring a priest, Alik responds by also demanding a rabbi. As a messenger of joy and savoir faire, Alik is nonpareil, for who else can say "life's excellent for me wherever I am" and mean it? Some loved ones may pine, but even that will end. The Russia of suffering is not for Alik, who is nonetheless wise. Ulitskaya's touching portrayal of Russian émigrés coming to grips with change transforms Alik's obsequies into liberation. For while Alik's magic "had built his Russia around him," when his dance of death ceases, his flock can conceive of anything. [Michael Pinker]

Ana Menéndez. *In Cuba I Was a German Shepherd.* Grove, 2001. 229 pp. $23.00.

This collection of short stories vividly captures the intense emotions experienced by Cubans, Americans, and all those caught in between during the long years since Fidel Castro's assumption of power in 1959. What was once thought to be a temporary political and economic situation in Cuba has evolved into heartbreaking tests of loyalty and faith, which Menéndez clearly shows will have no discernable resolution with Castro's passing. Most of her characters once belonged to Cuba's pre-Revolutionary elite and have now become the nearly invisible inhabitants of Miami's Little Havana. In the title story, a distinguished gentleman by the name of Máximo recalls his flight from Cuba two years after Castro took power and his belief that he and his wife would return with their children after only a few years. This is an unrealized dream, and Máximo is now old and widowed, with his grown children scattered across the country. In another story, a woman awaits news of her husband's arrival in Miami—a man she believes she married only to allow him entry into America. When she receives word of his unexpected departure from Havana on a raft, she must face not only the possibility of his death at sea but also reassess the powerful emotions concerning her long unseen husband. Stylistically, Menéndez's stories range between realistic, linear narrative and an unnerving magical realism; yet in each she masterfully re-creates characters imbued with a sense of pride, dignity, and family cherished by Cubans regardless of what city they call home. With Castro's hold on Cuba coming to what has seemed for many to be a nearly endless close, Menéndez's work highlights what it means to have a shared heritage and history and—for far too many—to have endured them for so long in the solitude of silence and memory. [Anne Foltz]

Haruki Murakami. *Sputnik Sweetheart*. Knopf, 2001. 210 pp. $23.00.

Sputnik Sweetheart, Haruki Murakami's seventh novel to be translated into English, is less dense and less referenced to pop culture than much of his other work; nonetheless, it touches on Murakami's usual themes, most particularly the idea of parallel realities. It does so deftly and lightly, in a way that is entirely accessible. For that reason, it serves as a strong introduction to Murakami's work. At the heart of the novel is Sumire, a woman obsessed with the Beat writers, who wants to be a novelist, and with whom the narrator is in love. Sumire, however, loves Miu, a Korean woman who runs an import business. Miu herself seems incapable of love, at least physical love, ever since an unusual experience has left her thinking that her self has been split, half of it lost in a parallel world. As the novel progresses, Sumire goes on vacation with Miu, propositions her and then, when her advances aren't accepted, vanishes. She is perhaps simply fleeing from a difficult situation or perhaps has entered another world herself by an act of sheer will. As the narrator investigates what might have happened to her, he discovers documents that give insights into her character without ever quite pinning things down, leaving all loves unrequited. *Sputnik Sweetheart* is remarkable in its simplicity and its ability to present in distilled form a distinctly Murakamian narrative. Yet this strength might also be considered a weakness. Those who have read Murakami's other books might well see *Sputnik Sweetheart* as a concession: Murakami lite. True, it is more simple, more basic, but at the same time there is enough to recommend it that it should be admired for what it is rather than being faulted for not being another *Wind-Up Bird Chronicle*. Indeed, *Sputnik Sweetheart* provides a model for incorporating the postmodern and the pastoral. It is a lucid work of fiction that is more interesting and perhaps more complicated than it initially seems. [Brian Evenson]

Pedro Juan Gutierrez. *Dirty Havana Trilogy: A Novel in Stories.* Trans. Natasha Wimmer. Farrar, Straus & Giroux, 2001. 392 pp. $25.00.

Pedro Juan Gutierrez's *Dirty Havana Trilogy* is a three-part collection of interconnected stories about its narrator Pedro Juan and his friends, lovers, and neighbors in 1990s Cuba. It doesn't pretend to be a grand narrative or an articulation of life's ultimate purpose, and yet it is that paradoxical thing: a truthful novel. The use of that author's name as that of the narrator is an indication of the book's mix of fact and fiction. The novel is a countertext both to the lie that Castro's Cuban revolution produced a utopia and also to the belief that elegant words, lofty ideals, and admirable situations are the best that literature has to offer. Despite Cuba's admirable educational and health programs, there remains racism, poverty, and misuses of official power—all of which encourage cynicism and even animal responses. Pedro Juan's voice is earthy, honest, intelligent, and self-critical as it speaks of blood, breasts, butts, cocks, misery, money, poverty, rage, semen, sweat, tears, and work. Pedro Juan, a journalist fired for trying to tell the truth, is forced into other forms of work—such as selling lobsters, meat, and tin buckets, pimping, and various kinds of hard physical labor—and he sometimes finds himself in jail. He gets drunk often and has sex just as often with women of all ages, colors, shapes and sizes. His wife has abandoned him for an art career in America. His acquaintances are busy with adultery, prostitution, matricide, gambling, murder, disease, and quick ways to make a dollar (or peso). One reads of Cuba but knows this is a human reality in every age. This is a fun book full of sad facts. [Daniel Garret]

Francesca Duranti. *The House on Moon Lake.* Delphinium Books, 2000. 192 pp. Paper: $13.95; *Left-Handed Dreams.* Delphinium Books, 2000. 176 pp. $20.00.

Francesca Duranti's protagonists are intuitive investigators, struggling to make sense of a world that tantalizes and frustrates with elusive, fragmentary meaning. Their actions are not the stuff of typical detective fiction: Fabrizio Garrone translates novels for a living in *The House on Moon Lake,* while Martina Satriano, the narrator of *Left-Handed Dreams,* works hard to negotiate the gap between her Italian roots and her current life as an American academic. But in both works, Duranti manages to coax drama from those small, subtle moments when the surface of everyday life is unsettled by the mysterious contingencies that shape it. Fabrizio, the son of a wealthy family fallen on hard times, is obsessed with claiming a legacy that he feels he was denied. He seems to get his chance when he runs across an essay collection containing a reference to *Das Haus am Mondsee (The House on Moon Lake)*, a novel by Fritz Oberhofer. Excited by the prospect of translating a great work by an obscure Viennese author, Fabrizio makes plans to track down the original. While eventually successful at finding and translating the novel, he runs into problems when his publisher assigns him to write a short biography of Oberhofer. Lacking information on the last years of the author's life—when he was supposedly writing *Moon Lake*—Fabrizio decides to make up the rest. This decision will have ominous implications, not just for the translator himself, but also for the line we take for granted between fact and fiction. Duranti is refreshingly uninterested in making Fabrizio a sympathetic character. His arrogance and distrust are unsparingly portrayed. And yet, over the course of the narrative, Fabrizio's obsessions become our own. Even something as simple as getting on a train to Vienna becomes an existential ordeal, one link in a tenuous chain of order that threatens to undo itself at any moment: "He felt horror at the thought that he was setting off on an adventure in which he would continually be forced to ask for help from rude, hurried strangers."

Martina, in *Left-Handed Dreams,* is on a more intensely personal quest. She arrives in Italy too late to say goodbye to her dying mother and too late to get answers about something that only her mother would know: Was Martina born left-handed but then forced to use her right? The question informs the rest of the novel, during which she tries to track down the only other person who might provide an answer. Her account of her search—

which takes the form of a lecture she gives to her students at NYU—is often digressive, but engagingly so. We learn, among other things, of her research with "the Machine," a device that Martina uses to record and study her dreams; of her dinners with Sebastiano Cerignola, an Italian intellectual who tries to lure her back home with a job offer; and of her impressions of the United States as compared to her native Italy. What ties together these disparate narrative strands is the poignant sense of a person trying to come to terms with what her life has become. As with all good fiction, Duranti produces distinct characters whose inner conflicts become recognizable as our own. [Pedro Ponce]

Haydn Middleton. *Grimm's Last Fairytale*. St. Martin's, 2001. 249 pp. $23.95.

Weaving together strands of biography, history, and fairy tale, Middleton creates a novel rich in allusion and mystery. Ostensibly, the book is about the last days of Jacob Grimm, the older of the two German brothers who collected and published their country's tales and legends. Grimm is being escorted by his niece Auguste and manservant Kummel to many of the places he knew as a child. This journey is not only a literal one, but a trip to his past where he recalls his mother, his beloved brother Willi, and the sacrifices he made to support his family after his father died. One of the most intriguing aspects of the novel is the seamless way that it slips between Jacob's present and his past, which often seems more real to him. He worked hard throughout his life for Germany, hoping for unification of the country, and saw their collection of fairy tales, as well as a German dictionary that he worked on until the day he died, as ways to bring the country together in spirit. "Story, story, story" is a constant refrain throughout the book, referring to the brothers' demands for stories when they were young, and then the collecting of tales in their travels. Auguste, too, wants a story, for she suspects that her uncle Jacob is really her father because they seem to be alike in so many ways. Even the mysterious Kummel has a story to tell Jacob, one of the last that he will hear before he dies. Woven into the narrative is a fairy tale about a peasant boy who becomes a prince, wakes a sleeping beauty, unites a kingdom, and then discovers that his mother is an ogre. The tale operates on several levels, commenting on Grimm's private and public lives, as well as Germany itself. *Grimm's Last Fairytale* is an engaging novel with many stories to tell. [Sally E. Parry]

Kay Boyle. *Process*. Ed. and intro. Sandra Spanier. Univ. of Illinois Press, 2001. 139 pp. $24.95.

Originally written in 1924 and 1925 and lost when sent to potential publishers in New York, *Process* has finally been published in an excellent edition and with a superb introduction by Spanier. Boyle's novel, a classic bildungsroman, takes its place alongside the other important coming-of-age stories of her contemporaries. In *Process* we find a main character sharing many of the same qualities and conditions as those found in Joyce's *A Portrait of the Artist as a Young Man*, McAlmon's *Village*, Anderson's *Winesburg, Ohio*, Lewis's *Main Street*, or Hemingway's Nick Adams stories. Kerith Day, a young woman living in Cincinnati, is acutely aware of the limitations of her surroundings, and she longs to find something more. Unlike many of the stories mentioned above, Kerith receives the support of her mother in her quest to flee Cincinnati. She tells Kerith, "I don't want you wasted here with them and what they can offer you. I want you away from here. I don't want little things absorbing you. . . . " Instead of those "little things," Kerith puts her energies into art and politics and emerges as a highly intelligent, observant woman. Her relationship with Soupault, a young French student, eventually leads to her epiphany and to her escape from Ohio to France, where she can fully engage with art, politics, and self. This novel is important for what it shows about Boyle's writing and how she adopts and adapts modernist language and techniques. While most of Boyle's work remains out of print, *Process* is a novel that deserves and demands a place in the modernist canon. Hopefully this novel will spur other attempts to see Boyle's work remain in print, for hers is a voice we must hear along with those authors already well-established in American modernism. [Jason D. Fichtel]

Patrick McCabe. *Emerald Germs of Ireland.* Harper Collins, 2001. 306 pp. $25.00.

If Alfred Hitchcock's *Psycho* were transplanted to Ireland, scored with a combination of folk and pop melodies, and given a comic twist, you'd have *Emerald Germs of Ireland*, the latest novel by Patrick McCabe. The Norman Bates of the novel is named Pat McNab, "one of life's unfortunates," who kills his mother because, like the stereotypical Irish mother—cooing either infantilizations or ball-crushing ridicule and humiliation—she'll never leave her son alone, especially after he murders his tyrannical father. Once she's gone, he misses her terribly. Luckily for him, she keeps reappearing to give him her sage advice and encouragement. Having dispatched his parents, Pat has a go at the neighbors, who disappear as quickly as cabs in a thunderstorm. When he turns his home into a bed-and-breakfast, the guests find checkout time comes a bit earlier than they expected. Still, no one ever gets suspicious about these missing people or the increasing number of bushes Pat plants at night in his back garden. *Emerald Germs of Ireland* is a slightly stale pastiche, purchased at the postmodern pasticherie for, I hope, half price. From early on in the novel—right after he kills Mrs. Tubridy, Pat's nosey and lascivious elderly neighbor—I was waiting for him to show up in his mother's clothes for one of the murders, and sure enough, about fifty pages from the end, he bludgeons his former schoolmaster, Mr. Halpin, in "a wig both sad and lifeless" while carrying "a once vivacious bouquet of flowers long since faded to the land of sepia." Hannah Arendt spoke of the banality of evil in regard to that other mass murderer Adolph Eichmann; Patrick McCabe shows us the drabness of insanity, for even Pat McNab's hallucinations are painfully unoriginal. [David Bergman]

James D. Houston. *Snow Mountain Passage*. Knopf, 2001. 317 pp. $24.00.

James D. Houston is, unfortunately, something of a secret to many readers. Each of his novels and many of his works of nonfiction, in particular *Californians* (1982), have attentively explored the landscape and culture of the Golden State. In *Snow Mountain Passage,* Houston examines the incident, two years before the Gold Rush, which burned California into the consciousness of the nation: the nightmare of the Donner Party. The novel traces that ill-fated journey from Illinois to the Sierra Mountains in 1846, centering on the experiences of James Frazier Reed, one of the leaders of the expedition. During a dispute with a teamster in Nebraska, Reed kills the man, is banished from the wagon train, and is forced to wander ahead of the party, arriving in California months before the others. There he is dragged into California's war of independence from Mexico and must delay for months the rescue of his family. Punctuating the narrative are chapters that emerge from the recollections of Patty, Reed's younger daughter, who at eighty-two years old looks back on her life and assesses her experiences with a critical eye: "[My father] was a dreamer, as they all were then, dreaming and scheming, never content, and we were all drawn along in the wagon behind the dreamer, drawn along in the dusty wake." These chapters are marvels of narrative presumption and conveyed with rich lyricism and wry insight. *Snow Mountain Passage* is Houston's most compelling novel for its sense of narrative sweep and luminous prose. The temporal shifts between 1846 and 1920 and pointed assessments of Californiana are deftly rendered. The novel is a testament to the powers of human will and the enduring ties of family devotion. [Dave Madden]

Halldór Laxness. *The Fish Can Sing*. Trans. Magnus Magnusson. Harvill, 2000. 246 pp. Paper: $15.00.

Awarded the Nobel Prize in 1955 "for his vivid epic power which has renewed the great narrative art of Iceland," Halldór Laxness writes in an idiom far removed from the hectic sensibility fostered by Hollywood (where Laxness, incidentally, sought employment after the First World War). One hurdle a contemporary reader faces in reading Laxness is the slow paced, bardic style of telling; another is the sheer geographical and cultural remoteness of the early-twentieth-century Icelandic community evoked. Against the backdrop of the homogenization of world culture, a process whose early stages are powerfully recorded here, the rootedness of the local community that Laxness describes seems almost shockingly exotic. I found myself marveling at the headway made by globalization since the initial publication of *The Fish Can Sing* (1957; first English translation 1966). Globalization is in fact a key theme of the novel, in which the narrator-protagonist's boyhood in a fishing cottage is contrasted with the cosmopolitanism of an Icelandic singer who wins fame and wealth touring the world's greatest opera houses. The juxtaposition serves to affirm what Laxness, in his Nobel acceptance speech, called "the humble routine of everyday life." The ecological didacticism and stubborn parochialism of the novel, together with its complete lack of spectacular effects and sentimentality, highlight, by sheer contrast, the pervasiveness of the thrill-seeking culture that has since prevailed. Magnus Magnusson's translation is exemplary. The importance of Laxness is not in question; whether he still has an audience is another matter. [Philip Landon]

Sigrid Undset. *The Unknown Sigrid Undset: Jenny and Other Works*. Ed. with intro. Tim Page. Trans. Tiina Nunnally and Naomi Walford. Steerforth, 2001. 406 pp. $30.00.

As Tim Page points out in his introduction, every used bookstore in America has copies of Undset's massive medieval opus, *Kristin Lavransdatter*, sitting untouched on dusty shelves. Though her Nobel prize came to her in 1928, there's a certain mustiness about her reputation, as though she'd lived in the era she most famously recorded. This publication blows away most of the cobwebs and proves her vitality is undiminished today. *Jenny*, originally published in 1911, fills almost three-quarters of the book, describing the travels and troubles of a Norwegian painter in her late twenties. Her concerns—career, love, family—wouldn't be unfamiliar even to Bridget Jones, but infusing all of them is a moral seriousness, a desire to live a just and truthful life. Although Undset isn't as frank as she could have been in our post-Joycean age, she undoubtedly benefitted from working outside of America's puritanical tradition, and there's a refreshing lack of coyness in the way she deals with Jenny's sexuality. It's not the heroine's erotic life but her intellect that's most notable, however. She perceives and can expound upon every nuance of every situation in which she finds herself, although her life isn't thereby made any less somber. The remainder of the volume consists of two short stories and a selection of Undset's own letters that serve mostly to complement *Jenny*. That novel by itself is a worthy addition to the all-too-small chorus of early-twentieth-century women's voices. [James Crossley]

Sylvia Townsend Warner. *The Music at Long Verney: Twenty Stories.* Ed. Michael Steinman. Foreword by William Maxwell. Counterpoint, 2001. 192 pp. $24.00.

This volume gathers previously uncollected stories, which, with one exception, were all published in the *New Yorker* over the last three decades of Warner's life (1893-1978). Given that Warner brought out ten collections during her lifetime and several more appeared posthumously—not to mention her novels, poetry and biography—one might expect this to be an assortment of odds and ends, so it is all the more impressive to discover the overall coherence and quality of the volume. These stories have the touch of a very sure writer who deftly presents striking situations and distinctive characters, then resists imposing a morally didactic closure, leaving them in a state of resonant irresolution (the "inside-out feeling," Warner calls it in one story). No doubt in part due to their targeted venue, Warner's leftist politics, lesbianism, and feminism are muted. Yet throughout, what at first appear to be perfectly conventional situations and characters are cast in a subtly askew perspective. Two children whose family is moving into a new house explore the overgrown garden and unsuspectingly drive another boy from his paradise and into resentment, quietly suggesting conflicts of class and property. A traditionally minded antiques dealer observes a young woman stealing a locket from his shop, but approvingly recognizes this as an act of defiance against her priggish husband. The one early story, "Stay, Corydon, Thou Swain," is a hilarious sendup of male erotic fantasizing, and is the only piece here to employ elements of the fantastic, which Warner explores extensively elsewhere. These typically bourgeois settings and characters have a tendency to veer toward the unexpected and to make offbeat associations, rather like the manic conversation of the mother in "Maternal Devotion," whose conventional and perplexed interlocutor is an unwanted suitor who has been dumped on the mother by her daughter. These stories should augment Warner's growing reputation as an outstanding writer of short fiction. [Jeffrey Twitchell-Waas]

Kathryn Hume. *American Dream, American Nightmare: Fiction since 1960.* Univ. of Illinois Press, 2000. 359 pp. $39.95.

The purpose of Kathryn Hume's volume is to juxtapose a series of postwar American novels in order to examine how they engage in what she calls "conversations" over a number of national issues. Following a method similar to that of Frederick R. Karl's *American Fictions 1940-1980,* she groups her selected texts under theme headings like "immigration" or "mythical innocence." To take two examples from her eight main chapters, under "immigration" she discusses Russell Banks's *Continental Drift* to establish that immigration is a global phenomenon, next includes Maxine Hong Kingston and Amy Tan to examine the gender dimension, and finally turns to Octavia Butler's Xenogenesis trilogy. This chapter is typical of the whole study in containing lively and shrewd insights into an impressive range of material. Butler, however, was an awkward choice for immigration since her trilogy explores the nature of otherness. Hume places N. Scott Momaday and John Updike under "Seeking Spiritual Reality" in order to establish those writers' criticism of the failure of the American Dream. She argues interestingly that Updike's Rabbit is a personification of white lower-middle-class America, whereas William Kennedy has devised for himself the role of "chronicler of Albany." It is a pity that she did not say more on those novelists who construct microcosms of the U. S. or depict nationally representative figures. In fact, the major reference point throughout this study is the American Dream, with the result that Hume's survey shows how much energy the tradition of the jeremiad still possesses in the U. S. Her avoidance of generic, ethnic and other categories was done to highlight the "visibility of common concerns" in her chosen writers. Inevitably, formal and historical issues tend to get flattened out into questions of theme. Nevertheless, this survey demonstrates how American writers continue to interrogate national values and makes a valuable contribution toward mapping out the variety of postwar fiction. [David Seed]

Mary Ann Caws, ed. *Manifesto: A Century of Isms.* Univ. of Nebraska Press, 2001. 713 pp. $35.00.

These days, when an interviewer suggests that an artist is part of some genre or movement, the preferred response seems to be, "I'm not consciously trying to work that way. I create for myself. I think the category was created by critics." It's a response that's both modest and strident, and shows how we elevate the image of the artist as an individualist, even a recluse. A century ago, the impulse was the opposite. The modern artist would issue a proclamation of intent, often composed with colleagues, often before any actual art was created. These broadsides, both major and obscure, are collected in Mary Anne Caws's anthology. While some of the tracts included are measured and still insightful, the charm of this book lies in the unhinged wail of the peak years, when all of society was in artists' crosshairs. Example: the dairy, Kurt Schwitters proposed, is unnatural. The solution? Attach rubber tubes to freely grazing cows, run the conduits for miles like gas lines, thus allowing a city dweller to milk a personal cow on demand, udder by udder. Enthusiasm is the common sentiment. The zeal of the early modernists overshadows the nationalism and callousness that darkens some manifestos, and it proves the sincerity of their declarations. In 1921, the Baroness Else Von Freytag-Loringhoven essayed on Joyce, designating him the paragon of modern writing, then admitted, "I have not read 'Ulysses.' As a story it seems impossible . . . to James Joyce's style I am not yet quite developed enough . . . no time now. . . . From snatches I have had shown me it is more worth while than many a smooth coherent story." This enthusiasm seems absent in our age of irony and expertise. It's as though a whole century's supply of exclamation points were used up. Even if the bellowing appears silly now, the manifesto can be more worthwhile than many a smooth coherent argument. [Ben Donnelly]

Denis Johnson. *Seek: Reports from the Edges of America & Beyond.*
HarperCollins, 2001. 238 pp. $27.00.

Johnson's reports, which on the surface are journalistic pieces on Montana,
Somalia, Liberia, and once-hallowed hippie retreats, confirms that his cos-
mic view is at the same time comic and bleak, angelic and demonic. His
prose is hallucinatory; it captures those ever-expanding pockets of hell that
are engulfing us. Almost every essay demonstrates that we live in bad—no,
apocalyptic—times. Johnson seems always to find himself in confusing
exotic locations. Two essays report from the Liberian civil war, in which
secrets overwhelm official information and statesmen rule without proper
procedures. A unit of small boys "are the soldiers Charles Taylor can trust
implicitly . . . because they love him as their father." Taylor is a kind of
ghostly ruler, speaking to interviewers in meaningless statements. Perhaps
one of the most amusing reports is Johnson's forced attempt—as the ten-
year-old son of a diplomat—to become a Boy Scout in the Phillipines. His
initiation is so bizarre that he becomes a kind of anti-Scout. He writes, "In
fact, if this had been a real army, one with an enemy, I would have joined
them and pinpointed this location on a map for their artillery." Elsewhere,
Johnson writes about the FBI's attempt to capture Eric Robert Rudolph,
the killer of abortionists, and the North Carolina community that shelters
and feeds him. Johnson views Rudolph as a survivor because he can find
some kind of peace in the caves of Nantahala National Forest, where he
hides. He quotes an anthropologist: "The cave is a maternal, matriarchal
aspect of the world. . . . To return to the cave, even in thought, is to regress
from life into the state of being unborn." The quotation seems to apply to
Johnson. He wants to get out of this world—he seeks salvation—but recognizes that even if he is saved, he won't know it. [Irving Malin]

Books Received

Adams, Hazard. *Home.* SUNY Press, 2001. $20.50. (F)

Alai. *Red Poppies.* Trans. Howard Goldblatt and Sylvia Li-chun Lin. Houghton Mifflin, 2001. $24.00. (F)

Albahari, David. *Bait.* Northwestern Univ. Press, 2001. Paper: $14.95. (F)

Albues, Tereza. *Pedra Canga.* Trans. Clifford E. Landers. Green Integer, 2001. Paper: $12.95. (F)

Appel, Allan. *Club Revelation.* Coffee House, 2001. Paper: $14.95. (F)

Arenas, Reinaldo. *The Color of Summer, or, The New Garden of Earthly Delights.* Trans. Andrew Hurley. Penguin, 2001. Paper: $15.00. (F)

Arnott, Jake. *The Long Firm.* Soho Press, 2001. Paper: $14.00. (F)

Barth, John. *Coming Soon!!!* Houghton Mifflin, 2001. $26.00. (F)

Bens, Jeff W. *Albert, Himself.* Dephinium, 2001. Paper: $13.00. (F)

Bialosky, Jill. *Subterranean.* Knopf, 2001. $23.00. (P).

Blair, J. H. *The Hot Spots: The Best Erotic Writing in Modern Fiction.* Berkley, 2001. Paper: $13.00. (F)

Botting, Fred, and Scott Wilson. *Bataille.* Palgrave, 2001. Paper: $19.95. (F)

Brecht, Bertolt. *Stories of Mr. Keuner.* Trans. and with an afterword by Martin Chalmers. City Lights, 2001. Paper: $9.95. (F)

Brenner, Wendy. *Phone Calls from the Dead.* Algonquin Books, 2001. $22.95. (F)

Bryson, Kathleen Kirk. *Mush.* Diva, 2001. Paper: $13.95. (F)

Buckley, Margaret. *The Commune.* Chrysalis, 2001. Paper: £6.99. (F)

———. *A Woman's Man & Family Portrait.* Chrysalis, 1993. Paper: £6.99. (F)

Burke, Henry, and Dick Crow. *The River Jordan: A True Story of the Underground Railroad.* Watershed, 2001. Paper: $14.95. (F)

Busch, Frederick. *War Babies.* New Directions, 2001. Paper: $12.95. (F)

Chaet, Eric. *People I Met Hitchhiking on USA Highways.* Turnaround Artist Productions, 2001. Paper: $15.00. (NF)

Chametzky, Jules, et al, eds. *Jewish American Literature: A Norton Anthology.* Norton, 2001. $39.95. (F, NF, P)

Choa, Carolyn, and David Su Li-quen, eds. *The Vintage Book of Contemporary Chinese Fiction.* Vintage, 2001. Paper: $14.00. (F)

Chaon, Dan. *Among the Missing.* Ballantine, 2001. $22.00. (F)

Cixous, Hélène. *Manna: For the Mandelstams for the Mandelas.* Trans. and intro. Catherine A. F. MacGillivray. Univ. of Minnesota Press, 2001. Paper: $18.95. (NF)

Cohn, Ruby. *A Beckett Canon.* Univ. of Michigan Press, 2001. $59.50. (NF)

Cokal, Susann. *Mirabilis.* Blue Hen/Putnam, 2001.$25.95. (F)

Czuchlewski, David. *The Muse Asylum.* Putnam, 2001. $23.95. (F)

Damle, Veena. *I Am Om.* Livingston, 2001. Paper: $12.00. (F)

Dean, Michael W. *Starving in the Company of Beautiful Women.* Kittyfeet, 2001. Paper: $13.99. (F)

De Krester, Michelle. *The Rose Grower.* Bantam, 2001. Paper: $12.95. (F)

Diski, Jenny. *Only Human: A Divine Comedy.* Picador, 2001. $23.00. (F)

Dörrie, Doris. *Where Do We Go from Here?* Trans. John Brownjohn. Bloomsbury, 2001. $24.95. (F)

Drewe, Robert. *The Shark Net.* Penguin, 2001. Paper: $14.00. (NF)

Duncan, Pamela. *Moon Women.* Delacorte, 2001. $23.95. (F)

Ellis, Rhian. *After Life.* Penguin, 2001. Paper: $13.00. (F)

Federman, Raymond. *The Voice in the Closet.* Preface by Gérard Bucher. Starcherone, 2001. Paper: $9.00. (F)

Fitzgerald, F. Scott. *Before Gatsby: The First Twenty-Six Stories.* Ed. Matthew J. Bruccoli with the assitance of Judith S. Baughman. South Carolina Univ. Press, 2001. Paper: $24.95. (F)

Fulk, Mark K. *Understanding May Sarton.* South Carolina Univ. Press, 2001. $29.95. (NF)

George, Elizabeth. *A Traitor to Memory.* Bantam, 2001. $26.95. (F)

Gerdes, Eckhard, ed. *Belighted Fiction: Journal of Experimental Fiction Four.* Writers Club Press, 2001. Paper: $13.95. (F, NF)

Gerdes, Eckhard. *Ring in a River.* Authors Choice Press, 2001. Paper: $9.95. (F)

Gilling, Tom. *The Sooterkin.* Penguin, 2001. Paper: $13.00. (F)

Greenlaw, Lavinia. *Mary George of Allnorthover.* Houghton Mifflin, 2001. $24.00. (F)

Greiff, Louis K. *D. H. Lawrence: Fifty Years on Film.* Southern Illinois Univ. Press, 2001. $39.95. (NF)

Guy, Rosa. *Bird at My Window.* Foreword by Sandra Adell. Coffee House, 2001. Paper: 14.95. (F)

Hamsun, Knut. *A Wanderer Plays on Muted Strings.* Green Integer, 2001. Paper: $10.95. (F)

Hannah, Barry. *Yonder Stands Your Orphan.* Grove, 2001. $24.00. (F)

Hartnett, P-P, ed. *The Gay Times Book of Short Stories: New Century, New Writing.* Gay Times, 2001. Paper: $13.95. (F)

Haxton, Brooks. *Nakedness, Death, and the Number Zero.* Knopf, 2001. $23.00. (P).

Heng, Liu. *Green River Daydreams.* Grove, 2001. $24.00. (F)

Herrera, Juan Felipe. *Giraffe on Fire.* Univ. of Arizona Press, 2001. Paper: $14.95. (P)

Heynen, Jim. *The Boys' House.* Minnesota Historical Society Press, 2001. $19.95. (F)

Hoban, Russell. *Angelica's Grotto.* Carroll & Graf, 2001. $25.00. (F)

Hoffman, Alice. *The River King.* Berkeley, 2001. Paper: $14.00. (F)

Hribal, C. J. *The Clouds in Memphis: Stories and Novellas.* Univ. of Massachusetts, 2001. $25.95. (F)

Hunt, Laird. *The Impossibly.* Coffee House, 2001. Paper: $14.95. (F)

Jarrand, Kyle. *Rolling the Bones.* Steerforth, 2001. $26.00. (F)

Jeyifo, Biodun, ed. *Conversatiosn with Wole Soyinka.* Univ. of Mississippi Press, 2001. Paper: $18.00. (NF)

———. *Perpectives on Wole Soyinka: Freedom and Complexity.* Univ. of Mississippi Press, 2001. $46.00. (NF)

Julavits, Heidi. *The Mineral Palace.* Berkeley, 2001. Paper: $14.00. (F)

Kermode, Frank. *Shakespeare's Language.* Farrar, Straus & Giroux, 2001. Paper: $15.00. (NF)

Klein, Richard. *Jewelry Talks.* Pantheon, 2001. $25.00. (F)

Knox, Elizabeth. *Black Oxen.* Farrar, Straus & Giroux, 2001. $25.00. (F)

Koeppen, Wolfgang. *Death in Rome.* Trans. and intro. Michael Hoffman. Norton, 2001. Paper: $12.95. (F)

Krouse, Erika. *Come up and See Me Sometime.* Scribner, 2001. $22.00. (F)

LaFarge, Paul. *Haussmann, or, The Distinction.* Farrar, Straus & Giroux, 2001. $24.00. (F)

Lavín, Mónica, ed. *Points of Departure: New Stories from Mexico.* Trans. Gustavo V. Segade. City Lights, 2001. Paper: $15.95. (F)

Leavitt, David. *The Marble Quilt.* Houghton Mifflin, 2001. $25.00. (F)

Lee, V. G. *The Comedienne.* Diva, 2001. Paper: $13.95. (F)

Lennon, J. Robert. *On the Night Plain.* Henry Holt, 2001. $23.00. (F)

Lewis, Barry. *Kazuo Ishiguro.* Manchester Univ. Press, 2001. $69.95. (NF)

Livesey, Margot. *Eva Moves the Furniture.* Henry Holt, 2001. $23.00. (F)

Lodge, David. *Thinks. . . .* Viking, 2001. $24.95. (F)

Lustig, Arnost. *The Bitter Smell of Almonds: Selected Fiction.* Northwestern Univ. Press, 2001. $25.95. (F)

Mackey, Nathaniel. *ATET A.D.* City Lights, 2001. Paper: $13.95. (F)

Makine, Andrei. *Requiem for a Lost Empire.* Trans. Geoffrey Strachan. Arcade, 2001. $24.95. (F)

Marcum, Carl. *Cue Lazarus.* Univ. of Arizona Press, 2001. Paper: $13.95. (P)

Marius, Richard. *An Affair of Honor.* Knopf, 2001. $26.95. (F)

Mawer, Simon. *The Gospel of Judas.* Little, Brown, 2001. $24.95. (F)

McAlexander, Hubert. H. *Peter Taylor: A Writer's Life.* Louisiana State Univ. Press, 2001. $34.95. (NF)

McCown, Clint. *War Memorials*. Mariner Books, 2001. Paper: $13.00. (F)

McCracken, Elizabeth. *Niagra Falls All over Again*. Dial Press, 2001. $23.95. (F)

Messud, Claire. *The Hunters: Two Short Novels*. Harcourt, 2001. $23.00. (F)

Moor, Margriet de. *First Gray, Then White, Then Blue*. Trans. Paul Vincent. Overlook, 2001. $25.95. (F)

Moravia, Alberto. *Two Women*. Steerforth, 2001. Paper: $16.00. (F)

Morris, Mary McGarry. *Fiona Range*. Penguin, 2001. Paper: $14.00. (F)

Mosher, Jake. *The Last Buffalo Hunter*. David R. Godine, 2001. $24.95. (F)

Munroe, Jim. *Angry Young Spaceman*. Four Walls Eight Windows, 2001. Paper: $13.95. (F)

Murray, Sabina. *The Caprices*. Mariner, 2001. Paper: $13.00. (F)

Nagel, James. *The Contemporary American Short-Story Cycle*. Louisiana State Univ. Press, 2001. $49.95. (F)

Nakell, Martin. *Two Fields That Face and Mirror Each Other*. Green Integer, 2001. Paper: $16.95. (F)

Nissenson, Hugh. *The Song of the Earth*. Algonquin Books of Chapel Hill, 2001. $24.95. (F)

Norton, John. *Re: Marriage*. Black Star Series, 2001. Paper: $10.00. (F)

Olds, Bruce. *Bucking the Tiger*. Farrar, Straus & Giroux, 2001. $25.00. (F)

Olson, Shannon. *Welcome to My Planet: Where English Is Sometimes Spoken*. Penguin, 2001. Paper: $13.00. (F)

Palahniuk, Chuck. *Choke*. Doubleday, 2001. $24.95. (F)

Pancake, Ann. *Given Ground*. New England Univ. Press, 2001. $24.95. (F)

Pap, Károly. *Azarel*. Trans. Paul Olchváry. Steerforth, 2001. Paper: $14.00. (F)

Parrinder, Patrick, ed. *Learning from Other Worlds: Estrangement, Cognition, and the Politics of Science Fiction and Utopia*. Duke Univ. Press, 2001. Paper: $18.95. (F)

Patell, Cyrus R. K. *Negative Liberties: Morrison, Pynchon, and the Problem of Liberal Ideology*. Duke Univ. Press, 2001. Paper: $18.95. (F)

Payne, Johnny. *North of Patagonia*. Northwestern Univ. Press, 2001. $25.95. (F)

Pederson, Laura. *Going Away Party*. Story Line, 2001. $22.00. (F)

Phillips, Max. *The Artist's Wife*. Henry Holt, 2001. $23.00. (F)

Polonsky, Antony, and Monika Adamcyk-Garbowska, eds. *Contemporary Jewish Writing in Poland: An Anthology*. Univ. of Nebraska Press, 2001. $60.00. (F, P)

Potok, Chaim. *Old Men at Midnight.* Knopf, 2001. $23.00. (F)

Pulaski, Jack. *Courting Laura Providencia.* Zephyr Press, 2001. Paper: $14.95. (F)

Reiner, Christopher. *Pain.* Avec, 2001. Paper: $11.00. (F)

Richler, Emma. *Sister Crazy.* Pantheon, 2001. $22.00. (F)

Rivas, Manuel. *The Carpenter's Pencil.* Overlook, 2001. $24.95. (F)

Roberts, Jenny. *Needlepoint.* Diva, 2001. Paper: $13.95. (F)

Roiphe, Katie. *Still She Haunts Me.* Dial, 2001. $23.95. (F)

Roth, Philip. *The Dying Animal.* Houghton Mifflin, 2001. $22.00. (F)

——. *Shop Talk: A Writer and His Colleagues and Their Work.* Houghton Mifflin, 2001. $23.00. (F)

Rucker, Rudy. *White Light.* Intro. John Shirley. Afterword by the author. Four Walls Eight Windows, 2001. Paper: $13.95. (F)

Ryan, Marie-Laure. *Narrative as Virtual Reality: Immersion and Interactivity in Literature and Electronic Media.* Johns Hopkins Univ. Press, 2001. $45.00. (NF)

Saipradit, Kulap. *Behind the Painting and Other Stories.* Trans. David Smyth. Silkworm, 2001. Paper: No price given. (F)

Sandler, Helen, ed. *Diva Book of Short Stories.* Diva, 2001. Paper: $13.95. (F)

Schickler, David. *Kissing in Manhattan.* Dial, 2001. $21.95. (F)

Schwartz, Daniel R. *Rereading Conrad.* Univ. of Missouri Press, 2001. Paper: $16.95. (NF)

Schwartz, Yigal. *Aharon Applefeld: From Individual Lament to Tribal Eternity.* Brandeis Univ. Press, 2001. Paper: $19.95. (NF)

Sheck, Laurie. *Black Series.* Knopf, 2001. $23.00. (P)

Sijie, Dai. *Balzac and the Little Chinese Seamstress.* Trans. Ina Rilke. Knopf, 2001. $18.00. (F)

Simon, Claude. *The Jardin Des Plantes.* Trans. and intro. Jordan Stump. Northwestern Univ. Press, 2001. $29.95. (F)

Southern, Terry. *Now Dig This: The Unspeakable Writings of Terry Southern.* Ed. Nile Southern and Josh Alan Friedman. Grove, 2001. $25.00. (NF)

Spitzer, Mark. *Chum.* Zoland, 2001. $21.00 (F)

Stanford, Ann. *Holding Our Own.* Ed. Maxine Scates and David Trinidad. Copper Canyon, 2001. Paper: $16.00. (P)

Stewart, Jeffrey. *Two Pink Horses.* Livingston, 2001. Paper: $12.00. (F)

Stewart, Leah. *Body of a Girl.* Penguin, 2001. Paper: $13.00. (F)

Sullivan, Evelin. *The Concise Book of Lying.* Farrar, Straus & Giroux, 2001. $25.00. (NF)

Tanning, Dorothea. *Chasm.* Turtle Point Press, 2001. Paper: $13.95. (F)

Tate, Linda. *Conversations with Lee Smith.* Univ. of Mississippi Press, 2001. Paper: $18.00. (NF)

Tyler, Natalie. *The Friendly Jane Austen: A Well-Mannered Introduction to a Lady of Sense and Sensibility.* Penguin, 2001. Paper: $16.00. (F)

Udall, Barry. *The Miracle Life of Edgar Mint.* Norton, 2001. $24.95. (F)

Vassanji, M. G. *Amriika.* McClelland & Stewart, 2001. Paper: $16.95. (F)

Vernon, John. *The Last Canyon.* Houghton Mifflin, 2001. $24.00. (F)

Villasenor, Daniel. *The Lake.* Penguin, 2001. Paper: $13.00. (F)

Vollmann, William T. *Argall: The True Story of Pochahontas and Captain John Smith.* Viking, 2001. $40.00. (F)

——. *The Royal Family.* Penguin, 2001. Paper: $17.00. (F)

Wachman, Gay. *Lesbian Empire: Radical Crosswriting in the Twenties.* Rutgers Univ. Press, 2001. $24.00. (NF)

Waldrop, Rosemarie. *The Hanky of Pippin's Daughter and A Form / of Taking / It All.* Northestern Univ. Press, 2001. Paper: $17.95. (F)

West, Paul. *Master Class: Scenes from a Fiction Workshop.* Harcourt, 2001. $24.00. (NF)

Wheeler, Elizabeth A. *Uncontained: Urban Fiction in Postwar America.* Rutgers Univ. Press, 2001. Paper: $22.00. (NF)

Wimmer, Dick. *Irish Wine: The Trilogy.* Penguin, 2001. Paper: $13.00. (F)

Wolf, Manfred, ed. *Amsterdam: A Traveler's Literary Companion.* Whereabouts Press, 2001. Paper: $13.95. (F, NF)

Wronsky, Gail. *The Love-Talkers: An Erotic Fable.* Hollyridge Press, 2001. $23.95. (F)

Young, Kevin. *To Repel Ghosts.* Zoland, 2001. (P)

Zukofsky, Louis. *Prepositions: The Collected Critical Essays.* Wesleyan Univ. Press, 2001. Paper: $16.95. (NF)

Contributors

DAVID ANDREWS has published criticism, interviews, fiction, and poetry in *Film Criticism, Leviathan: A Journal of Melville Studies, Nabokov Studies, Serpentine, Hunger, Bridge, Indefinite Space,* and *At Millennium's End: New Essays on the Work of Kurt Vonnegut.* In 1999 Edwin Mellen published his book *Aestheticism, Nabokov, and "Lolita."* Currently, he is working on a comprehensive study of the works of Gilbert Sorrentino and teaching at the University of Illinois—Chicago.

JOHN BEER teaches English and humanities at Robert Morris College in Chicago. He has published poems in *Colorado Review, Iowa Review,* and *Fine Madness.*

JOY CASTRO teaches fiction writing and modernist literature at Wabash College in Indiana. She is currently at work on a collection of short stories and a book on Margery Latimer. Her essay on Jean Rhys appeared in the Summer 2000 *Review of Contemporary Fiction.*

Annual Index

References are to issue number and pages, respectively

Contributors

Books Reviewed

Reviewers' names follow in parentheses. Regular reviewers are abbreviated: AH=Allen Hibbard; AT=Alan Tinkler; BE=Brian Evenson; BH=Brooke Horvath; CP=Christy Post; DB=David Bergman; IM=Irving Malin; JC=James Crossley; MP=Michael Pinker; PL=Philip Landon; SEP=Sally E. Parry; TH=Thomas Hove

THE GREENSBORO REVIEW

For Over 30 Years
A Publisher of Poetry & Fiction

Works from the journal have been anthologized or cited in *Best American Short Stories, Prize Stories: The O. Henry Awards, Pushcart Prize, New Stories from the South,* and other collections honoring the finest new writing.

Recent Contributors

A. Manette Ansay
Stephen Dobyns
Brendan Galvin
Richard Garcia
Rodney Jones

Jean Ross Justice
Thomas Lux
Jill McCorkle
Peter Meinke
Robert Morgan

Robert Olmstead
Dale Ray Phillips
David Rivard
Tom Sleigh
Eleanor Ross Taylor

Subscriptions

Sample copy—$5   One year—$10   Three years—$25

The Greensboro Review
English Department, UNCG
PO Box 26170
Greensboro, NC 27402-6170

Visit our website
www.uncg.edu/eng/mfa
or send SASE for deadlines
and submission guidelines

Produced by the MFA Writing Program at Greensboro

The Franchiser

a novel by

Stanley Elkin

Foreword by William H. Gass

A Lannan Selection
Fiction | $13.50

"Elkin's fiction runs on language, on parody, on comic fantasies and routines. Give him conventional wisdom and he will twist it into tomfoolery."
–Christopher Lehmann-Haupt, New York Times

"A frenzied parable, rather as though the Wandering Jew and Willy Loman had gotten together on a vaudeville act."
–John Leonard, Saturday Review

"Elkin is often drunk with words....The prevailing dialect of *The Franchiser* is free-wheeling and exuberant Jewish-American–a tribal dialect in which Elkin can achieve effects of S.J. Perelaman and Wallace Markfield."
–Robert Towers, New York Times Book Review

DALKEY ARCHIVE PRESS | www.dalkeyarchive.com

The Hive

a novel by

Camilo José Cela

1989 Nobel Laureate

Fiction | $12.95

"His best work…a carnivalesque reconstruction of the Spanish tradition, a nightmarish, surrealistic depiction of human endeavor."

–Julio Ortega

Banned for many years by the Franco regime, Cela's masterpiece presents a panoramic view of the degradation and suffering of the lower-middle class in the post-Civil War Spain.

"A web of sordid episodes in the lives of unimportant people, the dregs of society. A lover of crude realism . . . Cela is reminiscent of the Céline of *Journey to the End of the Night*."
–*New York Herald Tribune*

DALKEY ARCHIVE PRESS | www.dalkeyarchive.com